OUT OF THIS
WORLD

ARE UFOS

ALIENS, SPIRITS, OR PURE HOKUM?

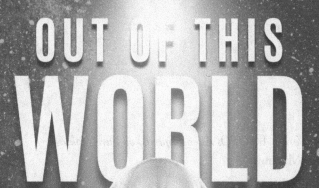

OUT OF THIS
WORLD

NORDIC   GRAY   REPTILIAN

LTC ROBERT L. MAGINNIS

DEFENDER
CRANE, MO

Out of This World: Are UFOs Aliens, Spirits, or Pure Hokum?
by Robert L. Maginnis

Defender Publishing
Crane, MO 65633

© 2024 Robert L. Maginnis
All Rights Reserved. Published 2024

ISBN: 978-1-948014-77-9

Printed in the United States of America.

A CIP catalog record of this book is available from the Library of Congress.

Cover designer: Jeffrey Mardis
Interior designer: Katherine Lloyd

Unless otherwise noted, images in this book were obtained through Unsplash and Pexels, online image services that provide art and photographs royalty-free and license-free for commercial and non-commercial use with no requirement of permissions or attribution. Licensing for use of these images are available at the following: "License," Unsplash, last accessed December 4, 2023, https://unsplash.com/license; "Legal Simplicity," Pexels, last accessed December 4, 2023, https://www.pexels.com/license/.

To the memory of Tom Horn, a dear Christian brother who supported my writing projects over the years and was especially excited about this book. May he rest in peace, and may his memory encourage others to walk with the Lord and boldly proclaim His truths to a lost world.

CONTENTS

Section Four:
Government Secrets about UAPs, UFOs, and ET Threats

Section Five:
What Have We Learned and What Should We Do?

Section Six:
Christians, Spirits, Aliens, and End Times

ACKNOWLEDGMENTS

gratefully acknowledge...

...my wife, Jan, who is always supportive of these writing efforts to address very tough issues, albeit at some sacrifice, given that throughout this writing effort I had a "day" job. She's a comfort and a supporter through these challenging times.

...my dear friend Mark Shaffstall, who provided welcomed recommendations, edits, and insights about the UFO phenomenon.

...finally, like all my previous works, my Lord Jesus Christ, who gave me the thoughts, skills, and breath to complete this effort, and I pray it serves His purpose. All the glory is to Him.

—Robert Lee Maginnis
Woodbridge, Virginia

OUT OF THIS WORLD:
ARE UFOS ALIENS, SPIRITS, OR PURE HOKUM?

The presence of unidentified space craft flying in our atmosphere (and possibly maintaining orbits about our planet) is now [June 1947], however, accepted as defacto by our military.[1]

—Dr. J. Robert Oppenheimer, American theoretical physicist known as the "father of the atomic bomb"

—Dr. Albert Einstein, German-born theoretical physicist and developer of the theory of relativity

PREFACE

F ew issues earn more attention and are less understood by a wide swath of the international public than unidentified flying objects (UFOs) and what is most often labeled an aspect of the paranormal. Are UFOs evidence of aliens from other worlds; markers of an Earth-bound phenomenon beyond our understanding; what some call "new" physics; spirits briefly lifting the veil of the unseen realm playing havoc with humankind; or just evidence of our vivid, crazed imaginations? Or, alternatively, are they just pure hokum? If they are real, can we expect that someday science and/or theology will come to explain them and that the government will reveal any secrets they may hold about invading aliens?

Records of UFO sightings date from ancient times, and, understandably, curious humans have always been fascinated by the prospect that there might be life beyond this tiny planet and/or visiting spirits—both the seen and unseen variety—that haunt our daily lives. The number of UFO sightings across history has been quite significant; perhaps more daunting are the many that remain inexplicable in spite of our best scientific efforts to diagnose their origins.

UFO characteristics that continue to confound any explanation and the scope of the issue follow:

- **Clocks freeze, strange sounds blast from heaven, and people claim to have seen alien visitors:** Those associated with geographical areas such as the Perm Anomalous Zone, an area known as Russia's Area 51, acknowledge troubling mysteries: wristwatches stop dead in the Zone, people hear rushing sounds emanating from the Zone's heavens, and visitors claim to have seen actual aliens in the vicinity. (Area 51 is America's top-secret facility in the Nevada desert, which allegedly [but denied by the US government] houses alien spacecraft.)

- **UFOs congregate near nuclear facilities and vessels:** UFO sightings appear more frequently near nuclear facilities and atomic-powered naval vessels than at most other locations. For example, most UFO sightings in Japan reportedly take place near the famous Fukushima Daiichi Nuclear Power Plant, which was severely damaged by an earthquake in 2011.

- **All things military attract UFOs:** Many UFOs are reported near military facilities or appear in the vicinity of ongoing military training exercises, such as those documented by a variety of airborne sensors operated by US Navy pilots over the oceans.

- **Millions claim to have seen UFOs, and many boast of alien encounters:** Millions of people across the world report having seen UFOs, and some indicate they have actually encountered alien beings. In fact, a subset of those people allege they were abducted by aliens, and yet other reports include bizarre descriptions of physical evidence of UFO incidents.

- **UFOs demonstrate extraordinary capabilities:** Many of the sightings made by totally reliable military pilots describe UFOs as having demonstrated extraordinary capabilities: anti-gravity propulsion; instantaneous acceleration to speeds more than thirty times the speed of sound; operations in a seemingly atmosphere-free environment; alleged alien craft details hidden from our best instruments; and the evident ease of transition some UFOs make through different mediums (air, water, space).

Documented and detailed descriptions of these and other bizarre UFO sightings with a few video descriptions and actual filmed footage are available in chapter 5, "The Inexplicable," and in appendix A.

No wonder that, given so many inexplicable UFO sightings over the past thousands of years, today more than eight in ten Americans (78 percent), according to a 2022 national survey, believe in the existence of aliens. Further, one in three believes aliens have abducted human beings, and more than one in three (37 percent) think the scientific community and government officials have already been in contact with alien life. Also, Americans are split regarding aliens' intentions, with half believing they "come in peace" and the balance thinking they seek our destruction.[2]

Alternatively, the skeptical among us tend to attribute UFO sightings to psychological influences or paranormal thinking. Specifically, some researchers explain that factors like dissociation, depression, and tendencies toward attention deficit contribute to a wide variety of paranormal beliefs and perceptions, including alleged sightings of the so-called Bigfoot, or Sasquatch, a mythical, hairy-like creature purported to inhabit forests in North America.

Of course, reports of strange objects in the sky or mysteries beyond our understanding could be evidence of secret government experiments, perhaps enemy nation spying (remember China's spy balloon that floated across our skies from January 28 to February 4, 2023?) or even out-of-control artificial intelligence entities. Such observations might also be manifestations of the spiritual world—the realm where angels and demons contest for souls as described in the Bible. The current amped-up reports of these incidents, such as those documented by the Pentagon's new All-Domain Anomaly Resolution Office (AARO) and the Office of the Director of National Intelligence could mean the increased paranormal activity means we are nearing the prophetic end times.

What Should We Believe?[3]

This volume explores UFO reports as well as other associated issues that typically capture the headlines of media outlets, stump government officials, and perplex scientists and common people across the world. Such unexplained phenomena have ancient roots, and a growing number of contemporary sightings defy our understanding of physics. They stir us up and frighten even the brightest among us, yet no one, not even our top government officials, can give a convincing explanation.

Out of This World explores the history of UFO and paranormal reports; the scientific assessment of the reported phenomena; what scientists, theologians, and philosophers have to say about these mysteries; and much more. It tries to answer tough questions like: Are these sightings mostly explainable phenomena? Does our understanding of the laws of physics need to become more sophisticated? Are UFOs evidence of government-created experimental craft? Are we alone in this massive universe? Are we being visited by more advanced beings, aliens from other galaxies, and might they already be among us? Do these "visitors" have other than peaceful aims? Alternatively, are these paranormal events evidence of a dimension not discernable by our five senses, the spirits—angels and demons—within the unseen realm?

Out of This World explores UFO reports
as well as other associated issues.[4]

In six sections, sixteen chapters, *Out of This World* explores the many dimensions of this intriguing phenomenon. We begin with section I to set the philosophical, historic, and spiritual context for exploring this controversial topic by defining key terms and considering what both ancient and religious history (especially the Bible) say about these inexplicable objects in our skies.

Section Two explores the contemporary—twentieth and twenty-first-century—manifestations of UFOs and otherwise paranormal events and how they are treated, as well as their frequency, locations, and descriptions. There is no standard for recording and assessing these sightings, which makes any scientific evaluation suspect.

The third section considers many attempts to answer questions about these mysteries, such as: Are UFOs and other paranormal events real or hokum? Here we explore what scientists say and what the religious communities discern, as well as consider arguments by those who attribute such sightings to psychological instability or mental illness, which presumably, according to some skeptics, includes even some of our Top Gun Navy pilots who report seeing UFOs.

Governments, starting with the United States and including many across the world, have weighed in on the issue—albeit too often, without being truly serious, which is explored in section four. What do international governments say about UFOs and, in particular, what have US government officials said and done regarding this phenomenon? What information about aliens might our government have sequestered away in secret facilities?

In section five, we review what we've learned in the first eleven chapters of *Out of This World* about the phenomenon—the "takeaways" that draw some conclusions (implications) and then suggest what, if anything, ought to be done by key communities. Specifically, I recommend that the US government publish a strategy, "Project UFO," and I recommend vigorously pursuing the topic with the full weight of government, suggesting what key public institutions like academia and the media ought to do as well.

I conclude *Out of This World* with a perspective for Christians interested in what this phenomenon means for our future, especially for the prophetic end times. In section six, we consider whether UFOs are really evidence of spiritual beings—angels and demons—or are a mixture of members of the unseen realm (spirits) and alleged aliens from places out of this world. Then I propose a biblically based, prophetic end-times scenario that demonstrates the role UFOs are likely to play in the future.

So, fasten your notional, psychologically attuned, and spiritually oriented seatbelt as we race through the facts, history, strange reports, and firsthand accounts; expose some suspect claims; and present possible explanations and insights into the growing mound of evidence and considerable speculation to consider who or what might be behind such events. This stirring and well-documented account of the paranormal, which sparks global curiosity, frightens the soberest among us and certainly challenges us all to get serious about what's happening before our eyes, especially considering that these events might actually be the manifestation of the unseen realm leading to the prophetic end times.

UFOS AND OTHER PARANORMAL EVENTS IN CONTEXT AND HISTORY

What is true, and I'm actually being serious here, is that there are, there's footage and records of objects in the skies, that we don't know exactly what they are. We can't explain how they moved, their trajectory. They did not have an easily explainable pattern. And so, you know, I think that people still take seriously trying to investigate and figure out what that is.[1]

—Barack Hussein Obama II,
forty-fourth PRESIDENT of the United States

We begin *Out of This World* with an overview of terms used and abused by detractors and advocates of the likelihood that extraterrestrials (ETs) have visited planet Earth.

Chapter 1 reviews terms like "paranormal," "metaphysical," "ufology," and other associated words used throughout this book. Unfortunately, they often elicit dramatically different definitions. These expressions cause some of us to attribute them to evil or insanity, yet others among us refuse to even consider the topics. However, the open-minded will embrace these terms as representing an ongoing challenge for science and theology.

Chapter 2 explores mostly ancient historical records to demonstrate that the notion of aliens from other worlds has interrupted our lives across dramatically different venues and reaches back thousands of years. Yes, modern science puts some of these reports into context by labeling them as natural astronautical or meteorological events, though many others continue to defy contemporary explanations.

Chapter 3 considers religious traditions, their scriptures, and art to reveal ancient thinking about UFOs and the potential regarding the likelihood that we've been visited by alien beings. Some readers will paint this testimony as pure myth, yet others, especially adherents of various faith groups, will accept them as factual but not necessarily conclusive. UFOs represent ancient events recorded over thousands of years and might indeed be evidence of extraterrestrials visiting Earth or spirits manifesting themselves, albeit briefly, to our senses. However, for the Christian, the Bible provides insights about strange events that some might attribute to aliens.

In summary, this section establishes a baseline for the balance of *Out of This World*. It demonstrates a philosophical foundation and affirms that the phenomena associated with UFOs are an ancient issue that has never been completely resolved and, in fact, continues to baffle our contemporary world.

1

THE "UNFATHOMABLES"
OF LIFE IN CONTEXT

I can assure you that flying saucers, given that they exist,
are not constructed by any power on Earth.[1]

—PRESIDENT HARRY S. TRUMAN,
Press conference, April 4, 1950

The God of the Bible states: "'For my thoughts are not your thoughts, nor are your ways my ways,' declares the Lord" (Isaiah 55:8, NIV). It is true that humankind often finds some things in life mysterious and unfathomable, and, as a result, people either speculate about their origin and purpose, or too often elect to ignore them by hiding their heads in the proverbial sand of thinking.

"'For my thoughts are not your thoughts,
nor are your ways my ways,' declares the Lord" (Isaiah 55:8, NIV).[2]

After all, these life mysteries defy our understanding of revealed science and/or are beyond the reaches of our five senses (sight, smell, touch, taste, and hearing). Therefore, many of us choose to ignore baffling events, while others—a few scientists and many theologians—commit considerable energy to unwrapping life's mysteries. Among the "unfathomable" events that cross the human's path are what have come to be known as unidentified flying objects (UFOs), which might include the alleged existence of extraterrestrial beings from far-away places, or spirits, ghosts, and the like.

This chapter defines terms associated with the UFO phenomena that try to explain these "unfathomables" that interrupt life. Admittedly, a significant sector of the world's population crams these mysteries into a notional box they label "foolishness," "lunacy," or "hokum," a topic serious people, they might argue—and, even more so, scientists—ought to ignore. That view is beginning to wane, though, especially as topics like UFOs and widespread interest in extraterrestrials/alien beings garner respectability among the contemporary scientific and media worlds. The details of that growing "respectability" and significant new findings about the phenomenon are addressed in this book.

Of course, many of the world's religious communities already accept the existence of what some label the "unfathomables," which they interpret as spirits, supernatural beings that are beyond the reach of modern science and our physical senses. For Jews and Christians, these spirits are biblically known as angels or demons that interact with humans in ways not widely understood, but that are not denied by true believers. We'll address this "unseen realm" of spirits in this volume and juxtapose them with the explosive interest in UFOs, especially alleged extraterrestrials.

Before building that case, however, I call attention to the significant prevalence of these "unfathomables" throughout our secular and religious history (chapters 2 and 3). Further, to help put this challenging topic into context, I begin this examination with the definition of some of these phenomena using terms and labels that are widely employed mostly in philosophy and pseudoscience, which should help our understanding of "unfathomables" like UFOs going forward.

Metaphysics and UFOs

Metaphysics explores the fundamental nature of reality, such as being or existence, identity, change, space, and time. Metaphysics, like ethics, logic, and epistemology, is one of the four main branches of philosophy. It studies questions that address the nature of consciousness and the relationship between mind and matter or potentiality and actuality.

The word "metaphysics" comes from writings by the ancient Greek philosopher Aristotle (384–322 BC). Although he never used the term, it was coined based on the four names for the branches of philosophy attributed to Aristotle: "first philosophy," "first science," "wisdom," and "theology." A century after Aristotle's death, the editor of his works titled them, *ta meta ta phusika*, or "the after the physicals." One view of the title's purpose is that it puts students of Aristotle's work on notice that they ought to first master "the physical ones" (so-called hard sciences like physics and chemistry) before venturing into the "metaphysics."[3]

Consistent with Aristotle's view of "the physical ones" that govern the physical world such as gravity, metaphysics is beyond the physics, not reachable by our senses. It addresses the nature and origin of reality, the immortal soul, and the existence of a supreme being.[4]

Many scientists tend to be skeptical about anything that isn't defined by the laws of physics—e.g., metaphysics, which very much includes the realm of UFOs, especially incidents presumed to be associated with alien beings. Consider a 1967 *Science* journal article by William Markowitz, a physics professor at Marquette University in Milwaukee, Wisconsin, who gives no credibility to the metaphysical, at least regarding extraterrestrials.[5]

Professor Markowitz explains that the laws of physics include "the elemental laws of celestial mechanics and physics, including special relativity," such as, "every action must have an equal and opposite reaction [Isaac Newton's third law of motion]." Then he addresses the "possible and impossible" to refute the proposition that "some people claim that nothing is impossible." However, Professor Markowitz states: "This is not so. The laws of mathematics and physics, if accepted, do provide limitations on what can be done [thus refuting the impossible]."[6]

Then Professor Markowitz addresses metaphysics, which is presumably anything that violates the laws of physics, with an eye on UFOs attributed to alien beings. He begins:

> Let us now consider the possibility that the laws of physics are not valid. One idea frequently suggested is that extraterrestrial beings have discovered gravity shields. This, however, would not solve the problem of propulsion because inertia would remain; reaction would still be needed to obtain acceleration.

The professor explains:

> If we could cancel gravity on the earth, an object would lift very slowly, because of the buoyancy of the air and because the object would begin traveling in a straight line whereas the earth would continue to revolve around the sun.

The professor at this point invokes fiction writer H. G. Wells' 1901 book, *The First Men in the Moon*, which creates a gravity-defying "shield" that cancels "the attraction of the Earth but not that of the moon." His point is under such a scenario that the acceleration of an object, like a "flying saucer" in Earth's atmosphere, would defy the imagination, "which is not that reported by UFOs."[7]

"We can reconcile UFO reports with extraterrestrial control by assigning various magic properties to extraterrestrial beings," writes Markowitz. He continues:

These include "teleportation" (the instantaneous movement of material bodies between planets and stars), the creation of "force-fields" to drive space ships, and propulsion without reaction. The last of these would permit a man to lift himself by his bootstraps. Anyone who wishes is free to accept such magic properties, but I cannot.[8]

Scientists like Professor Markowitz have little tolerance for those who entertain the possibility of aliens, attributing to them physics-defying capabilities like "teleportation" and "force-fields." He concludes:

We have been reminded that 21st-century science will look back on us. This is true. We, ourselves, look back on eras when many people believed in the existence of centaurs, mermaids, and fire-breathing dragons. I am afraid that 21st-century science will contemplate with wonder that fact that, in an age of science such as ours, the U.S. Air Force was required to sponsor repeated studies of UFOs [such as Project Blue Book].[9]

"I have no quarrel with anyone who wishes to believe that UFOs are under extraterrestrial control," writes Professor Markowitz. "As for me, I shall not believe that we have ever been visited by any extra-terrestrial visitors—either from the moon, from a planet of our solar system, or from any other stellar system—until I am shown such a visitor."[10]

In *Out of This World*, although I consider many UFO reports and government studies that indicate some presumed physics-defying capabilities, I remain skeptical, like Professor Markowitz, that we have been visited by aliens. But as you will see in greater detail in this work, I believe spiritual beings, not aliens from another stellar system, appear to be the metaphysical explanation for the UFO phenomenon.

Ontology and UFOs

Ontology, an arm of metaphysics related to concepts of existence and reality, traces its origin to what Aristotle called "first philosophy." The word "ontology" comes from the Latin *ontologia*—"science of being," which is attributed to German philosopher Jacob Lorhardus (1561–1609), but was first popularized by German philosopher Christian Wolff (1679–1754) in his 1730 writings, *Philosophia Prima, sive Ontologia*, translated "First Philosophy, or Ontology."[11]

Ontology addresses questions about how entities are grouped into categories such as substances, properties, and relations, and is most often contrasted with epistemology—the study of knowledge, which addresses how we can form knowledge. Specifically, ontology deals with the topic of religion in that it considers the question "Does God exist?" while epistemologists ask a very different question: "How could we know whether God exists?" Obviously, ontology deals with entities/realities outside the realm of current empirical (physical) science, like spirits and presumed alien beings.

The abstraction of ontology as an arm of metaphysics has taken on a modern look, juxtaposing philosophy and computer science in an attempt to describe everything that is for contemporary humans. A 2023 article by Dr. Ari Joury, a particle physicist, "How Ontology and Data Go Hand-in-Hand," illustrates that partnership. He explains that, a decade ago, if you searched online for the word "Paris," you'd get a list of links relevant to your query. He continues:

> Fast-forward to today: If you tap in 'Paris' now, your search machine recognizes that it is a city—and knows what a city is—and will propose data points pertaining to cities, like demographics, districts, and so on. It might also propose train lines that bring you to Paris because trains are things that bring you to Paris because trains are things that exist for ontologists, and because your relationship to Paris might be wanting to visit.

This example, according to Joury, is "ontology in action."[12]

Religion and UFOs

Religion is an aspect of the metaphysical, which describes the human's relation to what he or she regards as holy, sacred, absolute, spiritual, and divine. It is the means by which many people answer the ontological questions about life, death, the existence of god(s), supernatural beings, and our state of being.

Among the roughly 4,200[13] religions, churches, religious bodies, and related groups in the world today, most have nonscientific, spiritual practices that involve rituals, liturgies, ceremonies, and worship of deities that defy our senses. Further, a small number of those faiths embrace truly bizarre activities, such as mediumship (the practice of mediating communication between spirits of the dead and live humans), out-of-body experiences (episodes in which a person's conscious self leaves his or her body), near-death experiences (experiences of being at the imminent risk of death, such as a person's heart temporarily stops), reincarnation (from Latin meaning "entering the flesh again"; belief that every human continues to exist in another form after death), and other supernatural experiences.

David Weintraub, an astronomy professor at Vanderbilt University, considered the world's major religions and what they have to say about extraterrestrial life. In his book, *Religions and Extraterrestrial Life*, Professor Weintraub describes the beliefs of "more than two dozen major religions" such as Judaism, Roman Catholicism, several mainline Protestant sects, the Southern Baptist Convention, Islam, Hinduism, and the Bahá'í Faith. However, wrote Weintraub, "Very few among us have spent much time thinking hard about what actual knowledge about extraterrestrial life, whether viruses or single-celled creatures or bipeds piloting intergalactic spaceships, might mean for our personal beliefs [and] our relationships with the divine."[14]

Christianity and UFOs

Christianity is the world's leading major religion stemming from the life, teachings, and death of Jesus of Nazareth, which answer for believers

9

the key ontological questions about life, such as "Does God exist?" It recognizes the reality of spiritual beings like angels and demons and what many humans label as the "unfathomable."

The Christian philosophical view of metaphysics—reality in terms of ontology and cosmology—includes a set of beliefs including that there is only one God, the supreme source of all being and reality. The Creator God provides all meaning and purpose to life. Further, the Christian understands that God made us in His image and gave us the capacity to understand Him and His intelligent order. The Bible is full of many examples of spiritual beings, and the believer embraces them through faith and under the leadership of God's immaterial Holy Spirit.

We address in detail a biblical view of UFOs and the possibility of alien beings in chapters 3 and 15 of this book.

The above discussion of metaphysics, ontology, and religion is necessary to set the stage for what follows. Our world from ancient times has struggled to explain the unseen realm—God, spirits, and most anything that defies science and our senses. Events in life that can't be explained by metaphysics, especially by religion, tend to be categorized as *paranormal*, not scientifically explainable.

Paranormal

The term "paranormal" implies an event that denotes experiences outside the norm and are beyond our present scientific explanation. The secularist would label much of religion as paranormal, as well as reports of ghosts, extraterrestrials, and, of course, UFOs. However, occurrences of these events attract certain individuals, especially those within pop culture, and tend to be based on anecdote, testimony, and suspicion as opposed to scientific hypotheses, which are grounded in empirical observations and experimental data. One group that fits this characterization is ufologists.

Ufology

Ufology is the study of the possibility of extraterrestrial life, a branch of metaphysics often considered paranormal as well. Nevertheless, aspects of the possible existence of life beyond Earth have many scientists intrigued and are gaining considerable legitimacy. In fact, the scientific community is actively researching unicellular life across our solar system (what's called "astrobiology"), such as studies that send spacecraft to the surface of Mars and our examination of meteors for traces of life.[15] Other projects, such as the search for extraterrestrial intelligence, use giant radio antennas like China's Aperture Spherical Telescope to search the heavens for evidence of intelligent life outside our solar system.[16]

Two Ufology Camps

UFO followers, "ufologists," are segregated into two camps. First, the conservative UFO-ers want to label their sightings as meriting serious scientific examination. Thus, they call themselves "ufologists" to gain legitimacy, and they believe that, eventually, logical analysis—science—will validate extraterrestrial existence and perhaps visitations.

There are many self-identified ufologists across the world. Some are journalists, a few are scientists, and others are government personnel who pursue UFO research. However, most are none of these; they are just ordinary citizens pursuing knowledge about UFOs. Their research uses different methods, such as interviews and field investigations, to gather evidence that some UFO sightings may be caused by natural phenomena, while others in this camp host conferences, produce websites, and research the topic.[17]

The second camp of ufologists embraces a quasi-religious view about the possibility of extraterrestrial visitors. This group tends to be occultists (those with a "belief in or study of the action or influence of supernatural or supernormal powers")[18] or spiritualists (those with "a belief that spirits of the dead communicate with the living usually through a medium"),[19] and such people often coalesce around the New Age spiritual movement. In the context of religious thinking, there are ufologists who consider that humans have been abducted by alien beings, such as the 1961 event that impacted Betty and Barney Hill. Media reports indicate that while the Hills were driving through the

White Mountains of New Hampshire, they were abducted by aliens and taken to a distant star system; once they returned to Earth, they provided details about their journey to the star Zeta Reticuli.[20]

Understandably, allegations of alien abductions and generally claims of extraterrestrial visits are more often than not dismissed by much of the scientific community. Still, they are part of the paranormal events surrounding UFO sightings that warrant consideration.

Conclusions

The focus of this volume, *Out of This World*, is on UFOs, which have components of the paranormal, metaphysics, ontology, ufology (obviously), and religion. This is a complex milieu of abstract terms, albeit a controversial topic that explains in part its widespread human appeal.

After all, most humans legitimately want to know whether God—if they believe in a supreme being—made creatures other than we earthlings, and if so, they seek to know whether those aliens are visiting planet Earth. However, before exploring this and other related challenging topics, we next explore the presence of UFOs throughout both secular (chapter 2) and religious (chapter 3) history.

2

NOT MUCH DIFFERENCE BETWEEN ANCIENT AND MODERN UFO SIGHTINGS

*But any viable theory must reckon with the extraordinary
persistence and consistency of the phenomena [UFO sightings]
discussed here [on Earth] over many centuries.*[1]
—DR. RICHARD STOTHERS, astronomer and planetary scientist
Goddard Institute for Space Studies, National Aeronautics
and Space Administration

This chapter demonstrates that ancient UFO sightings are remarkably similar to contemporary events. The details shared by UFO observers thousands of years ago, reflected in script, art, and myth, are virtually carbon copies of many twenty-first-century UFO reports. That tells us what we are observing today is as old as humankind; this should spark our continued interest and ought to intrigue the scientific community.

My intent here is to briefly illustrate some of the past work done on ancient sightings. I won't break new ground, but will summarize previous efforts to reinforce current interest in the topic and perhaps spark renewed investigations into the mysteries that have always challenged humanity.

13

Petroglyph allegedly depicting an ancient astronaut.[2]

Oldest Recorded UFO Sightings

Perhaps the oldest recorded UFO sighting took place in 1440 BC and was reported by the royal scribe of an Egyptian pharaoh. That account states:

> In the year 22, of the 3rd month of winter, sixth hour of the day…the scribes of the House of Life found it was a circle of fire that was coming in the sky…. It had no head; the breath of its mouth had a foul odor. Its body one rod long and one rod wide. It had no voice. Their hearts became confused through it; then they laid themselves on their bellies…. They went to the Pharaoh…to report it. His Majesty ordered…[an examination of] all which is written in the papyrus rolls of the House of Life. His Majesty was meditating upon what happened. Now after some days had passed, these things became more numerous in the sky than ever. They shone more in the sky than the brightness of the sun, and extended to the limits of the four supports of the heavens…. Powerful was the position of the fire circles. The army of the Pharaoh looked on with him in their midst. It

was after supper. Thereupon, these fire circles ascended higher in the sky towards the south…. The Pharaoh caused incense to be brought to make peace on the hearth…. And what happened was ordered by the Pharaoh to be written in the annals of the House of Life…so that it be remembered for ever.[3]

This quotation is attributed to the Tulli Papyrus, named after Alberto Tulli, the then director of the Egyptian section of the Vatican Museum. Evidently, during his visit to Cairo, Egypt, in 1933, Mr. Tulli found a papyrus in an antique shop, but couldn't afford to buy it. He did make a copy of the text, which was then translated (above).[4]

The pharaoh in 1440 BC, the approximate date of the Tulli Papyrus, was Thutmose III, who reigned from 1504 BC to 1450 BC. The translation of the hieroglyphic record reveals that, around the year 1482 BC, Thutmose III first saw the fiery circles (disks) or UFOs mentioned above. In fact, Zecharia Sitchin, author of *The Stairway to Heaven*, speculated that at the time of Thutmose III, the pharaoh was also taken aboard an alien spacecraft (fiery circles).[5]

Views like that expressed by Mr. Sitchin, though, are understandably suspect. After all, his wild speculation that Thutmose III actually boarded an alien spacecraft is based on his interpretation of hieroglyphics written thousands of years ago and from an ancient cultural perspective explaining that most everything in society had a mystical aspect, including the popular view that the pharaoh was himself a god.

There is also reason to believe the Tulli Papyrus, as well as Sitchin's bizarre interpretation, are both fraudulent. In fact, the reliability of the document was questioned by Dr. Edward U. Condon (1902–1974), a former University of Colorado physicist who, later in his life, reported on UFOs for the US Congress. Dr. Condon wrote in his book, *Scientific Study of Unidentified Flying Objects*:

The Tulli papyrus and Ezekiel's wheel of fire [Ezekiel 1] show so many exact similarities of style, language and detail that one wonders whether, despite its alleged time priority, the "Tulli papyrus" may be taken from the King James version of the Book of Ezekiel. Or, if the "Tulli papyrus" is genuine, and its translation by Prince [Boris] de Rachewiltz is accurate, then the Book of Ezekiel may have been plagiarized from the Annals of Thutmose III.[6]

Evidently, Dr. Condon communicated with the Vatican Museum and then director of the Egyptian section of the Vatican Museum, Dr. Gianfranco Nolli, who wrote back to Dr. Condon:

> Professor Tulli had left all his belongings to a brother of his who was a priest in the Lateran Palace [the Catholic cathedral church in the city of Rome, which serves as the seat of the bishop of Rome, the pope]. Presumably the famous papyrus went to this priest. Unfortunately, that priest died also in the meantime and his belongings were dispersed among heirs, who may have disposed of the papyrus as something of little value.

Further, according to Condon, Dr. Nolli "intimated that Professor Tulli was only an amateur 'Egyptologist' and the Prince de Rachelwitz is no expert either. He suspects that Tulli was taken in and that the papyus is a fake." Prince de Rachewiltz reportedly studied Egyptology at the Pontifical Biblical Institute in Rome and later at Cairo University.[7]

Even though the Tulli papyrus is likely "fake," a growing cadre of contemporary historians and scientists continue to seriously study the topic of UFO sightings from ancient Egypt and come away from that experience still unable to eliminate the possibility that extraterrestrials have in fact visited Earth across the span of human history.

A Scientific View of Ancient Sightings

Richard Stothers (1939–2011) was an astronomer and planetary scientist with the Goddard Institute for Space Studies, a laboratory in the Earth Sciences Division of the National Aeronautics and Space Administration's (NASA's) Goddard Space Flight Center. He held a PhD from Harvard University and contributed to the modern understanding of the origin and evolution of stars. Later in his career, while working for NASA, Dr. Stothers examined ancient reports of UFOs and wrote an article, "Unidentified Flying Objects in Classical Antiquity," which was published in the peer-reviewed *Classical Journal*.[8]

"A combined historical and scientific approach is applied to ancient reports of what might today be called unidentified flying objects (UFOs)," wrote Dr. Stothers in his research article. He continued:

> Many conventionally explicable phenomena can be weeded out, leaving a small residue of puzzling reports. These fall neatly into the same categories as modern UFO reports, suggesting that the UFO phenomenon, whatever it may be due to, has not changed much over two millennia.[9]

Stothers states that most ancient UFO reports can be explained using modern science, however. Specifically, he wrote:

> There nonetheless remains a small residue of puzzling accounts, and regardless of what interpretation one places on them, these constitute a phenomenon that spans centuries of time and widely different cultures.[10]

Most UFO Reports Are "Explainable"

Dr. Stothers begins his survey of ancient sightings by explaining, "Today we can filter out the most obvious cases of conventional phenomena, in spite of the archaic terminology used to describe them." Specifically," he states "preliminary screening is relatively easy," because most of the sightings were solar and lunar eclipses or comets and new stars (nova). Further, he points out that aurorae ("natural light display that occurs in the sky, primarily at high latitudes or even on other planet")[11] were often determined by the ancient Greeks and Romans to be "chasms," "sky fire," and "night suns."[12]

There were also sightings associated with large volcanic eruptions, which Stothers explained made the sun appear dim, red, and sometimes haloed—often for months at a time. There were also examples of aerosol fallout from polar ice cores, which created an optical phenomenon that may have created ancient sightings.[13]

"For presentation purposes," Dr. Stothers explained, "I group the ancient reports [of UFO sightings] in four categories as defined by Hynek for modern UFO sightings." That presentation approach is attributed to Josef Allen Hynek (1910–1986), who once managed the US Air Force's efforts and claimed that military service underplayed the importance of UFOs. Dr. Hynek, an astrophysicist and ufologist, created the UFO classification system used by Stothers in this study, which was published in the *Classical Journal*. However, Stothers modified the Hynek criteria to adjust for the technologies available in ancient times. Therefore, he used four categories to identify UFOs, which he labeled "Distant Encounters," and then three other groupings, "Close Encounters of the First, Second and Third Kinds," which differed according to proximity, material remains, and whether the report indicated the presence of "occupants."[14]

To help the reader, Stothers profiled modern UFO sightings, believing that explanation would be helpful to better understand the categorization of the ancient record. Specifically, he wrote:

UFOs appear as disks or other extended objects, including vertical cylinders enveloped in "clouds" and associated with smaller disks. Depending on the viewing angles, their intrinsic shapes might be similar or even identical: a disk seen face-on looks circular, although edge-on it looks elliptical or oblong. Colors in the daytime are usually described as silvery or gray, and in the night as resembling red or multicolored lights. Estimated dimensions range from about one meter to hundreds of meters, with the scatter being probably intrinsic. UFOs are usually said to be noiseless. They are seen in the air or on the ground, hovering or stationary, or moving across the sky in a continuous fashion, even if erratically. Sometimes they suddenly appear or vanish.[15]

Distant Encounters

This category of UFO sightings addresses two subgroups: those described in military language, such as "flying armaments," and another in meteorological, astronomical language, such as "fiery globes."

Most UFO reports of the "flying armaments" subcategory are attributed to Roman historian Livy's prodigy lists, which are dated 123 BC and perhaps derived from the *Annales Maximi*, which were published by the Pontifex Maximus of Rome. Stothers argues that these reports tend to be regarded "as trustworthy and accurate." He cites three examples of this group taken from the Second Punic War (218–201 BC), and although the "observers are unknown," they "were probably many in number."[16]

Flying Armaments

- "At Rome in the winter of 218 BC 'a spectacle of ships (*navium* [Latin]) gleamed in the sky.'"
- "In 217 BC 'at Arpi round shields (*parmas*) were seen in the sky.'" Stothers explained that a "parma" was a small round shield made partly or wholly of iron, bronze, or another metal. He indicates the Roman prodigy lists describe these sightings as "double suns" or "triple suns."
- "In 212 BC 'at Reate a huge stone (*saxum*) was seen flying about.'" Stothers states that description means the object was a stony gray color and allegedly moved irregularly, which is likely why Livy described it as a bird or some kind of airborne debris.

Not all such sightings of flying armaments are attributed to Rome's Livy. For example, the most famous "sky army" was reported over Judea (present-day southern Israel) in the spring of AD 65 by historian Flavius Josephus (AD 37–100), a Roman-Jewish historian born in Jerusalem of priestly descent.[17] He wrote:

On the 21st of the month Artemisium, there appeared a miraculous phenomenon, passing belief. Indeed, what I am about to relate would, I imagine, have been deemed a fable, were it not for the narratives of eyewitnesses and the subsequent calamities which deserved to be so signalized. For, before sunset throughout all parts of the country [Judea], chariots were seen in the air and armed battalions hurtling through the clouds and encompassing the cities.

Josephus relied on eyewitness accounts to describe the event. Stothers writes, "The phenomenon does not seem to have been an aurora, cloud patterns or meteors, but does resemble the 'aerial fighting' of modern UFOs."[18]

Fiery Globes

The second subgroup of the "Distant Encounters" category is labeled "Fiery Globes." Stothers indicates the first cluster of these sightings happened during the Second Punic War.[19]

- "In 217 BC 'at Capena two moons rose in the daytime… and at Capua a kind of moon fell during a rainstorm." Stothers suggests the Capuan "moon" was likely evidence of "ball lightning." However, the "two moons" at Capena was possibly a "bolide [a meteor that exploded in the atmosphere] seen together with the real moon in the daytime." ["Ball lightning is a rare and unexplained phenomenon described as luminescent, spherical objects that vary from pea-sized to several meters in diameter."][20]

- "Seneca gives two examples from the eastern Mediterranean. In 168 BC, when L. Aemilius Paulus was waging war against King Perseus of Macedon, 'a ball...was the form of a fire that appeared, as large as the moon.' This could have been a bolide."

- Livy reports on two 91 BC sightings over central Italy. One over Rome took place "about sunrise a ball of fire shone forth from the northern region with a loud noise in the sky." Stothers indicates the sonic boom means it was probably a bolide.

- Historian Pliny reported on a nighttime incident: "A spark was seen to fall from a star and to grow as it approached the earth; after it had become as the moon, light was diffused all around as if on a cloudy day; then, retreating to the sky, the object changed into a torch." Stothers concludes, "Since no landing of the object was reported, it is simplest and most natural to interpret the event as the overhead passage of a bolide leaving a luminous train."

- Another "Fiery Globe" incident was reported AD 334 by a Byzantine annalist, Theophanes Confessor. He wrote: "At Antioch, in the daytime, a star was seen toward the eastern part of the sky, emitting smoke copiously as if from a furnace, from the third hour to the fifth hour."

Close Encounters of the First Kind

This category of UFOs represents those that include an "observation at close range" but fail "to interact with the observer" and do not "leave a physical trace."[21]

- In 74 BC, Roman commander L. Licinius Lucullus was preparing to wage battle with King Mithridates VI of

Pontus. Historian Plutarch wrote: "But presently...with no apparent change of weather, but all on a sudden, the sky burst asunder, and a huge, flame-like body was seen to fall between the two armies. In shape, it was most like a wine-jar (*pithdi*), and in color, like molten silver. Both sides were astonished at the sight, and separated. This marvel, as they say, occurred in Phrygia, at a place called Otryae." Stothers argues that this was not a meteorite and likely not a bolide. Therefore, he says, this incident is much like modern, classic UFO encounters.

- An AD 285 incident is recorded in the biography of St. Anthony, written by Athanasius, the bishop of Alexandria. The sighting took place near Fayum in the Egyptian desert. "Anthony saw on the desert floor a large silver disk that suddenly vanished like smoke." Stothers suggests the alleged sighting may have been a "desert mirage."

Close Encounters of the Second Kind

This category of sightings leaves a physical trace. There are numerous ancient-literature examples of UFO-like objects that leave either an imprint on the ground or a material residue. Most often the accounts of these sightings report a whitish gossamer substance dubbed "angel hair," glassy fibers left behind after a UFO leaves the ground.

- It's possible the Roman historian Cassius Dio picked up a sample of "angel hair" in AD 196. He wrote:

A fine rain resembling silver descended from a clear sky upon the forum of Augustus. I did not, it is true, see it as it was falling, but noticed it after it had fallen, and by means of it I plated some bronze coins with silver; they retained the same appearance for three days, but by the fourth day all the substance rubbed on them had disappeared.[22]

Close Encounters of the Third Kind

This category earns more attention than the others because it is associated with an occupant, "usually described as human or humanoid."[23]

- Livy wrote that, in 214 BC, "at Hadria an altar was seen in the sky; around it was forms of men dressed in shining white." Stothers indicates that four years earlier than this sighting, "in the district of Amiterum, in many places, forms of men dressed in shining white were seen at a distance; they did not approach anyone." Stothers indicates this incident is a classic UFO sighting that includes occupants and is similar to the instance of "a hovering, overhead craft as seen by Father Gill [a missionary] and his companions in 1959 off Papua New Guinea."

Dr. Stothers concludes that although many of the ancient UFO reports are explainable, there remains a small set that appears credible, yet inexplicable. From these reports, he summarizes a description of the UFO objects described from ancient history:

- Shape: discoidal or spheroidal
- Color: silvery, golden, or red
- Texture: metallic or, occasionally, glowing or cloudy
- Size: a meter to well over a meter
- Sound: usually none reported
- Type of motion: hovering, erratic, or smooth flight, with a rapid disappearance
- Occupants: covered in shiny, white clothing
- Time: daytime
- Location: rural areas

Stothers concludes that ancient scientific thinkers usually labeled these phenomena as "stars, clouds, atmospheric fires, light reflections

23

or moving material bodies." Even so, he writes, "Any viable theory must reckon with the extraordinary persistence and consistency of the phenomena discussed here over many centuries."[24]

Japan Investigated UFOs in 1235

Mack Maloney writes in *UFOs in Wartime: What They Didn't Want You to Know*, that the first known official investigation of UFOs was carried out in Japan in 1235:

> One night, a high officer named General Yoritsume and his army were settling down in their camp when they spotted mysterious lights in the sky. The general and his troops watched in astonishment as these lights performed amazing aerobatic movements, such as circling endlessly and flying in loops. Baffled by the bizarre aerial display, General Yoritsume ordered a scientific investigation of what he had just witnessed.... The explanation Yoritsume's scientists gave the general oozed with comfort and calm. "The whole thing is completely natural," Yoritsume was told about the mystery lights. "It is only the wind making the stars sway."[25]

UFOs and Ancient Art

Our ancient ancestors also recorded on cave walls and in their art astronomical or environmental phenomena. Some of those depictions remain inexplicable and fit the classic UFO report of the modern age.

The Wandjinas, the Australian aboriginal people, provide some interesting indictors of UFO sightings. Wanjina lands are found in the Kimberley region of northwestern Australia.

The Wandjinas are custodians of some of the most interesting figurative art paintings on rock in the world, which depict "people" with "white faces, devoid of a mouth, large black eyes, and a head surrounded by a halo or some type of helmet."[26]

These ancient paintings beg numerous interpretations. One view is they represent ancient astronauts or extraterrestrial beings who "visited earth tens of thousands of years ago and had direct contact with the inhabitants."[27] Of course, these paintings raise interesting questions: Why were dark-skinned people like the Wandjinas painting images of white-skinned beings? Why were the images painted without mouths and with disproportionate faces and noses?

Folklore indicates the Wandjina were really "sky-beings" or "spirits from the clouds" who came from a distant place to create the Earth and all its inhabitants. However, these "sky-beings" realized the enormity of the task and returned home.[28]

Much later, in AD 1538, what appears to be UFOs was woven into a tapestry known as *Summer's Triumph*. The tapestry depicts the ascension of a ruler to power and includes multiple objects in the sky that appear to be classic UFO-shaped craft. That tapestry is held today at the Bavarian National Museum in Munich, Germany.[29]

The top of the tapestry includes a number of "hat-shaped" flying objects in black and appear unrelated to any religious depiction of the time. However, it is possible the people of that era in the Flemish region of Belgium, the origin of the tapestry, associated flying saucers with divinity, possibly meaning they had seen such objects in the sky previously, which they associated with "godly phenomena."[30]

There are also medieval tapestries in France that include UFO-like craft "flitting" across the sky in the background. Those tapestries are found in the town of Beaune, which was constructed about AD 1120—1149. These tapestries date to the fifteenth century and depict the significant moments in the life of Mary, the mother of Jesus.[31]

UFOs in Ancient Mythology

Lastly, numerous ancient myths and legends speak of "sky gods," which might be what modern people call "spaceships." These reports come from many cultures across the world and tend to reflect current descriptions of UFOs as outlined by Stothers above.

The Egyptians, much like the initial report in this chapter, documented UFOs in their hieroglyphs, as did Central American civilizations such as the Quimbaya or Tolima.

Evidently, the Quimbaya or Tolima artifacts, dated to between AD 300 and AD 1000, are gold figurines found in what is present-day Colombia that may represent beings like ancient astronauts. Those figurines appear to depict ancient flying machines, "complete with aerodynamic features, stabilizers and fuselage."[32]

Of course, mythology is close to religion, the topic of the next chapter.

Conclusion

This chapter addressed the incidents of UFOs in ancient history. Most of those ancient reports can likely be dismissed because of our improved understanding of our world and the physical sciences. However, there remain many reports that defy even modern interpretation. They are indeed inexplicable for now, and, like some modern UFO sightings, they challenge us to learn more.

3

ANCIENT RELIGIONS AND UFOS

*There may be intelligent life on other planets—but if so,
the Bible doesn't mention it. If there is, it is because God
put them there (just as He put us here), and their purpose
is to glorify and serve God (just as ours is).*[1]

—WILLIAM "BILLY" GRAHAM (1918–2018),
American evangelist and Southern Baptist minister

This chapter considers the attention ancient religions paid to paranormal events. Of the world's 4,200-plus faith groups/religions,
paranormal phenomena like UFOs are addressed by many religions
either directly or indirectly, such as by the Hindu faith, which is very
specific about UFOs in that religion's ancient scriptures.

The Vedas, the oldest of the Hindu sacred writings, written in early
Sanskrit ("an ancient Indo-Aryan language that is the classical language of India and of Hinduism"),[2] contains guidance for the priests
of the Vedic religion. In that text, the term *vimana* is used, which is
translated "flying celestial vehicle."

The text with this term states:

When morning dawned, Rama, taking the Celestial Car Puspaka had sent to him by Vivpishand, stood ready to depart.
Self-propelled was that car. It was large and finely painted. It
had two stories and many chambers with windows, and was
draped with flags and banners. It gave forth a melodious sound
as it coursed along its airy way." (Ramayana).[3]

In another text, a *vimana* is described as:

...the Puspaka Car, that resembles the sun and belongs to my brother, was brought by the powerful Ravan; that aerial and excellent car, going everywhere at will, is ready for thee. That car, resembling a bright cloud in the sky, is in the city of Lanka." (Ramayana)[4]

Another Vedic script speaks of the liberation of a king named Dhruva who was picked up by a *vimana*, presumably a UFO, and taken on a journey. It states:

While Dhruva Maharaja was passing through space, he saw, in succession, all the planets of the solar system, and on the path he saw all the demigods in their vimanas showering flowers upon him like rain." (*Bhagavata Purana*)[5]

The prophet Ezekiel saw brightly lit extraterrestrials, wheels within wheels, and a carriage/chariot-like object (Ezekiel 1:4–5).[6]

Some bizarre accounts of UFOs across the world's religious communities explain what today we acknowledge is hard to discern, or others, like Dr. Stothers cited in the previous chapter, are quickly dismissed as weather events or solar eclipses and the like.

For the purposes of this chapter going forward, however, I will focus on Judeo-Christian Scripture (biblical) references regarding paranormal mysteries, especially in ancient times. I do this primarily because the vast majority of the readers of this book are familiar with biblical passages, especially some of the most popular accounts that might be labeled as associated with UFOs.

Therefore, we begin with Jewish views of UFOs based on their interpretation of the biblical Scripture and other Jewish literature. A Christian view will then follow as we examine selected biblical passages that appear to speak, though vaguely, of UFO-like craft and the possibly of extraterrestrial aliens.

Jewish View of UFOs/ETs in the Scriptures

The Holy Land (Israel) is no stranger to UFOs, and neither are the Jews. After all, the cornerstone of Jewish liturgy is found in Psalms 19:1 (NIV): "The heavens declare the glory of God; the skies proclaim the work of his hands." Some scholars understand this to mean that earthlings are not alone in the universe.

Noted Jewish Rabbi Benjamin Blech, an Orthodox rabbi and professor of Talmud (the central text of Rabbinic Judaism) at Yeshiva University in New York City, wrote:

> What is fascinating...is that a significant body of opinion in traditional sources not only validates the possibility for alien life on other planets but actually finds biblical and Midrashic [expansive Jewish biblical exegesis used to interpret the Talmud] confirmation for this view, even as it suggests that belief in an all-powerful God forbids placing any limitations on the extent of his creative powers.

Rabbi Blech's view is that we should not dismiss the possibility that our omnipotent God could have created other worlds and their creatures.[7]

David Weintraub, a professor of astronomy at Vanderbilt University in Nashville, Tennessee, who was introduced in the previous chapter and wrote the book *Religions and Extraterrestrial Life: How Will We Deal with It?*, wrote that Jewish theology requires a belief in extraterrestrials, because there are no limits to our omnipotent Creator. In his book, he agreed with Rabbi Blech that "for Jews to say that no life beyond the Earth could possibly exist would be unacceptable, as such an idea would appear to place shackles on God's creative power. The universe belongs to God and God can do what God wishes to do with the universe," a view most Christians would embrace as well.[8]

The account in Genesis (*Bereishis,* the first book of the Torah) speaks of beings who intermingle with humans, including "*B'ney Elohim* [sons of God]" and "Nephilim." Some Jewish scholars understand the "Nephilim" as the "fallen," and understand that to mean "fallen from the sky." One interpretation is these are nonhumans (aliens) who either came from another planet or are fallen angels, a topic we will explore in more detail later in this book.[9]

The eighteenth-century rabbi Pinchas Eliyahu Horowitz claimed there is Talmudic support for the view for life from another planet in the book of Judges 5:23 (NIV):

> "Curse Meroz," said the angel of the Lord. "Curse its people bitterly, because they did not come to help the Lord, to help the Lord against the mighty."

For Rabbi Horowitz, Meroz was one of many other worlds that God created.[10]

Twentieth-century Jewish scholar Rabbi Joseph B. Soloveitchik (1903–1993) expressed openness to the possibility of life on Mars and beyond. "It is possible that Hashem [the Hebrew term for God] created other life forms on other planets," wrote the American Orthodox rabbi, Talmudist, and modern Jewish philosopher. He continued:

It is no problem to Yahadus [a Hebrew curriculum]. The reason man likes to think he is the only created being in the entire universe is because of his egotistical nature. Even the concept of *am ha'nivchar*, [a] chosen nation, may only be relative to our world, our small section of the universe. The Torah is written from the viewpoint of our sun, moon, and stars. It would not detract from our being the *am ha'nivchar* in a distant galaxy.[11]

Rabbi Aryeh Moshe Eliyahu Kaplan (1934–1983) was an American Orthodox rabbi, translator of the Living Torah edition, a prolific writer, and professor of physics. He believed extraterrestrial life exists and claimed it was discussed in the Zohar, a foundational work in the literature of Jewish mystical thought known as Kabbalah. Kaplan wrote:

The Midrash [ancient commentary of Hebrew Scriptures] teaches us that there are seven earths. Although the Ibn Ezra [commentary] tries to argue that these [seven earths] refer to the seven continents, the Zohar clearly states that the seven are separated by a firmament and are inhabited. Although they are not inhabited by man, they are the domain of intelligent creatures.[12]

Certainly, these views reflect the opinion of a significant and respected cohort of Jewish scholars who embrace the possibility that God created living beings elsewhere in this massive universe.

For the reader interested in further understanding Jewish views about our role in the universe, especially about extraterrestrials, consider reading Rabbi Professor Dr. Norman Lamm's essays, "Man's Position in the Universe" and "The Religious Implications of Extraterrestrial Life," available in the book *Faith and Doubt: Studies in Traditional Jewish Thought*.

Christian View of Biblical References to UFOs and ETs

There is evidence that some notable early Christians were quite closed to the possibility that people existed on the other side of planet Earth, much less on other planets and galaxies. These skeptics called these hypothetical life forms on the opposite side of the Earth "antipodes."

In the third century AD, Roman Emperor Constantine's adviser, Lucius Caecilius Lactanctius (AD 250–324), a Christian author who wrote an apologetic treatise to establish the reasonableness and truth of Christianity to pagan critics, was among those skeptics of "antipodes." He wrote, "How is it with those who imagine that there are antipodes opposite to our footsteps?" Even St. Augustine of Hippo (AD 354–430), perhaps the most significant early Christian thinker after the Apostle Paul, had little interest in beings not within his line of sight.

Specifically, St. Augustine wrote:

As to the fable that there are antipodes, that is to say, men on the opposite side of the earth, where the sun rises when it sets on us, men who walk with their feet opposite ours, there is no reason for believing it. Those who affirm it do not claim to possess any actual information.... For Scripture, which confirms the truth of its historical statements by the accomplishment of its prophecies, teaches not falsehood; and it is too absurd to say that some men might have set sail from this side and, traversing the immense expanse of ocean, have propagated there a race of human beings descended from that one first man.[13]

Put such naivety aside to consider that the Bible includes at least one hundred passages depicting incidents that can be interpreted as UFOs or that suggest non-Earth beings or aliens. A few of those passages are highlighted below to illustrate the point, but not to necessarily agree with the proposition that alien beings exist.

Does "Us" mean God has alien help? Genesis 1:26–28 (NIV) speaks in terms of "Us" as planning to create human beings:

> Then God said, Let Us make mankind in our image, in our likeness, so that they may rule over the fish in the sea and the birds in the sky, over the livestock and all the wild animals, and over all the creatures that move along the ground.

Some people will infer from the use of the word "Us" that God is speaking of Himself with aliens or angels. Yet, many Bible scholars, such as the respected Matthew Henry (1662–1714), known for his six-volume biblical commentary *Exposition of the Old and New Testaments*, indicate this is a reference to the Trinity—Father, Son, and Holy Spirit—rather than alien beings.

Alternatively, Dr. David Schrock of the Occoquan Bible Church in Woodbridge, Virginia, addressed the "Us" in a sermon titled, "Beholding the Glory of God." He affirmed there is one Creator, *Elohim*, in the Hebrew (see Genesis 1:1), and the "Us" in Genesis 1:26 is a reference to this one God who created all things by His Spirit (Genesis 1:2) and His Word (Genesis 1:3).[14] In the fullness of time, the Apostle John made the connection between the one God and His three persons.[15] He wrote:

> In the beginning was the Word, and the Word was with God, and the Word was God. He was with God in the beginning. Through him all things were made; without him nothing was made that has been made. In him was life, and that life was the light of all mankind. (John 1:1–3, NIV)[16]

With the light of John's Gospel, which reveals God as Father, Son, and Spirit, we can return to Genesis 1 and the statement, "Let Us make mankind in our image." God the Father is the architect of creation;

God the Son is the Word by which the Father spoke the universe into existence; and God the Spirit is the giver of life who brings into being all the Father spoke by way of the Son. Therefore, the "Us" can be understood as God the Creator, who is Father, Son, and Spirit.[17]

Are Job's "morning stars" aliens? Job 38:7 (NKJV) states, "When the morning stars sang together, and all the sons of God shouted for joy." Are Job's "morning stars" and "sons of God" extraterrestrials, or, as *Ellicott's Bible Commentary* suggests:

> The context seems to suggest that by the stars are meant the angels entrusted with their guardianship, from whence Milton has borrowed his conceptions.[18]

Evidently, the author of Ellicott's commentary believes seventeenth-century British poet John Milton borrowed the concept of time and the role of angels from this verse, which he uses in his best-known work, *Paradise Lost*. Specifically, "rebel angels in Paradise Lost rise from the lake of fire and light on the fiery land of hell…an impressive myth created mainly out of Biblical accounts in the Old Testament [Job 38:7]," according to Ellicott.[19]

Are the Nephilim of Genesis 6:4 and Numbers 13:33 aliens? There are at least four theories from Christian scholars about the Nephilim mentioned in Genesis 6:4 and Numbers 13:22.

1. Fallen angels (or perhaps aliens) had relations with the "daughters of men," resulting in part-supernatural beings— Nephilim. One passage used to defend this view is Jude 1:6–7 (NIV), which speaks of "angels who did not keep their proper positions but abandoned their proper dwelling… gave themselves up to sexual immorality and perversion."
2. Demons or fallen angels possessed men and had relations with the "daughters of men," resulting in the Nephilim.
3. The Sethite view is that the Nephilim came from the

lineage of Seth who disobeyed God and married women from the wicked line of Cain. Evidently, those women "followed other gods and rejected full allegiance to God. The offspring [Nephilim], as a result, 'fell away' and turned to the system of the world."[20]

4. The "sons of God" were simply fallen men who married ungodly women. The interpretation here is that the term "Nephilim," from the Hebrew word *naphal,* means "to fall." Simply, these men were among the pre-Flood offspring of the "fallen men."[21]

I will say much more in chapter 16 of this book about the possible role played by the potential descendants of the Nephilim in the prophetic end times.

Was Ezekiel swept away by an alien spacecraft? Much speculation surrounds the account of that prophet's vision, which fuels the view that alien astronauts visited Earth in antiquity. In Ezekiel 1 we learn that the prophet saw brightly lit extraterrestrials, wheels within wheels, and a carriage/chariot-like object. The text states:

And I looked, and, behold, a whirlwind came out of the north, a great cloud, and a fire infolding itself, and a brightness was about it, and out of the midst thereof as the colour of amber, out of the midst of the fire. Also, out of the midst thereof came the likeness of four living creatures. (Ezekiel 1:4–5, KJV).

Moshe Greenberg (1928–2010), a former American rabbi, Bible scholar, and professor at the Hebrew University of Jerusalem, wrote in his commentary on the subject:

Virtually every component of Ezekiel's vision can thus be derived from Israelite tradition supplemented by neighboring iconography—none of the above cited elements of which need have been outside the range of the ordinary Israelite.

Therefore, if Greenberg is correct, then the Israelites in exile with Ezekiel in Babylon, present-day Iraq, at the time would have easily understood the vision. Author Tim Callahan writes in his article, "Ezekiel's Spaceships," that it's "modern readers' unfamiliarity with the iconography of the ancient Near East, that makes it possible for us today to mistake angels for spaceships."[22]

Ezekiel clarified his vision when he concluded that what he saw was God's glory, not aliens:

> As the appearance of the bow that is in the cloud in the day of rain, so was the appearance of the brightness round about. This was the appearance of the likeness of the glory of the Lord. And when I saw it, I fell upon my face, and I heard a voice of one that spake. (Ezekiel 1:28, KJV)

Did Elijah ride a spaceship into heaven? In 2 Kings 2, we read about Elijah being taken to heaven in a celestial vehicle, as witnessed by his son Elisha:

> And it came to pass, as they still went on, and talked, that, behold, there appeared a chariot of fire, and horses of fire, and parted them both asunder; and Elijah went up by a whirlwind into heaven. (2 Kings 2:11, KJV)

Once again, like in the case of Ezekiel, was Elijah's disappearance attributed to an alien spacecraft, or was it God's way of expediting the prophet's trip to heaven?

The Bible doesn't state whether or not aliens exist; it is silent on the matter. However, it does leave open the possibility. After all, in Matthew 19:26 (KJV), Jesus declared, "With men this is impossible; but with God all things are possible." This being said, it appears that here Jesus was explaining to His disciples that salvation is possible even for the rich, a cohort considered unworthy of salvation in that day. Yet nothing is impossible for an omnipotent God, a view most Christian and Jewish theologians will embrace.

Although the Scriptures don't eliminate the possibility of extraterrestrial aliens and spacecraft, Christian art, especially from both the Middle Ages and the Reformation period, confuse the issue with troubling displays of iconic biblical stories accompanied by what appear to be aliens and their spacecraft.

Ancient Christian Art and UFOs

Historic Christian art clearly shows UFOs nested in divine settings. One analysis examines classic pieces of artwork that suggest the existence of UFOs.[23]

In 1486, Italian artist Carlo Crivelli painted *The Annunciation with Saint Emidius,* which depicts the Virgin Mary shortly before she was told she would give birth to Jesus the Christ. The halo displayed above Mary's head in the painting is projected from a saucer-like object (perhaps a UFO) in the sky, which some argue is consistent with modern-day alien abductions. The painting has been housed in the National Gallery in London since 1864.[24]

The painting *The Crucifixion of Christ,* which hangs above the altar of the Visoki Decani Monastery near Dečan, Kosovo, shows Jesus on the cross with two airborne, spacecraft-like figures at both upper corners of the painting. The craft appear to be piloted by human-like beings outfitted in space suits.[25]

The 1710 painting *The Baptism of Christ* by Dutch artist Aert de Gelde shows a saucer-shaped object shining four beams of light upon the baptismal scene. Speculation is that Gelde had "secret knowledge" of the event thanks to his access to the Vatican's art archives. The painting hangs in the Fitzwilliam Museum in Cambridge, United Kingdom.[26]

A fifteenth-century painting, *The Madonna with Saint Giovannino,* is attributed to artist Jacopo del Sellaio or Sebastiano Mainadri. It shows a flying craft above the left shoulder of the Madonna. Rays of light call attention to the object, and in fact it appears that the Madonna is shielding the children from it. The work currently hangs in the Palazzo Vecchio in Venice, Italy, and is part of the collection known as the Loeser Bequest.[27]

The fresco *The Crucifixion of Christ*, found at the Svetishoveli Cathedral in Mtskheta, Republic of Georgia, shows two flying objects on either side of Christ. Each object includes a face, as if someone is piloting the craft. This interpretation makes sense, because it is consistent with ancient astronaut theories that claim Jesus was an alien-human hybrid.[28]

Conclusion

The purpose of this chapter is to summarize some of the ancient religious material used to advance the view that aliens played a role in both secular and especially religious/biblical history. The consistency of these reports over recorded history to the present justifies continued investigation even though most, but not all, of these events seem to be explained by modern science or theology.

SECTION TWO

UFO SIGHTINGS
SINCE WORLD WAR II

If aliens visit us, the outcome would be much as when Columbus landed in America, which didn't turn out well for the Native Americans. We only have to look at ourselves to see how intelligent life might develop into something we wouldn't want to meet.[1]
—STEPHEN HAWKING (1942–2018),
British theoretical physicist and cosmologist

This section scopes out the UFO challenge by carefully considering sightings since World War II, the beginning of the era of nuclear weapons, ballistic missiles, and space exploration. Although there are significant records of UFO sightings prior to the Second World War, as demonstrated in chapter 2, the numbers of such reports have increased significantly in recent years, and many entities, both official and civilian, have built impressive databases that capture those reports. Of course, numerous factors contribute to the surge of UFO sightings: civilian and military aviation, the Cold War accompanied by the nuclear threat and space exploration, pop culture's science-fiction craze, a general fascination with the supernatural (paranormal), changes in media technologies, and media's proclivity to hype and obfuscate the phenomenon.

In three chapters, this section considers the characteristics, classification, and collection of UFO sightings based on numerous significant databases. Subsequent sections address the legitimacy of these sightings, some of which require further investigation.

Chapter 4 summarizes the characteristics of some unexplained sightings across the various databases. Specifically, this chapter answers the following questions: What are the general locations and notable human activity in the vicinity of the sightings? Who reported the sightings and how many other people reported a similar account? What technology (such as radar and cameras), if any, was involved in the sightings? What characterized the reported object(s) in terms of ambient light at the time, the size and shape, color, and behavior?

Chapter 5 examines the number of unexplained sightings using the classification system attributed to Josef Allen Hynek, first addressed in chapter 2 of this volume. Further, this chapter calls out some of the hardest-to-understand UFO sightings, the truly inexplicable.

Chapter 6 summarizes the many efforts to account for UFO sightings, both by US and foreign governments, as well as by civilian-led efforts across the world.

4

SIGHTING THE UNIDENTIFIABLE

*"I think it's horrible that just because I'm from New Jersey, you asked
me about unidentified flying objects and Martians," said former
New Jersey Governor Chris Christie to laughter. "We're different,
but we're not that different," explained the 2024 Republican
presidential candidate. However, Christie acknowledged, "The job
of the President of the United States is to level with the American
people about everything [and that includes UFOs]."*[1]

—GOVERNOR CHRIS CHRISTIE,
Republican presidential debate, August 23, 2023

This chapter profiles the characteristics of UFO/UAP ("unidentified anomalous phenomena") sightings. Although the cause of
most sightings eventually is identified, we seldom see profiles of
the many that are beyond current science, the truly inexplicable.
Therefore, what follows is an attempt to answer key questions about
those enigmatic sightings by profiling what we think we know about
most sightings and then trying to parse whether anything is missing. Specifically, are trends and/or patterns present, such as common
locations, reliability of the reports, technology observed, physical
descriptions, and more?

Of course, we begin this effort by acknowledging that bringing new
information to the UFO issue is a high hurdle, given our record. After
all, multiple American presidents have long promised to be honest about
the government's knowledge of UFOs, what the current administration

officially labels UAPs. In fact, in August 2023, Pentagon spokesman Brigadier General Patrick Ryder (US Air Force) promised at a press briefing, "The [D]epartment [of Defense] is committed to transparency with the American people on AARO's work on UAPs."[3]

UFO sightings since World War II have skyrocketed, which corresponds with the era of nuclear weapons, ballistic missiles, and the space race.[2]

The Pentagon's All-domain Anomaly Resolution Office (AARO) officially announced on August 31, 2023, the launch of a new website that promises to provide the public with declassified information about UAPs. The spokesman indicated the site will serve as a "one-stop" shop for information, and AARO will regularly update its website with all recent UAP findings when new information is cleared for public release.[4]

The new site follows the release of more than 1,500 pages of UFO-related material in 2022 (addressed later in this chapter) about the Pentagon's now-defunct Advanced Aerospace Threat Identification Program (AATIP). That program, which ran from 2007 to 2012, became publicly known in 2017, after the resignation of former program director Luis Elizondo and the release of videos of several now-infamous UAPs moving in seemingly impossible ways.[5]

The Pentagon's new UAP effort, AARO, came into being quickly on the heels of members of Congress demanding details about alleged secret Pentagon programs that retrieve crashed UAP and then supposedly reverse engineer the crafts' technology. Those revelations became public thanks to UFO whistleblower David Grusch, who, in his July 26, 2023, testimony before a US House of Representatives oversight committee, asserted there was government secrecy around UAP incidents. He claimed at the hearing that he knows personnel injured while reverse engineering UAP technology and said the government "absolutely" has had UAP technology and "biologics" of "non-human origins" since the 1930s. However, he provided no evidence to back up that allegation, at least in that open hearing.[6]

Of course, the US government is seldom forthcoming about sensitive information, as indicated by the case of former AAITP director Luis Elizondo. After all, anyone who has ever served in a sensitive government position understands that much of its work, especially in the national security realm, is intentionally classified to keep it out of the public eye, purportedly to conceal what we know from our enemies. Therefore, what the government posts on its AARO website has been thoroughly vetted by government minders and likely has long been suspected by the public. As a result, the information offers little help toward understanding whether UAPs are a legitimate national security threat, much less verifies if the government does possess UFO technology and "biologics."

Don't Shy away from the Inexplicable

We must not go into this effort with our minds made up about UAPs. After all, the US government claims it is just now getting serious about the growing number of inexplicable UAP sightings, and with good reason. Further, our scientific community is getting serious about solving this mystery as well, or at least that's the claim.

Keep in mind that for the past sixty years NASA has sent spaceships to the moon, landed others on Mars, slipped by Jupiter, orbited Saturn, and investigated the former planet Pluto. What might be especially eye-opening for some readers is that our Voyager 1 and Voyager 2 space probes, launched in 1977 to study the outer solar system and interstellar space, carried golden records on their outer shells etched with coded sounds and pictures of planet Earth. Yes, these modern messages in a "bottle" were meant for unknown (alien) civilizations that might one day encounter these Earth-launched spaceships and be curious about their origin and the associated "alien" species that sent them deep into the universe.

So, yes, we are once again getting serious about UAPs. In July 2023, the US Congress decided it was time to take another close look at the growing plethora of unexplained craft spotted in Earth's atmosphere. A congressional committee hosted hearings to learn more about the most recently announced and inexplicable UAP sightings, objects described by military pilots as bobbing, weaving, hovering, diving, quickly changing direction, moving at deadly g-forces, and more.

One US military pilot reportedly said in a 2015 audio recording about his UAP sighting: "Look at that thing, dude!" Then he said, "Oh my gosh. There's a whole fleet of them. They're going against the wind! The wind's 120 knots [135 mph] west!"[7]

Granted, those objects could be the product of a yet-to-be-identified natural phenomenon, a new technology developed by the communist Chinese, or extraterrestrials that read the message on our Voyager spacecraft and decided to get a closer look at planet Earth and the aliens that inhabit this blue-looking planet in the orbit of the star Sol, the Greek name of our sun.

What's clear at this moment is that the US government and the scientific community want answers about these curious sightings. Congressman Andre Carson (D-IN) said at the July 2023 hearing, "UAPs are unexplained, it's true." However, he continued, "But they are real."[8]

That's why NASA is now involved in efforts to explain UAPs. In May 2023, the agency set up a sixteen-member expert panel to conduct a preliminary analysis of the UAP data and recommend a "road map" to contribute to NASA's study of the issue in the coming years.

NASA hired astrophysicist David Spergel, a former chair of the astrophysics department at Princeton University, to lead that effort.

"The current data collection efforts about UAPs are unsystematic and fragmented across various agencies, often using instruments uncalibrated for scientific data collection," Spergel said.[9]

To better understand and describe UAPs, NASA needs "better, targeted data collection, thorough data curation and robust analysis," he said. "Even then there's no guarantee that all sightings will be explained."

Spergel continued, "One of [the panel's] goals is to remove the stigma, because there is a need for high-quality data to address important questions about UAPs."[10]

Going forward, NASA acknowledged "there is no evidence [that] UAPs are extraterrestrial in origin." But the agency's officials continue to argue that the "absence of evidence…is not evidence of absence… [and they acknowledge] that anything is possible and that they will follow the findings, wherever they might point."[11]

"NASA believes that the tools of scientific discovery are powerful and apply here also," said associate NASA administrator Thomas Zurbuchen. "We have the tools and team who can help us improve our understanding of the unknown. That's the very definition of what science is. That's what we do."[12]

Profile of UFO/UAP Data

A number of studies and reports about UFO/UAP sightings provide useful information. These efforts are based either on the analysis of large databases (civilian and government), released government documents, and/or the experience of those involved in the issue over many years. They profile UFO/UAP sightings and, although they may not be conclusive, they are quite useful in our effort to better understand the phenomenon.

Data Analysis of UFO Sightings: Treemaps, Lollipop Charts, and Network Diagrams

One effort to analyze UFO-sighting data was made by Travis Greene, in "Data Analysis: Everything You've Ever Wanted to Know about UFO Sightings." Greene's study considers eighty thousand National UFO Reporting Center (NUFORC) sightings, employing a variety of tools, including treemaps, lollipop charts, and network diagrams to characterize UFOs and draw some conclusions.[13]

Words Used to Describe UFOs

At the time of the study, Mr. Greene was a PhD student in business analytics at the Institute of Service Science, National Tsing Hua University in Hsinchu City, Taiwan. He used treemaps to identify the most common words used to report on UFO sightings. "Treemapping" or "link analysis" is an information-visualization method for displaying hierarchical data using nested figures, usually rectangles. Below is a summary of Mr. Greene's findings.[14]

- The words most frequently used to describe the speed of a UFO include "incredible," "fast," "rapid," "steady," "amazing," "extreme," "tremendous," and "constant."
- The words most frequently used to describe the movement of a UFO include "erratic," "strange," "unusual," "rapid," "impossible," "odd," "fast," "abrupt," "zag," "steady," "odd," "jerky," and more.
- The words most frequently used to describe the shape of a UFO include "cigar," "triangular," "oval," "diamond," "disc," "saucer," "egg," "changed," "sphere," and more. Disk-related sightings were especially significant in the 1950s. Cigar shapes died out in the 1960s, while triangles were at the top

of the most frequently reported shapes in the late 1980s. Meanwhile, spheres and circles remained stable, reported in 10 percent of all sightings across the database.

- The words most frequently used to describe the color(s) and light intensity of a UFO include "bright," "white," "orange," "white," "red," "orange," "green," "blinking," "strange," "flashing," "moving," "yellow," "amber," and more.

Location of UFO Sightings in the United States

Mr. Greene used what's called a "lollipop" chart to create a visual of the states and cities most associated with UFO sightings. His chart includes fifty-one cities, with Seattle, Washington, reporting the most sightings and Atlanta, Georgia, reporting the least. Almost half (twenty-four) of the cities were in the Mountain West and thirteen, or a quarter, were on the West Coast: California, Oregon, and Washington. Seattle and Phoenix, Arizona, stand out among all fifty-one cities as having the most sightings in any given year, but their numbers began to decline in 2008. California, Washington, and Florida led all states in the aggregate number of UFO sightings, which also correlates with large populations.

An important, totally logical conclusion from the data is that the number of UFO reports is a function of the size of the city/state population. In other words, there are fewer sightings in unpopulated areas and more sightings where there are more people. The data demonstrates that conclusion, but that doesn't necessarily mean the distribution of all UFOs is necessarily larger in one area than another.

A more recent study (2022) of the phenomenon by MyVision. org, which consulted the National UFO Reporting Center Database, identified America's historical UFO hot spots. That study found a shift in UFO sightings in the past five years, with the top five states with the most observations being Idaho, New Hampshire, Montana, Vermont, and New Mexico. Today, according to that study, California now ranks forty-first in the number of sightings per one hundred thousand residents. The only explanation for the alleged shift among the states is "these alien visitors may be changing their flight paths," according to MyVision.org.[15]

Years of the UFO Sightings

The aggregate numbers of UFO sightings have radically increased in the United States over time. The data shows there were few sightings in 1940, and the number of sightings spiked in about 2012, with more than six thousand reports. That tally then declined to almost two thousand by 2015. The number of sightings began to steeply increase around 1995, and that trend mostly continued until 2012 before a precipitous decline.

Timing of UFO Sightings

Mr. Greene used what's called "lubridate," a method for using date-time data. He found the peak number of sightings takes place between June and July in almost every year and tends to occur around nine to eleven in the evening, with daytime sightings being very rare.

The distribution of sightings across the twenty-four-hour clock demonstrates that one-third occur between midnight and three in the afternoon, while the majority (nearly 50 percent) occur between eight in the evening and midnight. Also, Saturdays and Sundays are the most popular days for sightings; that's likely because most people have more leisure time on the weekends to gaze into the sky.

It's not surprising that the biggest annual spikes in UFO sightings occur around two holidays, the Fourth of July and New Year's Eve, which are both associated with fireworks in the night sky.

RAND Study: "Not The X-Files"

In February 2023, after a Chinese surveillance (spy) balloon sailed unimpeded across the United States to be downed by a US Air Force Sidewinder missile in the Atlantic Ocean, the Pentagon asked the RAND Corporation to study what the government knows about objects that fly over our estimated 5.3 million square miles of airspace and adjoining oceanic airspace. This interest was capped by growing public concern about such objects vis-à-vis the Chinese balloon episode. That RAND research was published in a 2023 report, titled "Where People Are Reporting Unidentified Aerial Phenomena (UAPs) across the United States."[16]

The RAND Corporation, whose name is derived from the phrase "research and development," is an American nonprofit global policy think tank, research institute, and public-sector consulting firm. It operates three federally funded research-and-development centers sponsored by the Department of Defense.[17]

The RAND team obtained data on reported UAP sightings from all fifty states and the NUFORC database, which includes common phenomena not reported. Specifically, the RAND team considered 101,151 UAP sightings from 1998 to 2022 as part of this project.[18]

RAND identified 751 statistically significant clusters of UAP sightings from that data. Those clusters varied from 1.2 UAP sightings up to more than 100 sightings per cluster. Some of the most persistent clusters were along the coasts of Washington and Oregon.[19]

The report states:

Our statistical models predicted two outcomes of interest: the total number of UAPs over time and the total number of UAPs in clusters that accounted for a significantly higher number of reports relative to the rest of the country. Both of these models found inconsistent results in the relationship between the nearest military installations and self-reports of UAP sightings. For example, there was a higher likelihood of UAP reports in areas that were within 60.1 km [kilometers] to 120 km of a Marine Corps installation, as compared with 30.1 km to 60 km, but there was some evidence that reports were less likely in areas within 30 km of these same installations.[20]

RAND also found:

...inconsistent results when we examined the association between proximity to weather stations with reported launches of government weather balloons and self-reports of UAP sightings. We also found negative associations in our models for UAP reports within 30 km of weather stations, within 60 km of civilian airports, and in more-densely populated areas. One possible explanation for this pattern of findings is that people located in more densely populated areas, near airports and near weather stations, are more aware of the types of objects that fly overhead and nearby and are therefore less apt to report aerial phenomena.[21]

"The most consistent—and statistically significant—finding from our models was for reports of UAP sightings in areas within 30 km of MOAs [military operations areas]," states RAND. The Federal Aviation Administration indicated that "MOAs are established to contain nonhazardous, military flight activities," which include air combat maneuvers, air intercepts, and low-altitude tactics. RAND concludes that some of the "self-reports of UAP sightings to NUFORC are authorized aircraft flying within MOAs."[22]

This result isn't conclusive, but indicates that UAP sightings appear to be more common near military installations than perhaps other areas.

Five UFO/UAP Traits That Defy Explanation

Luis Elizondo ran a team at the Pentagon investigating military-based UAP reports until his resignation in 2017. Therefore, his characterization of the common "traits" of inexplicable UAP, what Elizondo called the "five observables," is important to consider in this chapter.[23]

When Elizondo ran the program known as the Advanced Aerospace Threat Identification Program, or AATIP, he compiled a list of extraordinary, logic-defying capabilities associated with UAP. Those "five observables" are paraphrased from multiple sources below.

Anti-gravity propulsion: Aircraft require a propulsion system, which, according to our understanding of physics, means an engine and flight surfaces (such as the rudder and wing elevators) to operate through Earth's atmosphere. Even so, most UAPs demonstrate both unconventional shapes and flight characteristics—disk shape, with no wings or visible propulsion system. These characteristics defy our understanding of how these craft could overcome Earth's gravity and atmospheric conditions.

AATIP's conclusion was that these craft have an anti-gravity propulsion system, which explains their ability to travel at significant speeds and quickly disappear or hover silently. It would also explain how those ships would travel from distant galaxies, if that's indeed their origin. Of course, such an anti-gravity propulsion system is at present well beyond our existing technology.

Sudden and instantaneous acceleration: The 2004 UAP Nimitz UAP incident indicates the observed craft was tracked by radar operators as it dropped from the sky at more than thirty times the speed of sound. Also, Commander Fravor, a Nimitz-based fighter pilot who was introduced earlier in this book, described the craft's side-to-side movements as being like a ping-pong ball. Commander Fravor, a graduate of the Navy's Strike Fighter Tactics Instructor Program, more popularly known as Top Gun, and the commanding officer of the Black Aces squadron at the time, said he looked down and "saw a roiling shoal in the water and, hovering above it, a white oval object the resembled a large Tic Tac." The commander "estimated it to be about forty feet long, with no wings or other obvious flight surfaces and no visible means of propulsion," adding, "it appears to bounce around like a Ping-Pong ball."[24]

Evidently, according to advanced SPY-1 radar operators on the USS Princeton, which was part of the Nimitz carrier group at the time, the "Tic Tac" object accelerated from a hovering position to traveling sixty miles in a minute, or thirty-six hundred miles an hour, or Mach 3. By comparison, a Boeing F/A-18 Super Hornet fighter's maximum speed is twelve hundred miles an hour. Lieutenant Commander Jim Slaight, who participated in the Nimitz incident, said the UAP experienced "about 1350 Gs," which would turn any human body into paste.[25]

Hypersonic speeds without signatures: Human pilots and observers are aware that aircraft flying faster than the speed of sound leave vapor trails, or condensation trails, when flying at high altitudes, and they create sonic booms. Therefore, the lack of these signatures makes us presume these UAPs are operating in an atmosphere-free environment—a vacuum, further evidence they use an anti-gravity propulsion system.[26]

UAP hidden details: It's especially puzzling for us to understand why UAP sightings, even those caught on radar or by gun cameras, are never clear and detailed. It's as if they have a field—glow or haze or cloud—around them that prevents acquiring a clear image. That's why the majority of sightings describe UAPs as being either bright lights or bright glows, and they never include much detail.

Easily navigate across different mediums—space, air, water: Once again, such capabilities defy our understanding of the laws of physics. Evidently, according to UAP sightings, these craft move easily in and between different environments/mediums—space, Earth's atmosphere, and even our oceans. In the Nimitz incident, witnesses claim a UAP hovered above the Pacific Ocean just above a churning "disturbance" in the water below. A radar operator aboard the USS Princeton at the time, Gary Vorhees, confirmed that sonar in that area recorded a craft moving underwater at a speed of more than seventy knots, which is twice the speed of our best submarines.[27]

Each of these traits associated with UAP sightings defies our laws of physics and aerodynamics. The capabilities displayed are virtually unattainable by any US military and are certainly incomprehensible at this time. However, that's what many pilots describe, and we can't explain why.[28]

Flight Dynamics of Four UAP Profiles

The National Aviation Reporting Center on Anomalous Phenomena (NARCAP) profiled the flight dynamics of four UAP-shaped craft:

balls of light, disks, cylinders, and spheres. For example, for each of these craft types, the study considered attitudes, movements, and velocities that appear inconsistent with and often exceed the capabilities of airplanes and other known aerial phenomena.[29]

Pilot reports on these types of UAPs included descriptions with words like "suddenly," "instantaneously," and "disappeared" to describe the craft's movements. Further, the accounts called out sudden movements, angular changes of direction, "instantaneous" reversal of direction, extreme accelerations, sudden full stops, and hovering in space.

NARCAP concluded the four profiles of UAPs are "distinctly different from any aircraft or known aerial phenomena." In fact, they concluded that these UAPs are not "flying" in the sense of aerodynamic lift associated with known aircraft propulsive systems, because they do not have aerodynamic forms and therefore do not generate lift. Evidently, they are not dependent on balancing forces of thrust, lift, drag, gravity, and other factors normally associated with atmospheric resistance to perform movements. Further, these UAPs "are not affected by environmental forces and factors like drag, gravity, and atmospheric resistance." Also, the UAPs show no apparent resistance to changes in direction or velocity. Therefore, inertia is reduced or irrelevant.

Thus, NARCAP went into its analysis based on the assumption that an object operating within Earth's environment must be subject to all known physical laws. However, if this assumption is not correct, then UAP movements will appear to be unusual to us; thus, the above-mentioned environmental factors—weather, gravity, and material mediums—will be absent from and inconsistent with known principles of flight and physical laws. To wit, they are out of this world, alien.

UAP Sightings Near Nuclear Facilities

There are reports of a higher-than-expected number of UAP sightings near nuclear facilities. What might that mean? Although this material is anecdotal, it is relevant to this chapter, because we are considering the correlation of UAP sightings with particular, sensitive locations, and nuclear facilities or atomic test sites fit that description.

It is suggested that, since the end of World War II (1945) and the beginning of the nuclear age, our military has reported UAPs near sites associated with nuclear power, weaponry, and technology, especially nuclear test sites and areas with active nuclear naval fleets.

Luis Elizondo, who quit in 2017 as the head of the Pentagon's Advanced Threat Identification Program (AATIP), said in a press interview there "were geographical 'hot spots'—sometimes around nuclear facilities and power plants—which emerged during AATIP's investigations, as well as common facts between UFO sightings."[30]

"All of the nuclear facilities—Los Alamos, Livermore, Sandia, Savannah River—all had dramatic incidents where these unknown craft appeared over the facilities and nobody knew where they were from or what they were doing there," said George T. Knapp, an award-winning American television investigative journalist and noted conspiracy theorist known for his investigation of UFO claims. Evidently, Mr. Knapp has collected UFO sightings files through Freedom of Information Act requests from the Departments of Defense and Energy.[31]

Robert Hastings, who wrote *UFOs and Nukes: Extraordinary Encounters at Nuclear Weapons Sites,* claims to have interviewed more than 160 veterans who witnessed UAP near nuclear sites over a period of decades. "You have objects being tracked on radar performing at speeds that no object on earth can perform," he said.[32]

Journalist Knapp claims to have interviewed dozens of workers from the Nevada desert atomic test site, the location where the US government detonated nuclear devices after World War II. He claims those workers told him UFO activity was commonplace at the test facility.[33]

Other nuclear-related sites that experienced an inordinate number of UAP sightings included Malmstrom Air Force Base in Montana, a storage site for nuclear-tipped intercontinental ballistic missiles. Evidently, in 1967, a former Air Force captain, Robert Salas, claimed several of the missiles became inoperative just as a red, glowing object about thirty feet in diameter hovered above the front gate of the base.[34]

"And just as I [contacted my commander]," said Captain Salas, "our missiles began going into what's called a no-go condition, or unlaunchable. Essentially, they were disabled while this object was still hovering over our site."[35]

It would be easy to dismiss these reports by attributing them to UFO conspiracy theorists. However, our government has been silent about such matters for much too long; besides, these reporters and former service members stake their reputations on the truthfulness of their stories.

Pentagon UAP Files Indicate Health Damage to Humans

A British newspaper gained access to fifteen hundred pages of Pentagon UAP files using a Freedom of Information Act request. Those files came from the AATIP program that was previously led by Luis Elizondo. Those documents, according to the newspaper, reveal that UAP encounters "left Americans suffering from radiation burns, brain and nervous system damage, and even 'unaccounted for pregnancy.'"[36]

The article regarding the cache of AATIP documents includes information "on the biological effects of UFO sightings on humans, studies on advanced technologies such as invisibility cloaks, and plans for deep space exploration and colonization."[37]

One of the Pentagon documents is a report titled, "Anomalous Acute and Subacute Field Effects on Human and Biological Tissues," dated March 2010, which alleges injuries to "human observers by anomalous advanced aerospace systems." Further, that report describes forty-two cases of medical files and another three hundred "unpublished" incidents in which humans sustained injuries after supposed encounters with anomalous vehicles. In fact, the documents indicate burn injuries or other conditions were associated with electromagnetic radiation and some are suggested to have been inflicted by "energy related propulsion systems."[38]

The report, which includes "a list of alleged biological effects of UFO sightings on human observers between 1873 and 1994," concludes there is sufficient evidence "to support a hypothesis that some advanced systems are already deployed, and opaque to full US understandings."[39]

Conclusions

I conclude this chapter by reminding you what NASA acknowledged. It is true that "there is no evidence [that] UAPs are extraterrestrial in origin." Yet, as NASA officials stated, the "absence of evidence…is not evidence of absence," "anything is possible," and "they will follow the findings, wherever they might point."[40]

That is where the next section of this book begins. It seeks to answer the pregnant question by following the science: What are we to conclude about all this material? Are there really aliens roaming our skies, or are the reports just hokum? But first, we will review some of the most inexplicable sightings in chapter 5.

INEXPLICABLE UFOS AND CLASSIFYING THEM FOR ANALYSIS

The limited amount of high-quality reporting on unidentified aerial phenomena (UAP) hampers our ability to draw firm conclusions about the nature or intent of UAP.[1]

—OFFICE OF THE DIRECTOR OF NATIONAL INTELLIGENCE
"Preliminary Assessment: Unidentified Aerial Phenomena," 2021

Most UFO sightings are eventually explained as having been a mistaken identity, such as an aircraft; a weather-related incident; or a natural phenomenon, like a meteor. However, those that remain inexplicable should be studied and classified for further scientific investigation to confirm and eliminate the possibility that we are being visited by extraterrestrials.

This chapter introduces the reader to a few UFO incidents that continue to baffle the scientific world. Examining these events helps illustrate the need for a scientifically useful UFO classification system, because, to date, many of the efforts associated with these mysteries are hampered by inexact science, especially when in the hands of those who don't take the sightings seriously, like the people involved in most of the past US government projects.

Inexplicable UFO Incidents

America has a long history of UFO incidents. One of the earliest unexplainable, documented "New World" UFO sightings is recorded in the diary of John Winthrop, the governor of the Massachusetts Bay Colony. In March 1639, Governor Winthrop reported:

> James Everell, a sober, discreet man, and two others saw a great light in the night at Muddy River. When it stood still, it flamed up, and was about three yards square; when it ran, it was contracted into the figure of a swine: it ran as swift as an arrow... up and down about two or three hours.[2]

In the interest of brevity, I will only address some of the most enigmatic UFO sightings over the last seventy-five-plus years. These continue to baffle our best minds and toughest cynics, and they fuel the persistent belief among many people across the world that UFOs are a serious security threat, which the US and other governments so far have failed to properly address.

It is true that most UFO sightings end up being mistaken identities: astronomical objects like meteors, weather balloons, satellites, birds and the like, according to Seth Shostak, a senior astronomer at the SETI Institute, which explores the origins of life and intelligence in the universe. (SETI is an acronym for Search for Extraterrestrial Intelligence. The SETI Institute is a not-for-profit research organization that began in 1984 with just one project, NASA's SETI program, and today it has a portfolio that searches for understanding of life beyond Earth. It has one hundred scientists and specialists on staff.)[3]

Just because we don't have an explanation for an event doesn't necessarily mean it is a visit by extraterrestrials. Mr. Shostak illustrated the problem of identifying some UFO events with a practical, down-to-earth illustration: "There's no explanation for about one-third of the murders in New York City," he explained. "Nonetheless, that doesn't mean that they weren't committed by people." Arguably, said Shostak, the same logic applies to unsolved incidents in our skies.[4]

The age-old reports of humans spotting mysterious objects in the sky persist, and by some accounts, the number of sightings has increased in the twenty-first century. Below is a chronological listing of some of the most notable examples of UFO incidents since the end of World War II that, frankly, haven't been solved. However, we begin this list with perhaps the best-known American UFO incident to indicate that it has been likely solved, but was so amped up by the media that both the phenomenon and the location associated with it became household words.

Reports of mysterious objects in the sky persist; some say the number of sightings has increased in the twenty-first century.[5]

Some of these examples are replicated in more detail at appendix A, which includes links to videos that provide pictures and more context.

Roswell "flying saucer" incident, 1947: Arguably, the UFO mania that gripped America beginning in the late 1940s began with the sighting associated with a 1947 incident that took place about seventy-five miles north of Roswell, New Mexico. The story of that occurrence, especially about the missteps by US government officials, is quite revealing and, as a result, directly influenced the public's anxiety about UFOs and trust in their government's explanations of the phenomenon.

According to the *Washington Post*, reports of "flying saucers" sighted in ten states in June and early July of 1947 prompted all US intelligence agencies to look into the matter. "Army experts," wrote the

Post, "suggested, as a bare possibility, that some civilian inventor had been making experiments of some kind." Further, the Army Air Force spokesman at the Pentagon said, "If some foreign power is sending flying discs over the United States, it is our responsibility to know about it and take the proper action."[6]

Within days of the report in the *Washington Post*, the unexplained event got completely out of hand. In hindsight, the Roswell occurrence was related to the mischaracterization by the US Army Air Force (USAAF) report of debris from a highly classified balloon-spying project meant to detect atomic bomb tests over the Soviet Union.

The facts are that a ranch worker named William Brazel collected material from the downed balloon on both June 14 and again on July 4. Then, on July 5, Brazel, after learning about flying disks in the news, wondered whether what he previously gathered were remnants of the flying disks. So, on July 7, Brazel took the gathered debris with him to inform local authorities. After hearing the report and seeing the debris, Roswell Sheriff George Wilcox reported the findings to the USAAF base in Roswell.[7]

Major Jesse A. Marcel, the intelligence officer of the 509th Bombardment Group at the USAAF base, accompanied Sheriff Wilcox back to the sheriff's home where the major retrieved the debris. Subsequently, Marcel went to the Brazel ranch to recover the balance of the debris.[8]

The recovery of the debris prompted the public information officer at Roswell Army Air Field, Lieutenant Warren Haught, to release a statement to the press. It stated:

> The many rumors regarding the flying disks became a reality yesterday when the intelligence office of the 509th (Atomic) Bomb Group of Eighth Air Force, Roswell Army Air Field, was fortunate enough to gain possession of a disk through the cooperation of one of the local ranchers and the sheriff's office of Chaves County.[9]

The next day, the story of the "flying saucer" appeared in the local paper, the *Roswell Daily Record*, with the headline: "RAAF Captures Flying Saucer on Ranch in Roswell Region." The news item stated that no details "of the saucer's construction or its appearance had been revealed," but after the local office inspected the debris, it was flown to "higher headquarters."[10]

Soon, Brigadier General Roger Ramey, commander of the Eighth Air Force at Fort Worth, Texas, described the debris from Roswell as "apparently some sort of tin foil." Further, General Ramey indicated the debris was then shipped to the Air Force Research Center at Wright Field near Dayton, Ohio.[11]

A day later, the *New York Times* picked up the story. It reported that "celestial crockery had the Army up in the air several hours yesterday before an Army officer explained that what a colleague thought was 'a flying disk' was nothing more than a battered army weather balloon." The report also noted, "This denouncement closes the New Mexico chapter in the 'flying saucer' saga that already had contributions from forty-three other states in the union as well as from Australia, England, South Africa, Mexico, and Canada."[12]

On July 11, 1947, the *Washington Post* ran an opinion piece about the "saucer" debacle. The article stated:

> We don't want to be uppity about this business, but it seems to us that the boys have only themselves to blame that the story has got out of hand. Some of them are pretty bitter about Lieut. Warren Haught, USA, official press agent for the Army Air Forces command near Roswell, N. Mex., because he sent out a story beginning, "The many rumors regarding the flying disk became a reality yesterday when" it seems to us that Lieutenant Naught [deliberate misspelling] was only doing his job according to his lights, and, after all, he got the name of Roswell Field into the first pages of almost every newspaper in

the country before the thing that was found there turned out to be some kind of meteorological kite.[13]

Evidently, news of the Roswell incident led to many other flying saucer reports across the world. Days after Roswell, UFO accounts poured in from forty-four US states, Canada, the Netherlands, the United Kingdom, Chile, Iran, Australia, Manchuria, France, and other countries. The Roswell episode became the butt of a diplomatic joke by Soviet deputy foreign minister Andrei A. Gromyko, who stated at a United Nations meeting:

> Some attribute [saucer reports] to the British for exporting too much of their [S]cotch whisky into the United States. Some say it is a Russian discus thrower training for the Olympic games who does not realize his own strength.[14]

Once the Roswell report achieved international fame, it was impossible to contain. By the fall of 1947, the US Air Force officially labeled the "flying saucers" as "unidentified flying objects" (UFOs) and recognized they represented a possible threat to national security and concerned the public. Then, on December 30, 1947, the Air Material Command at Wright-Patterson Air Force Base was ordered to establish a project to collect and analyze the facts surrounding the sightings. That effort became known as Project Sign, which will be profiled in chapter 6 of this book.[15]

Although the Roswell incident sparked the UFO mania, many other sightings came in its wake. Some of the most notable accounts, unlike the Roswell balloon story, remain inexplicable today and are summarized below.

Flying saucer near Mount Rainier, 1947: On June 24, 1947, civilian pilot Kenneth Arnold was flying his personal aircraft, a single-engine CallAir A-2 out of Chehalis, Washington, when he saw a flash of light he described as "like a saucer skipping across water."

Further, the "saucer," which appeared in the vicinity of Mount Rainier, south of Seattle, moved at an incomprehensible speed before Arnold saw eight more "saucers" arrayed in a "V" formation. Mr. Arnold described the craft as moving as "a saucer," words the media, as in the Roswell case, repeated to formulate the term "flying saucer."[16]

Men in black at Maury Island, Washington, sighting of donut-shaped aircraft, 1947: On June 28, 1947, Harold Dahl was on the shore of the Puget Sound's Maury Island when he noticed six donut-shaped objects thousands of feet above him. He reported that one of the craft fell nearly fifteen hundred feet, then Mr. Dahl and his son were pelted with metallic debris. One of the objects killed his dog. Mr. Dahl took photographs of the aircraft and told his supervisor, Mr. Fred Crisman, what he had seen. Mr. Crisman returned to the spot of the sightings and also observed the aircraft. The very next day, Mr. Dahl was visited by a man in a black suit, who reportedly instructed Mr. Dahl to not tell anyone about what he had witnessed; otherwise, he threatened, negative consequences would happen. Two things are noteworthy here. First, Maury Island isn't very far from the Hanford nuclear reactor, which produced plutonium for the first nuclear weapons. Also, this episode seeded the idea for the *Men in Black* movie series (1997–2019) about an unofficial government agency that investigates alien encounters.[17]

Eastern Airlines flight encounter with "spaceships" while flying to Atlanta, Georgia, 1948: In the midafternoon of July 24, 1948, at five thousand feet over southwest Alabama, Eastern Airlines pilots Clarence S. Chiles and John B. Whitted saw something they described as "spaceships from other worlds." The two pilots of the twenty-passenger commercial aircraft said:

> It was clear there were no wings present, that it was powered by some jet or other type of power, shooting flame from the rear some 50 feet. There were two rows of windows, which indicated an upper and lower deck, [and] from inside these

windows a very bright light was glowing. Underneath the ship, there was a blue glow of light.

Evidently, given this report, the US government opened a top-secret investigation.[18]

US soldiers' engagement with a UFO during Korean War, 1951: In May 1951, near Chorwon, North Korea, an artillery unit was preparing to engage a nearby village just as they saw a strange sight in the hills—"a jack-o-lantern come wafting down across the mountain." The pulsing, "attacking" light made its way down into the village as the artillery air bursts sounded. "We further noticed that this object would get right into...the center of an airburst of artillery and yet remain unharmed," explained Private Francis P. Wall, who reported his story to the Center for UFO Studies.[19]

Private Wall said the object next turned and changed colors from orange to a pulsating, blue-green, brilliant light. At that point, Wall fired his rifle at the object and heard the distinctive metallic "ding" as the bullets bounced off the craft. Next, Wall said:

> We were attacked, swept by some form of a ray that was emitted in pulses, in waves that you could visually see only when it was aiming directly at you. That is to say, like a searchlight sweeps around and the segments of light...you would see it coming at you.[20]

The light from the craft gave him a burning, tingling sensation all over his body. The men quickly moved to underground bunkers and watched from small windows as the craft first hovered above them and then shot off at a forty-five-degree angle. "It was there and was gone."[21]

Days later, Wall's entire unit was evacuated because they were suffering from dysentery and extremely high white-blood-cell counts. Richard F. Haines, a UFO researcher and former NASA scientist, said the soldiers "had symptoms that sounded like the effects of radiation."[22]

Mount Palomar alien contact, 1952: Perhaps the most controversial and bizarre account was of an incident said to have occurred on November 20, 1952, between George Adamski and an alien visitor from "Venus" in the Mojave Desert of California. It is noteworthy that, by that year, Edwards Air Force Base, near the Mojave Desert, was operational and was a site where the US conducted significant sensitive military tests, such as of the SR-71 "Blackbird," a long-range, high-altitude, Mach 3+ strategic reconnaissance aircraft.

Mr. Adamski claimed he and a group of friends saw a gigantic, cigar-shaped, silver craft that eventually rocketed out of sight. However, a few minutes later, a smaller craft appeared and landed near Mr. Adamski. As he approached the object, Adamski saw what looked like a man.

"The beauty of his form surpassed anything I had ever seen," Adamski claimed. The humanoid-like figure was tall and blond, with smooth-tanned skin. It wore a brown one-piece suit with a broad belt and red shoes. Adamski said he shook hands with the being, and they communicated using telepathy and sign language. The alien's name was Orthon from Venus, according to Adamski.[23]

Mr. Adamski wrote several books, such as *Flying Saucer Farewell*, in which he claimed the Soviet Luna 3 (1959) probe brought back photographs of the lunar surface. Another Adamski claim was that on his space travels he saw "billions and billions of fireflies...flickering everywhere," while on the dark side of the Moon while aboard a Venusian craft. Surprisingly, US astronaut and eventual US Senator, John Glenn, an early space traveler, reported seeing "fireflies" as well while in orbit around the Earth.[24]

Mr. Adamski certainly had some outlandish stories that made him a lot of money and earned him considerable notoriety in the 1950s. However, there is good reason to believe he was a consummate con man, at least according to Daniel Loxton, the editor of *Junior Skeptic*, who wrote an article, "Flying Saucer 'Space Brothers' from Venus!?,' about George Adamski. Mr. Loxton spoke with people close to Mr.

Adamski who seriously discredited the man. For example, Desmond Leslie, a coauthor with Adamski, said, "Some of his claims take a lot of swallowing." Adamski's ghostwriter, Carol Honey, recalled that he "wrote one thing one month and changed it a few weeks later. He did this numerous times." She said he sometimes "made statements that contradicted others made a few days before."[25]

Evidently, Adamski was quite persuasive in person. "To look at the man and to listen to his story you had an immediate urge to believe him," said Edward Ruppelt, a ufologist who spent time with Adamski. Mr. Ruppelt admitted Adamski "radiated an aura of humility and goodwill." Even James Mosely, an Adamski critic, said, "He also had a way of gazing upon his listeners that gave each of them the flattering sense that he was speaking directly and almost only to each of them."[26]

Grotesque incident blamed on "compelling natural force," 1959: On February 1, 1959, near Dyatlov Pass, "Dead Mountain," Russia, nine experienced hikers were found dead, frozen in various stages of undress. Their tents were mostly destroyed, some of the corpses were missing eyeballs or tongues, and one body registered high levels of radiation. Although the Russian investigation concluded the victims were killed by a "compelling natural force," others believed the deaths were associated with UFO activity.[27]

"Egg-shaped craft" over New Mexico desert, 1964: On April 24, 1964, police sergeant Lonnie Zamora drove down a New Mexico dirt road when, all of a sudden, he saw to his front an "egg-shaped craft" peering out from an *arroyo* (Spanish for a "dry creek bed"). Soon he saw a blue flame and heard a loud roar from the *arroyo* just as the object rose into the sky. Evidently, five local tourists reported seeing the same craft.[28]

"Charlie Redstar's" nightly appearances over Canada, 1975: In 1975, hundreds of people in the southern Manitoba, Canada, region reported seeing what they described as a glowing, red-orange object that soared through the sky every night for several months. It was nicknamed "Charlie Redstar" because it performed aerial maneuvers in a "mischievous" and "playful" manner.[29]

Iranian fighter jet's loss of all electronics in UFO encounter, 1976: On September 19, 1976, Iranian F-4 fighter jet pilot Lieutenant Yaddi Nazari chased a UFO craft at a high speed. That encounter became known as the "Tehran UFO incident." Pilot Nazari reported that, as he approached the UFO, his entire suite of electronics—including his communications device—blacked out, forcing him to abort his mission. A second F-4 assumed the mission and achieved radar lock on the object. Still, that pilot reported the UFO released a glowing object, which the F-4 pilot assumed was a missile headed at him. Almost immediately, the Iranian pilot's instruments failed to function, much like the first aircraft, and he, too, witnessed a bright object being released from the UFO. It wasn't until he returned to the airfield that his equipment miraculously started functioning once again.[30]

Iran, on good terms with the United States at the time, contacted the US military to help with the UFO investigation. Subsequently, a US Air Force memorandum concerning the Iranian incident outlined a number of possible explanations for the events, such as the planet Jupiter, a history of electrical problems with the F-4, and a malfunction of the radar. Regarding the "alien missiles," the USAF said they were likely a meteor shower that might likely have accounted for the sightings.[31]

Pilot and aircraft disappearance after UFO encounter, 1978: On October 21, 1978, twenty-year-old Frederick Valentich was flying a small aircraft near Bass Strait, Australia, when he reported over the radio, "It is hovering, and it is not an aircraft." He continued, saying the hovering aircraft was "playing a game" with him. Then the ground station lost all contact with the pilot and airplane, and not a trace of either Valentich or his aircraft has ever been found.[32]

British "Roswell" incident in the Rendlesham Forest, 1980: In December of 1980, the US Air Force reported sightings of strange, colorful lights above the Rendlesham Forest northeast of London. A man who investigated the forest area from which the lights came discovered what he described as a "spacecraft." Others returned to the site the next day to confirm damage to nearby trees and a high level of radiation at the site.[33]

Days later, US Lieutenant Colonel Charles Halt recorded his observations, as he, too, had observed the lights. However, the British Ministry of Defence, which oversaw UFO incident reports, failed to find any credible threat to the nation based on the report. Today, UFO tourism is common in the Rendlesham Forest, and a hiking trail was created specifically for spacecraft tourists.[34]

Burn marks left from a whistling UFO in France, 1981: On January 8, 1981, Renato Nicolaï was working at his farm when he heard a whistling sound and immediately saw a disk-shaped object launch and disappear above the tree line. He investigated the launch site and found burn marks on the ground. The French UFO project *Groupe d'Etudes et d'Information des Phenomenes Aerospatiaux Non Identifies,* or Unidentified Aerospace Phenomenon Research and Information Group, claimed the ground had been heated to over five hundred degrees Fahrenheit.[35]

Low-flying black triangles in Belgium, 1989–90: For five months spanning the years 1989–1990, 13,500 citizens of Belgium claimed to have seen low-flying, black, triangle-shaped UFOs equipped with three orange headlights hovering in the sky. A few months after the initial sightings, new events with multiple objects were confirmed by military radar, and two F-16 fighter jets investigated the anomalies but could not see anything—even though the pilots were able to lock onto their targets with radar. Some skeptics said this UFO was evidence of a mass delusion. The Belgian air force offered no explanation and reached out to the United Kingdom to help investigate, but the British refused to look into the incident because it didn't appear to present a threat.[36]

Silvery UFO spotted by thousands in broad daylight, Mexico City, 1993: Perhaps one of the most spectacular UFO sightings took place on January 1, 1993, over Mexico City, an incident seen by thousands and reported by many media outlets. Evidently, such appearances began in July of 1991 during a total eclipse of the sun. At that time, many people videotaped a metallic, disk-shaped object hanging motionless below the eclipsed sun. Those videos show a "hockey-puck-shaped" object that turned counterclockwise. The following year, on March 4, 1992, air-traffic controllers in Mexico City recorded on their radar screens other UFOs that stayed for forty minutes.[37]

UFO invasion of Israel, 1996: On September 17, 1996, Tel Aviv motorists watched as a UFO hovered above the city. *Mai'ariv*, one of Israel's largest newspapers, reported "the event was witnessed by police along with hundreds of motorists at the scene." David Ronen, a reporter for *Mai'ariv*, wrote in the newspaper that such UFO incidents had previously been restricted to deserted areas. In 1997, in the British journal *UFO Reality*, Ronen said:

> All at once, UFOs have begun to appear in the centre of Israel and in other areas throughout the country, as well as simultaneously in Iran and Australia. At precisely the same time (August 1996) a tide of eyewitness reports came in, this time not from individual people, but involving a wave of mass reports, including an intervention by the police and the army. The succession of reports is so staggering that it is already impossible to keep track of the hundreds and thousands of eyewitness reports that pour in each day.[38]

The New Jersey Turnpike lit up by UFOs, 2001: Just after midnight on July 14, 2001, drivers on the New Jersey Turnpike saw strange, orange and yellow lights in a V formation streaking across the Arthur Kill waterway between Staten Island and Carteret, New Jersey. A Carteret police officer, Lt. Daniel Tarrant, witnessed the formation, as did other residents from the area of the Throgs Neck Bridge on Long Island and Fort Lee, New Jersey. A group known as New York Strange Phenomena investigated the sightings and reviewed the Federal Aviation Administration (FAA) radar data that corroborated the incident.[39]

"Tic Tac"-shaped UFO southwest of San Diego, 2004: On November 14, 2004, one hundred miles from San Diego out in the Pacific Ocean, US Navy F/A-18F fighter pilots operating off the USS Nimitz, an aircraft carrier, engaged a white aircraft described as a massive "Tic Tac" about the same size as a Hornet aircraft—forty feet long—with no wings. It was surrounded by a glowing halo and was moving three times faster than the speed of sound. The audio recording of the pilots at the time included the statement: "There's a whole fleet of them."[40]

Pilot Navy Commander David Fravor said of the incident, "I have no idea what I saw." He continued, "It had no plumes [exhaust], wings or rotors and outran our F-18s." Although the pilots tried to intercept the craft, it accelerated away, reappearing moments later on radar sixty miles away. Two weeks prior to these sightings, the Navy had tracked objects that appeared at eighty thousand feet and then plummeted to hover right above the surface of the ocean.[41]

The number of inexplicable UFO sightings like those described above is persistent. The US Department of Defense's Airborne Object Identification and Management Synchronization Group, as recently as June, 2022, determined there were more than 140 "unidentified aerial phenomena" (UAP) incidents it couldn't explain. So, the problem isn't going away.[42]

A 2023 US government report indicated it received more than five hundred UAP sightings since 2021, yet hundreds remain unexplained. Of those explained, twenty-six were drones, one hundred sixty-three were balloons, and six were aerial objects such as birds, weather, or debris. However, one hundred seventy-one remain inexplicable, and "some of these uncharacterized UAP[s] appear to have demonstrated unusual flight characteristics or performance capabilities, and require further analysis."[43]

It would be appropriate to ask: Why don't we know more about UFOs/UAPs, given so many sightings over the centuries? Frankly, part of the issue is that the topic is seldom taken seriously, and rigorous science hasn't been applied.

Ineffective Scientific and UFO Classification Efforts

UFO classification methods are not standardized and, as a result, tend to be almost useless for meaningful scientific investigation. Further, the challenges of documenting and scientifically studying the phenomenon are also made quite difficult by the diversity of incidents over thousands of years and across many cultures and languages, as illustrated in chapters 2 and 3 of this book.

Before considering the most popular methods of cataloging UFO sightings, it is helpful to consider what the US Office of the Director of National Intelligence (DNI) told us about the challenges in its 2021 report entitled *Preliminary Assessment: Unidentified Aerial Phenomena*.[44]

That publication outlines four difficulties associated with cataloging, that is, characterizing potential UFOs/UAPs. Past efforts to gather high-quality data on UAPs "hampers our ability to draw firm conclusions about the nature or intent of UAP[s]," according to the DNI's report. The Unidentified Aerial Phenomena Task Force (UAPTF), the Pentagon's office prior to the current AARO, states in the report this effort "considered a range of information on UAP[s] described in U.S. military and IC (intelligence community) reporting, but because the reporting lacked sufficient specificity, ultimately recognized that a unique, tailored reporting process was required to provide sufficient data for analysis of UAP events."[45]

The DNI report identified four conclusions (below) regarding its limited effort to acquire a secure grasp on UAP sightings with the intent of conducting meaningful scientific analysis. Before introducing those conclusions, the report acknowledges there are multiple types of UAPs requiring different explanations based on discernable characteristics. Specifically, the report states that UAPs fall into five categories: airborne clutter, natural atmospheric phenomena, government or industry development programs, foreign adversary systems, and a catchall group it labels as "other." Presumably, the "other" category includes potential extraterrestrial craft and/or alien beings and paranormal activities such as spirits in the unseen realm.[46]

Further, cataloging UAPs, admits the DNI, across the federal government is problematic because there is a lack of standardized reporting, and limited analysis of collected data to eventually allow for sophisticated evaluation "to deepen our understanding."

The DNI report outlines the following specific shortfalls in the US government's process of cataloging and analysis of UAP data.

"Available Reporting Largely Inconclusive":

First, "available reporting [is] largely inconclusive," because of "limited data and inconsistency in reporting are key challenges to evaluating UAP," according to the DNI report. It admits the UAPTF (the Pentagon's program until 2023) mostly heard anecdotal information, and it never captured that data in a formal or informal manner.

Just how immature is the US government's UAP collection and analyses processes? According to the DNI's report, it considered 144 UAP accounts—all witnessed firsthand by military aviators—but only a single UAP was identified with "high confidence." Clearly, we have collection challenges, which the report delineated.

Most importantly, according to the DNI, there are "sociocultural stigmas and senor limitations" that limit the collection of UAP information. Specifically, there is a social stigma associated with reporting "flying saucers" (UAPs) because would-be reporters of sightings don't want to be labeled as "kooks" or "wackos." So, as a result, those pilots or other professionals remain silent and the data on UAP sightings remains lost to the databases. However, the stigma associated with reporting UAPs has "lessened as senior members of the scientific, policy, military, and intelligence communities engage on the topic seriously in public." In the past, "reputational risk [has kept] many observers silent, complicating scientific pursuit of the topic."[47]

There is also the technical aspect of reporting. Evidently, "the sensors mounted on U.S. military platforms are typically designed to fulfill specific missions." Therefore, those sensors are often less than optimally suited to help identify UAPs. Further, there is the issue of vantage points by a number of sensors that happen to be used to observe UAPs that might contribute to, or not prove useful for, gathering information about sightings.

There is also a factor the DNI called "collection bias." Evidently, many UAP sightings cluster around US military training and testing locations, which may bias the collection of information and confound our latest generation of sensors.

The report also indicates that, of those UAPs analyzed, only a handful demonstrated advanced technologies characterized by special movement patterns or flight characteristics. Specifically, some UAPs remained stationary in winds aloft, maneuvered abruptly, or moved at considerable speed—all without any discernable means of propulsion. Other UAPs demonstrated radio frequency energy, which remains inexplicable.

"UAP[s] Probably Lack a Single Explanation"

Second, "UAP[s] probably lack a single explanation," because "the UAP[s] documented in this [DNI 2021 report] limited dataset demonstrates an array of aerial behaviors, reinforcing the possibility there are multiple types of UAP[s] requiring different explanations.'"

The report categorizes these sightings into the five groups introduced above.

Airborne clutter: This likely includes birds, balloons, recreational unmanned aerial vehicles or drones, and airborne debris—all of which muddle the aviator's ability to specifically identify the object.

Natural atmospheric phenomena: This may include ice crystals, moisture, and thermal fluctuations that register on sensors.

US government—or industry—development programs: Some UAPs might be attributable to experimental and classified platforms.

Foreign adversary systems: Some UAPs might be technologies developed and deployed by adversaries like China or even a nongovernment entity and employed for spying or other nefarious purposes.

Other: The DNI report indicated that most UAPs in its database remain unidentified because of limited information or challenges in collection or analysis. Therefore, this grouping awaits better scientific advances to understand. The report, though, doesn't mention the possibility of extraterrestrials or entities from the unseen realm in this category.

"UAP[s] Threaten Flight Safety and, Possibly, National Security"

Third, "UAP[s] threaten flight safety and, possibly, national security," because they "pose a hazard to safety of flight and could pose a broader danger if some instances represent sophisticated collection against U.S. military activities by a foreign government or demonstrate a breakthrough aerospace technology by a potential adversary."

The report indicates there are ongoing airspace concerns. Evidently, aviators who encounter safety hazards are required to report those concerns. Of the one hundred forty-four incidents considered in this report, eleven were documented instances in which pilots reported having near misses with a UAP.

The DNI admits it lacks sufficient data to attribute any of the UAP incidents to foreign collection programs, especially a "major technological advancement by a potential adversary." This factor is important, because some UAP activity is detected near military facilities "or by aircraft carrying the USG's most advanced sensor systems."

"Explaining UAP[s] Will Require Analytic, Collection and Resource Investment"

Finally, "explaining UAP will require analytic, collection and resource investment" because the "UAPTF's long-term goal is to widen the scope of its work to include additional UAP events documented by a broader swath of USG personnel and technical systems in its analysis."

The report also calls for the standardization of UAP reporting. It states, "The UAPTF has begun to develop interagency analytical and processing workflows to ensure both collection and analysis will be well informed and coordinated."

Further, the UAPTF seeks to expand the collection of UAP data and then standardize to "mitigate the collection bias in the dataset." The DNI indicates it has plans to "update its current interagency UAP collection strategy."

Finally, the DNI calls for increasing investment in UAP-related research and development to further the study of the phenomenon.

Hynek's UFO Classification System

The best-known UFO classification system was developed by Josef Allen Hynek, a now deceased astronomer, defense researcher, and director of the Ohio State University's McMillin Observatory. A modified version of Hynek's system was used in the categorization model employed by NASA's Dr. Stothers in his analysis of ancient UFOs referenced in chapter 2 of this book.

In the 1940s, Hynek studied UFO reports and found that about 20 percent couldn't be identified. Then, in 1973, he investigated a Pascagoula, Mississippi, UFO case in which two men reported being abducted by aliens, prompting him to classify UFO sightings—a system outlined in his 1972 book, *The UFO Experience: A Scientific Inquiry*.[48]

In that book, Hynek identified three classes of "close encounters." They are:

Close encounter of the first kind: Someone simply observes a UFO but it leaves no evidence.

Close encounter of the second kind: A UFO leaves physical traces it was present, such as burns on the ground or broken branches.

Close encounter of the third kind: A person makes contact with a UFO or other life form.

After Hynek died in 1996, others added to his classification system. Specifically, they added a "close encounter of the fourth kind," which covers: "Alleged alien abductions[,] while a close encounter of the fifth type includes communication exchange between humans and non-earth creatures."[49]

Evidently, among many ufologists, Hynek's is the most popular classification system. However, there are other systems and additions made to his approach. For example, the Rio Scale is attributed to the 51st International Astronautical Congress, 29th Review Meeting on the Search for Extraterrestrial Intelligence in 2000. It uses factors like reliability and quality of reporting, whereby a zero rating means a "totally insignificant encounter" and a rating of ten "indicates an 'extraordinary' sighting worthy of serious study."[50]

On reflection, it is understandable to ask: Why bother to classify UFO encounters? Dr. Barna Donovan, a professor at Saint Peter's University in Jersey City, New Jersey, and a skeptic about UFOs, said, "About 90 percent of sightings are misidentified aircraft, weather phenomena or sleep disorders [like sleep paralysis] of people reporting abduction experiences and experimentation upon by aliens." The professor stated UFO sightings are one of two things: They are either legitimate extraterrestrial presence or some type of phenomenon that science can't explain. That's why we need to classify sightings and then investigate those that at present remain inexplicable.[51]

Conclusion

What's clear from the information presented in this chapter is that there remain many UFO/UAP sightings modern science has yet to explain; some that seem wacky, and others that make one truly wonder about the origin. Efforts to properly categorize the baffling events and then expose them to rigorous scientific analysis have been, at best, haphazard to this point. That must change if we're to find the truth about these events, especially if the growing number of inexplicable incidents is a threat to our national security.

6

REVIEW OF UFO PROGRAMS

*The agency's [Central Intelligence Agency] understandable interest
in concealing its role in some of the early U.F.O. investigations
ultimately proved to be counterproductive, that it just fed into
later charges of conspiracy and cover up.*[1]

—Dr. David Robarge, chief CIA historian

This chapter profiles many past and current efforts to account for
UFO sightings. Part of that effort has been the creation of a variety
of databases and/or clearinghouses for all things inexplicable. Today,
much of that data is available to the public, yet conclusions drawn from
the avalanche of information remains mixed. Although the causes of
most UFO sightings are eventually identified—the focus of section
three of this book—a significant percentage remains unknown, which
feeds global curiosity and speculation about the topic.

In recent decades, there has been a surge in UFO sightings, perhaps
in part thanks to the advent of the modern age, which was ushered
into the present with America's use of nuclear weapons, the now-common
use of ballistic missiles, and manned space flight. Accompanying
those advances have been new sophisticated detection devices as well
as a flurry of reports of unexplained objects in our skies and troubling
details from government whistleblowers about alleged closely held
secrets concerning aliens and their spacecraft.

Beginning shortly after the Second World War, waves of UFO
sightings, accompanied by debates about the existence and gestalt of

extraterrestrial life, gained prominence. Those discussions were fueled by reports such as that of a young airman at Ellsworth Air Force Base in Rapid City, South Dakota, on July 17, 1952.

The airman was peering into the early evening sky when he saw something he had never seen before at an estimated altitude of between twelve thousand and fifteen thousand feet: a series of orange-colored disks, glowing like light bulbs, traveling at several times the speed of a jet fighter, and lasting five or six seconds before disappearing over the eastern horizon. He reported the incident to his superiors, who initiated an official inquiry.[2]

An Air Force intelligence officer interrogated the airman and filled out an "Air Intelligence Information Report" that was forwarded to Wright-Patterson Air Force Base at Dayton, Ohio. The report noted the airman worked in armaments and electronics and was considered reliable.[3]

At Wright-Patterson, the information from that report was transferred to a standard form known as the White Project 10073 Record Card, which captured the details of the account. An official studied the material on the card and subsequently classified the incident as "unknown," indicating there was insufficient evidence for confirmation and identification. However, that reviewer concluded, "Reports similar to this have turned out to be ducks." That ended the investigation into the sighting. The clerk filed the results, which were classified for three years and later downgraded. The incident became known as Case 1479 in the US Air Force's Project Blue Book.[4]

The postwar anxiety about sightings of objects such as Case 1479 were fueled in part by fear that our nuclear peer, the Soviets, would drop an atomic bomb on America. The collective nervousness further spiked when the Kremlin became the first nation to put a satellite into orbit, the Sputnik 1 in 1957. At about the same time, pop culture went into overdrive about all things associated with UFOs. Specifically, "interest in flying saucers shot up around the same moment it became plausible that humans would visit space," wrote Katharine

Coldiron, author of *Plan 9 from Outer Space [Midnight Movies Mono-graph]*, an analysis of the 1957 movie by the same name, which is often called the worst film of all time.

In 1961, anxiety about threats from outer space continued to mount when Soviet astronaut Yuri Gagarin orbited the planet—another space first for the Soviets. That accomplishment encouraged then President John F. Kennedy to announce on May 25, 1961, before a joint session of Congress: "I believe that this nation should commit itself to achieving the goal, before this decade is out, of landing a man on the moon and returning him safely to the earth." At that point going forward, the world's attention was captured by the mysteries of space flight, adding to the general anxiety about Soviet space advances, the nuclear missile threat, and, of course, the growing number of UFO sightings.[5]

Hollywood helped fuel the anxiety by creating nightmarish films about fictional attacks by space aliens, such as the 1956 motion picture *Earth Versus the Flying Saucers*. Television acted as an accelerant as well, with its 1966 space-drama series, *Star Trek*, which featured the *USS Enterprise*, a strange-looking, saucer-shaped space vehicle with legs extended to the rear. Arguably, filmmakers like George Lucas, perhaps the best at igniting interest in outer space, released a host of blockbuster films that caught the public's imagination, further spiking our fears and feeding our fascination with the subject beginning in 1977 with his *Star Wars* series.

The wide-screen and television were accompanied in the saucer mania beginning in the 1950s and accelerating in the 1960s when legitimate news agencies fanned the craze with accounts of the latest UFO sightings, accompanied by what seemed to be endless reporting about the space competition between the US and Russia. Meanwhile, pop culture piled on with books like Donald E. Keyhoe's *The Flying Saucers Are Real* and Frank Scully's *Behind the Flying Saucer*. Comic books such as *Saucer Attack*, *Ringworld*, and *The Martian Chronicles*, as well as magazines like *Starlog* and *Imagination* were part of the mania as well. Even the mainstream edition of

Life magazine published an article in April 1952 entitled "Have We Visitors from Space?" that opened the door for other notable media outlets to embrace the topic.

The political class in Washington was mostly caught off-guard as demands for answers about space aliens and UFOs rose to a fever pitch, pressuring Congress and the administration to address the perceived threat. At that point, the US government and other national governments across the globe scurried to set up task forces promising their public they would find answers about the sightings of strange objects in the skies. Those efforts included the creation of UFO data-collecting offices and institutions to study the phenomenon.

In recent decades, the amped-up interest in UFOs waned after space launches to Earth's orbit became almost routinized with the United States' Space Shuttle program, the Russian Soyuz spacecraft series, and the International Space Station, as well as the perceived threat of a nuclear holocaust being diminished with the demise of the former Soviet Union (1991). However, over the past few years, we've experienced a renewed interest in the topic, perhaps in part because government whistleblowers who told the public the truth about UFOs is being kept from them by government.

One such whistleblower is the earlier-mentioned Luis Elizondo, a career military intelligence officer lauded in 2016 for managing a highly classified Pentagon program "in a manner that protects our national security interests on a global scale." This praised official resigned in 2017 and warned in his resignation letter to then defense secretary James Mattis that "bureaucratic challenges and inflexible mindsets" had prevented "anomalous aerospace threats" from being taken seriously by the Pentagon. He said there was "overwhelming evidence" of these threats and, in fact, that there were "many instances" of "unusual aerial systems interfering with military weapon platforms and displaying beyond-next-generation capabilities."[6]

More recently, the Pentagon began removing the stigma often associated with reporting UFOs in the past, because what the public knows as UFOs could be a national security threat. "Our goal is to eliminate this stigma by fully incorporating our operators and mission personnel into a standardized data-gathering process," said Ronald Moultrie, the undersecretary of defense for intelligence and security. He made that statement May 17, 2022, during the first congressional hearing into UFOs since the 1960s.[7]

At the same hearing, Scott Bray, deputy director of the Office of Naval Intelligence, told the House Intelligence Subcommittee, "The message is now clear: if you see something, you need to report it."[8]

At the time of that hearing, subcommittee panel chair, Representative Andre Carson (D-IN), said people reporting incidents should be treated "as witnesses, not as kooks." He noted broad public interest in the topic, and continued: "The American people expect and deserve their leaders in government and intelligence to seriously evaluate and respond to any potential national security risks—especially those we do not fully understand."[9]

"Since the early 2000s," Bray testified, "we have seen an increasing number of unauthorized and unidentified aircraft near military control training areas and ranges, and other designated airspace. Reports of sightings are frequent and continuing," but fleeting. Further, Director Bray explained, most of the contemporary incidents are observed by US military personnel and are registered on technical sensors. Nevertheless, there is still insufficient data on the sightings to draw meaningful conclusions.[10]

US Government UFO Databases and Research

The US government leads the world in terms of the number of past and current official projects to collect UFO-related data. That effort began in 1948 with Project Sign, the government's response to the 1947 "flying saucer" incident near Roswell, New Mexico.

Almost overnight, the incident prompted the stand-up of the US Air Force's Project Sign (1948), which just as quickly concluded that the things people reported seeing, such as at Roswell, were "real," but at least "some of the incidents may be caused by natural phenomena," which were presumably related to domestic or foreign aircraft.

Roswell, New Mexico, became famous in 1947 after the local paper reported a "flying saucer" crashed nearby.[11]

Project Sign ended in late 1948 and was quickly replaced by another short-lived effort, Project Grudge, which itself morphed into the now-famous Project Blue Book in 1951, an effort based at Wright-Patterson Air Force Base near Dayton, Ohio. It is notable that Project Grudge had a special unit, Project Twinkle, that studied mysterious fireballs over New Mexico's atomic facilities. The project determined those incidents were natural phenomena.[12]

Project Blue Book became the government's main repository for UFO sightings, and its unstated true purpose was to reassure the public there was no threat, but it essentially failed at that task. Over the project's eighteen years of existence, the staff investigated thousands of UFO reports, often interviewing those who rendered the reports about alleged flying saucers, cigar-shaped rockets, and displays of bizarre nighttime lights. It is noteworthy, according to Project Blue Book's final report, that the incidents of sightings rocketed from 170 reports per year during Projects Sign and Grudge to 1,501 sightings annually in 1952 alone.[13]

In July of 1952, Washington, DC, experienced a taste of the UFO mania. At that time, a series of unusual blips appeared on radar screens at local airfields, prompting the US Air Force to launch fighter jets to intercept the "bodies." According to the pilots, they saw the lights dancing through the night sky, "but were unable to catch them."[14]

In the wake of that incident, the US Air Force hosted a press conference, at which time Major General John Samford assured the journalists the government was continuing to investigate the reports made by "credible observers of relatively incredible things." However, he cautioned that the events over the nation's capital were likely "temperature inversions," and he assured the audience that UFOs did not threaten the United States.[15]

At the time, President Harry Truman expressed concern about the UFO issue, which evidently panicked many citizens and choked federal communications. In fact, the Central Intelligence Agency, according to one report, evidently believed the Soviets might have staged a UFO incident to "help screen an attack on the United States." That suspicion led to the agency's 1953 decision to convene a group of experts under the direction of California Institute of Technology physicist H. P. Robertson to review the UFO issue.[16]

The so-called Robertson Panel concluded that most of the UFO sightings were harmless optical illusions, such as weather-related phenomena. However, the panel suggested that, to prevent further public unrest, the US government needed to discredit the UFO reports with a public-relations campaign. Specifically, the report stated:

> The "debunking" aim would result in reduction in public interest in "flying saucers" which today evokes a strong psychological reaction.... Such a program should tend to reduce the current gullibility of the public and consequently their susceptibility to clever hostile propaganda."[17]

The proposed campaign would use "mass media, celebrities, and even the Walt Disney Company to ridicule and discredit UFOs."[18]

Subsequently, civilian astronomer Josep Allen Hynek, a Project Blue Book investigator, spent many years debunking UFO sightings as either natural phenomena or hoaxes. As a result, thousands of cases were cleared. However, even though Dr. Hynek was one of the leading debunkers, he later wrote, "The entire Blue Book operation was a foul-up."[19]

He continued, "Not enough attention was paid to the subject to acquire the kind of data needed even to decide the nature of the UFO phenomenon." He further said, "For many years the Blue Book operation had very low priority as far as the Air Force was concerned. And it was sloppy, just kid's stuff, actually."[20]

An example of the Blue Book Project's cavalier attitude came to a head after word of a UFO sighting in Michigan caused considerable media attention. Evidently, on March 14, 1966, at least one hundred residents near Dexter, Michigan, reported seeing lights and football-sized shapes hovering at low altitudes. Dr. Hynek went to that community, which was rocked by "near hysteria." At a follow-up press conference, he said the sightings were nothing more than the moon and stars veiled behind "swamp gas," the product of decomposing vegetation. Predictably, the locals rejected that explanation.[21]

Project Blue Book's rush-to-judgment approach in Dexter caught the attention of future president Gerald Ford, then a Michigan congressman. Ford called "foul" regarding the project's conclusion about the 1966 UFO sightings in Michigan blamed on "swamp gas." Ford called for a "full-blown" congressional investigation to "allay any apprehensions" of a cover-up.[22]

Congress contracted with the University of Colorado to investigate the issue for three hundred thousand dollars. The study was led by Edward U. Condon, a physicist and the person who debunked the legitimacy of the Tulli Papyrus addressed in chapter 2. Evidently, the "swamp gas" investigation was noteworthy for infighting, especially after a memo written by the project coordinator, Dr. Condon, proposed the effort focus on the psychological and social circumstances of UFO believers.[23]

The Condon project, which began in 1966, published its findings in a 1968 report, *Scientific Study of Unidentified Flying Objects*. That publication stated: "Our general conclusion is that nothing has come from the study of UFOs in the past twenty-one years that has added to scientific knowledge." It continued, "On the basis of present knowledge, the least likely explanation of UFOs is the hypothesis of extraterrestrial visitations."[24]

Dr. Condon's report was labeled "biased" by some, and the physicist himself later admitted his effort was really a "fiasco" and "damned nonsense." Meanwhile, a 1967 report prepared for the US Air Force stated, "The history of Project Blue Book alone has shown that the UFO phenomena is mainly that of a public relations project" and was never serious science.[25] Perhaps that is why on December 17, 1969, the Secretary of the Air Force shuttered Project Blue Book, announcing it "no longer can be justified either on the ground of national security or in the interest of science."[26]

The postmortem on Project Blue Book indicated it analyzed 12,618 cases of UFOs in American skies and 701 remained "unidentified." However, a decade later (1979), then President Jimmy Carter suggested that NASA look into the subject, something the agency at the time considered unwarranted.[27]

Of course, the 1969 termination of Project Blue Book was hardly the end of the government's efforts regarding UFOs. For example, a decade prior (1960), Project Ozma was created as an effort to search for radio signals from outside our solar system. That endeavor, funded by the National Science Foundation, a government agency, ran the National Radio Astronomy Observatory in Green Bank, West Virginia. The project—named after the imaginary land of Oz in the 1900 book by L. Frank Baum, *The Wonderful Wizard of Oz*—was launched to examine the stars Tau Ceti in the constellation Cetus and Epsilon

Eridani in the constellation Eridanus. Evidently, those stars were monitored for six hours a day for four months in 1960 using the eighty-five-foot antenna tuned to the frequency of the twenty-one-centimeter emission line of interstellar hydrogen. No signal was found, though, except "an early false alarm caused by a secret military experiment," according to the Search for Extraterrestrials Institute (SETI).[28]

Beginning in the 1970s, NASA also conducted research into the search for extraterrestrial intelligence using the Arecibo and Goldstone antennas. Evidently, that program was canceled in 1993 just after it was renamed the "High-Resolution Microwave Survey Program," what one source indicated was done to hide the fact that it was actually a search for extraterrestrial intelligence. However, similar projects continue at universities around the world today, such as the Allen Telescope Array, an effort partially funded by Microsoft cofounder Paul Allen and located in Shasta County, 290 miles northeast of San Francisco, California.[29]

NASA's research into extraterrestrial intelligence includes spaceships that have traveled to other planets such as Mars. The organization's press release dated August 6, 1996, claimed: "NASA Scientists Find Evidence of Life on Mars." The next day, President Bill Clinton announced:[30]

This is the product of years of exploration and months of intensive study by some of the world's most distinguished scientists. Like all discoveries, this one will and should continue to be reviewed, examined and scrutinized. It must be confirmed by other scientists. But clearly, the fact that something of this magnitude is being explored is another vindication of America's space program and our continuing support for it, even in these tough financial times. I am determined that the American space program will put its full intellectual power and technological prowess behind the search for further evidence of life on Mars....

Today, rock 84001 speaks to us across all those billions of years and millions of miles. It speaks of the possibility of life. If this discovery is confirmed, it will surely be one of the most stunning insights into our universe that science has ever uncovered. Its implications are as far-reaching and awe-inspiring as can be imagined. Even as it promises answers to some of our oldest questions, it poses still others even more fundamental.

We will continue to listen closely to what it has to say as we continue the search for answers and for knowledge that is as old as humanity itself but essential to our people's future.

The Mars "rock 84001" announcement earned considerable skepticism at the time. Months later, that statement was followed by NASA's claim that it had discovered liquid water on Europa, one of Jupiter's moons. The press release said:

> Tantalizing new images of Jupiter's moon Europa from NASA's Galileo spacecraft indicate that 'warm ice' or even liquid water may have existed and perhaps still exists beneath Europa's cracked icy crust. Europa has long been considered by scientists and celebrated in science fiction as one of the handful of places in the solar system (along with Mars and Saturn's moon Titan) that could possess an environment where primitive life forms could possibly exist.[31]

NASA's continued efforts to find life on other planets drew accusations that it was hiding the truth from the public. Specifically, in 2022, a researcher from Buckingham University claimed NASA is hiding evidence of alien life on the surface of Mars. Barry DiGregorio, with the Center of Astrobiology at the University of Buckingham, United Kingdom, claimed NASA is aware of the discovery, but is hiding the facts from the public.[32]

NASA alleged DiGregorio's discovery is likely crystals. However, Mr. DiGregorio responded:

The crystals theory does not add up. The crystals do not branch or twist. We are talking about something that could have been similar to the Ordovician period on Earth.[33]

Dr. John Brandenburg, a plasma physicist at Morningstar Applied Physics, LLC, indicated that Mars was once home to complex alien life, but not like the soft-bodied creatures proposed by DiGregorio.[34]

The excitement about possible microbiological finds on other planets led to the creation of NASA's Astrobiology Institute, which opened in 1998 and continues operation today. It examines under what circumstances life, from microbial to intelligent, could arise. NASA's Astrobiology Institute (NAI) conducts interdisciplinary research to tap the expertise of different scientific research institutions and universities across the country to answer daunting questions such as: Is life possible on icy moons? What kind of microbes could survive the extreme conditions of Mars?[35]

Even though the Pentagon officially closed Project Blue Book in 1969, it couldn't resist creating, albeit secretly, a UFO monitoring program in 2007 that officially closed in 2012. That program was known as the "Advanced Aviation Threat Identification Program," or AATIP. It reportedly tracked reports of UFOs, including descriptions of some strange aerial activities, such as those reported by two US Navy pilots in 2004. The former head of AATIP, Luis Elizondo, introduced previously, made it clear to various media outlets that we may not be alone in the universe. Specifically, he told CNN, "My personal belief is that there is very compelling evidence that we may not be alone."[36]

The CIA also maintained records of UFO sightings, as evidenced by the release of a trove of documents in 2016, reports collected between the 1940s and the early 1990s. Media reports state the CIA's released documents contain "unsubstantiated UFO sightings in the foreign press and intra-agency memos about how the agency handled public inquiries about UFO sightings." The files have names such as "Flying Saucers in East Germany" and "Police officers spot UFO; rapid reaction force alerted."[37]

In August 2021, the Pentagon once again announced it formed yet another task force to study UFOs or UAPs known as the Unidentified Aerial Phenomena Task Force (UAPTF). A Department of Defense spokesperson at the time confirmed "the Department of the Navy, under the cognizance of the office of the undersecretary of defense for intelligence and security, will lead the UAPTF."[38]

The UAPTF's database as of May 2022 included about four hundred incidents, according to congressional testimony by Scott W. Bray, the deputy director of naval intelligence. Mr. Bray told lawmakers they have not uncovered anything "non-terrestrial in origin."[39]

In October 2023, the Pentagon's new UAP effort, All-Domain Anomaly Resolution Office (AARO), published its first report to Congress in conjunction with the Office of the Director of National Intelligence. That report covered the period of August 31, 2022, to April 30, 2023, which addressed 291 UAP sightings, 274 that occurred during the reporting period, and 17 others from 2019–2022.[40]

Most of those accounts came from sightings over restricted military airspace, which were reported by military personnel and sensors. However, some reports were generated by commercial pilots, and all incidents were primarily US-centric.[41]

The AARO report indicates some of the incidents presented "potential safety of flight concerns, and there are some cases where reported UAPs have potentially exhibited one or more concerning performance characteristics such as high-speed travel or unusual maneuverability."[42]

AARO states it is making progress at standardizing reports and working to improve "sensor placement and calibration to better collect against UAP[s]." However, there continue to be "gaps in domain awareness," thanks to "insufficient data secured by radar, electro-optical (EO)/infrared (IR) sensors; the presence of sensor artifacts, such as IR flare; and optical effects, such as parallax, that can cause observational misperceptions."[43]

Of the 291 UAP reports, all but one were within the air domain. The one was in the maritime domain. One hundred of those sightings were from the FAA and took place over the US and its adjacent waters. Most concerned unidentified lights without specific shape at a variety of altitudes, and none of these UAPs "were exhibiting anomalous characteristics, maneuvering to an unsafe proximity to civil aircraft, or posed a threat to flight safety to the observing aircraft."[44]

In November 2023, in an attempt to be forthcoming about its efforts, the AARO at the Pentagon announced its website has begun hosting a new online tool to report government activity related to UAPs. This is where those claiming "firsthand knowledge of a U.S. Government program/activity related to UAP[s]" can submit a report to the government.[45]

Currently, the form is limited to current or former US government employees, service members, and contractors, according to Sean Kirkpatrick, AARO's director. However, Mr. Kirkpatrick said, "We are exploring methods for how the public can do so in the forthcoming third phase of the secure reporting mechanism."[46]

AARO will gather information on UFO incidents dating back to 1945, said Mr. Kirkpatrick. That data will become part of the congressionally mandated report to help UAP investors research past government programs.[47]

The form used to report UAP-related information "will be protected as personal and confidential," according to Kirkpatrick. Further, it is different from past efforts because it establishes reporting measures such as sightings by both military and civilian pilots.

However, "operational reporting is different," Kirkpatrick explained. "That is, [a] pilot's flying around, and he sees something in his airspace, and he needs to report it. That goes through operational channels."[48]

Other federal agencies, such as the National Security Agency and the Federal Bureau of Investigation, allegedly either collected data or kept UFO-related files, reportedly secured by citizens using the

Freedom of Information Act. The released files are available at many websites by searching UFO-related documents, and some are referenced in appendix B.

Many of the US government's older documents about UFOs are available at the National Archives, a treasure trove of materials for researchers. One of those sets of documents includes those surrendered by the US Air Force, the Project Blue Book records that include reports of a total of 12,618 sightings.[49]

Evidently, UFO lore excites people from all backgrounds, not just those here in the United States, which may explain why many other governments spend their tax money to document UFO sightings as well. According to the website Muckrock, there are publicly available UFO-related files from governments across the world, including Australia, Brazil, Great Britain, Canada, Denmark, France, New Zealand, Panama, and Spain.[50]

Consider a review of some other countries' UFO programs, past and present.

UFO Foreign Government Programs

Peru: The Peruvian air force created an office to investigate UFOs, *Oficina de Investigacion de Fenomenos Aereos Anomalos* (OIFAA). That decision followed a series of UFO sightings over the capital city of Lima that caught the attention of officials who were looking for any possible national security threats from aerial anomalies.[51]

Australia: The Australian government opened its first-ever official UFO investigation in 1930 to look into mystery aircraft over the Bass Strait at Warrnambool, Victoria. In 1994, the Royal Australian Air Force discontinued all UFO research and, in 2001, the Ministry of Defence announced it would no longer handle cases of "unusual aerial sightings."[52]

France: After the Second World War, the French government demonstrated considerable interest in UFO sightings and analysis beginning in the 1960s under the guidance of Atomic Energy

Commission scientist Jean-Luc Bruneau. That effort was proposed by the staff of President Charles de Gaulle, who expressed concern about a 1954 UFO sighting. Still, the initiative was overcome by political upheavals in 1968 and never got off the ground.[53]

After a wave of UFO sightings in the 1970s, the French space agency persuaded the government to create the group *d'Etudes Des Phenomenes Aerospatiaux Non-Identifiees* (GEPAN) to investigate credible and strange UFO sightings. That remained active until 1989 before being replaced by the *Service d'Expertise des Phenomenes de Rentrees Atmospheriques* (SEPRA). That new effort continued UFO work, mostly behind the cover of investigating satellite and rocket debris, before closing in 2005. Almost immediately, in 2006, *Groupe d'Etudes et d'Information des Phenomenes Aerospatiaux Non Identifies* (GEIPAN) came into being and was led by Yves Sillard, the former assistant secretary general for environmental and scientific affairs for NATO. He defended the need for the serious study of UFOs by taking a swipe at America's UFO research efforts.[54]

Mr. Sillard wrote:

> I think that the Americans practice on the subject much higher efforts of investigation than those of any other country, they practice a deliberated policy and had deliberately orchestrated misinformation. It is total misinformation. What for? Is it the fear to see their supremacy challenged if one day they face a much more advanced external civilization? Is it their concern of keeping potential technological assets to themselves? Or... or any other explanation, who knows?[55]

Former Soviet Union: UFO-related actions by the former Soviet Union provide an interesting bit of history. Back on September 20, 1977, witnesses at Petrozavodsk, a city of three hundred thousand in Russia's northwest, saw a massive pulsating object like a red star or jellyfish appear over their city. People as far away as Finland saw the same sight, causing a flood of inquiries to Moscow's Academy of Science. Soon, the Military-Industrial Commission called on the Ministry of Defense to conduct "research of paranormal atmospheric and space phenomena and their influence on the operation of military technical equipment and personnel." That program ran until the Soviet Union collapsed in 1991.[56]

Russia's UFO research program was kept secret, and the underlying conclusion about the objects was that they were somehow related to military weapons tests. Meanwhile, in parallel with that program was a KGB (the Soviet's state security police) effort to collect UFO reports as well and to train especially missile crews to avoid acting in a manner that might provoke an aggressive response from the presumed UFOs.

Retired FSB (Federal Security Service) general and Academy of Sciences researcher Vasily Yeremenko was involved in an experiment to allegedly attract UFOs. Evidently, UFOs were drawn to "heightened tension," such as periods during weapons tests and military exercises. The researchers concluded, according to General Yeremenko, that UFOs were one of three things: an unknown natural phenomenon, American reconnaissance platforms, or extraterrestrial objects.[57]

Civilian UFO Groups

Governments around the world aren't the only entities that keep records on UFO sightings and try to explain their origins. Many civilian, mostly nonprofit, organizations host databases of UFO sightings and publish reports. A few are highlighted below for context.

National UFO Reporting Center: This American organization, founded in 1974 by UFO investigator Robert J. Gribble, receives, records, and tries to corroborate reports of possible UFO-related events. It claims to have processed over 170,000 reports and published many reports on its findings.[58]

Mutual UFO Network (MUFON) is a US-based nonprofit organization originally established in 1969, in Quincy, Illinois, to study UFO sightings. The group's stated goals on its website are: (1) "Investigate

UFO sightings and collect the data in the MUFON Database for use by researchers worldwide; (2) Promote research on UFOs to discover the true nature of the phenomenon, with an eye towards scientific breakthroughs, and improving life on our planet; (3) Educate the public on the UFO phenomenon and its potential impact on society."[59]

Other active US-based UFO organizations that monitor sightings include the Center for Study of Extraterrestrial Intelligence, the Center for UFO Studies, and the International UFO Congress.

There are numerous other nongovernmental UFO organizations across the world in countries including Belarus, Estonia, Sweden, Russia, and the United Kingdom. (See also appendix B, UFO Resources.)

Conclusion

The number of UFO sightings has waxed and waned across the post-World War II period. The US and many other national governments have created programs to document UFO sightings and attempt to identify them, hoping to assuage their citizens' fears regarding any potential threat. Similarly, many civilian organizations complement ongoing government efforts to study and explain the phenomenon. However, at this point, a significant portion of all UFO sightings remain inexplicable.

Section Three will explore what a variety of experts and the general public say about the UFO phenomenon.

WHAT DO THE EXPERTS SAY ABOUT UFOS/UAPS?

Given the millions of billions of Earth-like planets,
life elsewhere in the Universe without a doubt, does exist.
In the vastness of the Universe we are not alone.[1]

ALBERT EINSTEIN (1879–1955), German theoretical physicist
and one of greatest scientists of all times, best known for
developing the theory of relativity

Are UFO events real or hokum? There is a lot of skepticism among the scientific community and even some among the religious communities about the phenomenon. However, that debate is becoming mainstream and is no longer just relegated to the "wacko" corner of society. A growing number of respected scientists and theologians don't immediately dismiss these events as attributable to natural phenomena, conspiracy theories, or pure nonsense.

This section in three chapters examines what three cohorts of experts with a stake in the issue have to say: scientists, theologians, and ufologists. We also consider what the general population says about UFOs.

Chapter 7 answers the question: What do scientists say about UFOs and the possible alien paranormal? There is a group of scientists who completely dismiss the issue as pure hokum, yet a growing number of scientists are publishing their findings about UFOs in peer-reviewed journals that create considerable questions about the origin of this phenomenon.

Chapter 8 surveys the realm of the religious who are also split, but who aren't as skeptical about UFOs as the scientific community. For many in this camp, they see the possibility that so-called UFOs are really evidence of either the unseen spiritual realm (spirits) or accept that the Creator of the universe is quite capable of conceiving beings other than the narcissistic bunch known as "earthlings."

Chapter 9 addresses the demographic profile and motivation of citizens who tend to believe UFOs are alien beings, as well as considers the cohort of UFO experts known as ufologists and their beliefs. The chapter also addresses fringe groups, the UFO cults and those who allege to have been abducted by aliens.

SCIENTISTS GETTING SERIOUS ABOUT UFOS

"I, for one, am not so immensely impressed by the success we are making of our civilization here that I am prepared to think we are the only spot in this immense universe which contains living, thinking creatures," Winston Churchill wrote in a 1939 essay, "or that we are the highest type of mental and physical development which has ever appeared in the vast compass of space and time."[1]

—WINSTON CHURCHILL (1874–1965), British prime minister
"Are We Alone in the Universe?"

This chapter begins by setting the stage via my personal experience with the aerospace scientific community, then elaborates on some inside criticism about their past failure to take the UFO/UAP phenomenon seriously. We also consider the particulars of our new era of openness about scientific investigation, identify areas that require better focus/collaboration, and then conclude with a warning about avoiding the inevitable professional and divisive jealousies among our experts that could sideline progress.

It is my view that space scientists (astrophysicists) and rocket engineers tend to be an odd lot: unquestionably bright, maybe not the most social group, but incredibly focused on their discipline, perhaps to a fault. At least that was my understanding after having spent my youth among America's space community near Cape Canaveral (later

Cape Kennedy, where many US spacecraft are launched), Florida; near a number of space-related research centers in California; and at the Marshall Space Flight Center in Huntsville, Alabama, during the mid-1960s leading up to the 1969 Apollo Moon mission.

My Huntsville neighbors were involved in the space program at the Marshall Center, including a number of Germans who came to America with rocket technologist Wernher von Braun. It was von Braun who built the Nazi Regime's V-2 rockets that were used to attack Great Britain toward the end of World War II. Prior to 1958, von Braun and the nearly fifteen hundred German rocket engineers brought to America after the war acted as advisers to American rocket engineers.

However, that all changed with the Soviet launch of Sputnik 1 in 1957, the first artificial satellite put into Earth orbit. Soon, von Braun was called upon to create the Jupiter series of rockets and, within a year, America placed its first satellite in orbit. The Jupiter became the prototype for the Saturn rockets America eventually used to launch the 1969 Apollo Moon mission.

Those were exciting times to live in among some of the nation's brightest scientists focused on the new frontier: outer space. Leading up to the 1969 Moon launch, it was my view that our scientific community worked well together to overcome seemly insurmountable obstacles presented by space flight. They deserved the heartfelt applause of a grateful nation once astronaut Neil Armstrong descended a ladder from the Apollo landing module on July 20, 1969, towards the surface of the Moon to declare: "That's one small step for man. One giant leap for mankind."[2]

That was a proud day for our science community. It was the result of many years of hard work and genuine collaboration. Unfortunately, that same community quickly turned its back on a new challenge, and now for decades they have defaulted when it comes to discovering the truth about UFOs.

Science in Default

Perhaps the best argument for the scientific community to get serious about the UFO phenomenon was made by Dr. James E. McDonald, former professor of atmospheric science at the University of Arizona. In his 1969 article, "Science in Default: Twenty-two Years of Inadequate UFO Investigations," Dr. McDonald points out:

> Despite continued public interest, and despite frequent expressions of public concern, only quite superficial examinations of the steadily growing body of unexplained UFO reports from credible witnesses have been conducted in this country or abroad.

Much can be said about the dearth of UFO-related research today as well, now more than fifty years after Dr. McDonald's initial (1969) admonition—and our progress still remains marginal at best.[3]

"In my opinion, the UFO problem, far from being the nonsense problem that it has often been labeled by many scientists, constitutes a problem of extraordinary scientific interest," wrote Dr. McDonald. Then he lambasted prior tepid efforts, mostly US government studies outlined in a previous chapter, as being "either devoid of any substantial scientific content, or else have lost their way amidst the relatively large noise-content that tends to obscure the real signal in the UFO reports."[4]

"I believe science is in default," argues Dr. McDonald, "for having failed to mount any truly adequate studies of this problem, a problem that has aroused such strong and widespread public concern during the past two decades [1950s–1960s]." Then he blames the creation of a stigma surrounding UFO investigations on a "long series of inadequate studies," such as the one conducted for the US government's Project Blue Book (1951–1969), and another under the direction of Dr. E. U. Condon at the University of Colorado. After all, Dr.

Condon's report, profiled earlier in this book, was eventually labeled by him of all people as a "fiasco" and "damned nonsense."[6]

Many scientists have avoided UFO research because of the stigma associated with what they label "pseudoscience," the investigation of the unidentified flying objects.[5]

Dr. McDonald identifies two regrettable results of the stigma that came to be associated with the UFO phenomenon, something he attributes to Dr. Condon and others of his ilk. The first, according to Dr. McDonald, is that "the most credible of UFO witnesses are often those most reluctant to come forward with a report of the event they have witnessed." Second, "only a very small number of scientists have taken the time and trouble to search out the really puzzling reports that tend to be diluted out by the much larger number of trivial and non-significant UFO reports."[7]

Dr. McDonald's conclusion is "that there still exists no general scientific recognition of the scope and nature of the UFO problem."[8]

Hopefully, given recent events in the United States, such as the July 2023 congressional hearing on the subject, the lack of "general scientific recognition...of the problem" will quickly change, and our scientific community will begin to step up to the challenge of finding answers to our concerns about UFOs.

Scientists Understandably Skeptical

The scientific community, however, remains skeptical about the phenomenon. Yet, it is willing to consider tackling the issue, albeit under certain conditions, especially now it appears the US government is serious about finding answers regarding the origin of UFOs.

Dr. Don Lincoln, a senior scientist at the Fermi National Accelerator Laboratory and author of *Alien Universe: Extraterrestrial Life in Our Minds and in the Cosmos*, wrote, "The government is [now] taking the sighting of UFOs very seriously." Dr. Lincoln, though, like many other scientists, wants to avoid the stigma long associated with the issue by clarifying his view of UFOs. He dismisses the view that they are "flying saucers and little green men"; rather, according to Lincoln, they are "simply something in the air that is not explained."[9]

He calls for the scientific community to "break the mental link between UFOs and extraterrestrial life, then the idea of a UFO sighting seems more plausible." Of course, as Dr. Lincoln warned, "One can't rule out the possibility of outright hoaxes." (See appendix C for examples of UFO hoaxes.)[10]

Dr. Lincoln rhetorically responds to the question: "So, what do I think about UFOs and LGM [little green men]?" He explained with an evolutionist's perspective:

As a scientist, I think that extraterrestrial life is common in the universe. After all, astronomers have discovered thousands of exoplanets and chemistry is chemistry. Given the right conditions, life will arise from the same chemical reactions...we see here on earth; and other chemical combinations are also possible. Indeed, it boggles my mind to think that life has not evolved elsewhere. I think it's likely that intelligent extraterrestrial life is relatively rare.[11]

As an aside, Dr. Lincoln demonstrates blind faith to believe in something like evolution without evidence. The evolutionist must believe that nonliving substances spontaneously generated life. However, although many scientific experiments "have been conducted over the centuries testing the hypothesis that spontaneous generation could occur...every one of them has resulted in the same conclusion: in nature, life only comes from life," wrote Jeff Miller, who holds a PhD in biomechanical engineering and serves as the full-time science writer at Apologetics Press.[12]

Any scientist, even an astronomer like Lincoln who is rational and follows the evidence to its logical conclusion, should determine that, across the vast universe, life cannot come from nonlife. Unfortunately, much of the modern scientific world has opted instead for irrationality, blind faith, to embrace the view that life can come from nonlife. Rather, scientists should swallow their pride and dismiss faulty concepts like Charles Darwin's theory of evolution to understand that life comes from a supernatural source—God, who "gives everyone life and breath and everything else" (Acts 17:25, NIV).[13]

Dr. Lincoln surmises that "most (probably all) UFOs are not observations of extraterrestrial craft...but I'm open to being proven wrong." He favors funding for programs that search for extraterrestrial life, but admits:

> I also want to get to the bottom of UFO phenomena. If it's advanced weapons from other countries, we should know. And nobody would be more excited than I would be to find out that we're not alone in the cosmos and we're being visited.[14]

Yes, there is a growing collective of scientists willing to agree with the famous poster that shows a flying saucer and boasts the caption: "I want to believe." That poster became popular because it hung on the wall above the desk of FBI special agent Fox Mulder, the fictional character in the mid-nineties hit series, *The X-Files*. The storyline in the series has Agent Mulder and his partner, Dana Scully, uncovering a grand conspiracy "that the U.S. government has been collaborating with extraterrestrials in an alien-human hybrid program."[15]

Of course, the problem for Dr. Lincoln and other like-minded scientists regarding the phenomenon is that they "want to believe," but they need incontrovertible proof, which remains elusive.

Dr. Lincoln isn't alone in seeking "incontrovertible proof," but he wants to distance himself from some of the wacky UFO/UAP ideas and theories bubbling out of our culture. For example, Lincoln likely agrees with astrobiologist Jacob Haqq Misra of the Blue Marble Space Institute of Science in Seattle, Washington, who said, "We don't know what [UAPs] are, and that's what makes them interesting." However, Dr. Misra clarified that UAPs are "a little different from the term UFO in the sense that a phenomenon could be something that's not necessarily a physical solid object. So UAP is maybe a more all-encompassing term."[16]

Astrobiologist Ravi Kopparapu is with NASA's Goddard Space Flight Center in Greenbelt, Maryland. He supports the scientific investigation of UAPs as well:

> We conduct scientific studies of unknown phenomena all the time. This [UAP issue] should not be any different. The most critical point to remember is that when conducting those studies, we should not let our speculations drive the conclusions. The collected data should do it.[17]

"As scientists," explained Dr. Misra, "what we should do is study things that we don't understand."

He continued:

> With UAP[s], there seem to be some anomalous observations that are difficult to explain. Maybe they're a sign of something like new physics, or maybe it's just instrumental artifacts that we don't understand or things that birds are doing.[18]

"Ultimately," Dr. Misra said, "I realized for a scientist who wants to understand what's going on with this UFO thing, there's a lot of noise to sift through."

He stated further:

There's a lot of public discourse about other topics like crop circles, alien abductions and paranormal stories that muddy the waters, and the more we can be clear about the specific aerial anomalies that we're talking about, the more we can actually solve the problem.[19]

US Academics More Welcoming of Research

It may surprise the reader that our American academic community is becoming far more receptive to investigating the UFO phenomenon. Specifically, a 2023 study shows that UFO research is reaching into mainstream academia. In fact, over a third (37 percent) of all US academics indicate they are interested in researching UFOs, and a large minority (19 percent) have witnessed or know someone who has witnessed a UFO.[20]

The 2023 study of US academics, which found significant interest in UFO research, was published in the peer-reviewed *Journal of Humanities and Social Sciences Communications*. This evident awakening to the subject by the academic community may be attributed in part to a resurgence in public interest and some rather tantalizing signs of possible alien life.[21]

Understandably, the academic community avoided the issue in the past because of the stigma as well as government secrecy. However, now the matter has been rebranded to "UAPs" and not as a search for extraterrestrials (alien beings), the science community appears far more receptive to investigating the topic than at any time in the past five decades.

As an aside, the view that aliens exist is held more widely among academics than is often acknowledged. Alexander Wendt of Ohio

State University and Raymond Duvall of the University of Minnesota conducted a study of the issue. They stated in their report, titled *Sovereignty and the UFO*, that "society is perhaps not yet ready to accept that a different, much more superior species exists which is why most of learned society accepts only the possibility that there are UFOs but no aliens."[22]

Wendt and Duvall claim:

UFOs have never been systematically investigated by science or the state, because it is assumed to be known that none are extraterrestrial. Yet in fact, this is not known, which makes the UFO taboo puzzling given the ET possibility.... The puzzle is explained by the functional imperatives of anthropocentric [humankind as the most important element of existence] sovereignty, which cannot decide a UFO exception to anthropocentrism while preserving the ability to make such a decision. The UFO can be "known" only by not asking what it is.

Evidently, purposeful blindness to the possibility that aliens exist has kept the scientific community mute about the issue, a modern example of the Japanese pictorial maxim of three monkeys: "See no evil [eyes covered], hear no evil [ears covered], speak no evil [mouth covered]."[23]

Returning to the survey, the authors found that more than half of the academics (55 percent) said they "would be more likely to conduct research into [UFO/UAP issues] if they had funding for it, and nearly half (43 percent) said they would be more likely to do so if there was a reputable academic scholar in their field who did too."[24]

Fortunately, a number of notable scientists are already pursuing UAP-related research. Among that group is Israeli-American astrophysicist Dr. Avi Loeb, the former head of Harvard's astronomy department. In 2021, Dr. Loeb launched the Galileo Project, which searches for alien life from a scientific perspective. So far (2023), the project's scientists have published eight peer-reviewed scientific articles that seek to advance our understanding of UFOs/UAPs.[25]

Dr. Loeb indicates the Galileo Project, which is privately funded, will search for ET technology.

He stated:

I established the Galileo Project to examine two things. One of those is unidentified aerial phenomena. And the second is objects like "Oumuamua that enter the solar system. They may very much be the same thing; they may be related."[26]

The Galileo Project is "like a fishing expedition where you don't know what kind of fish you will find," said Loeb in an interview.

He continued:

Even if we don't find anything, if we bring in only sardines, objects with mundane explanations, so be it. Whatever we find we will report. The data will be open. The analysis will be transparent.[27]

Dr. Garry Nolan, a prominent researcher at Stanford University, is very active in the study of UAPs as well. Dr. Nolan has collaborated with the US government and published peer-reviewed articles on his work. Further, Nolan told a SALT[28] iConnections conference in New York he believes advanced and intelligent alien life has "'100%' not only already visited earth, are still here, and have 'been here for a long time.'"[29]

As an aside, there is significant evidence, despite what the skeptics say, that a small part of the scientific community has long taken the UFO issue seriously, albeit while many still hold to a nonscientific, anthropocentric-sovereignty perspective. Specifically, there are many dozens of scholarly and academic articles in peer-reviewed journals that address the issue. Although some of those pieces cast a jaundiced eye at ufology, a considerable number takes a rigorous scientific look at the realm. An updated list as of January 2022 is found at "Scientific and Scholarly Articles about UFOs."[30]

A partial listing of peer-reviewed journal articles and other investigations and resources on UFOs is provided in appendix B.

"Getting Serious" about UFOs/UAPs: What Does That Look Like for the Scientific Community?

We are entering a bold new era of interest in all things space, in which robust scientific studies hopefully will replace decades of fruitless speculation and stigmatization of anyone remotely interested in the UFO/UAP topic. Whether this new period of concern is due to renewed attention given by the US Congress, the reports by the Director of National Intelligence, and/or the Pentagon, no matter; what's important going forward is whether these efforts bear fruit, and that outcome will depend on the diligence of our scientific community. Otherwise, all the renewed attention could once again go dormant like it did after the 1969 lunar mission.

There are a number of things the scientific community must seek in order to meet this challenge.

Better equipment is needed. The scientific community must acquire better data regarding the UAPs. "A million blurry images are worthless, compared to a single high-resolution video that resolves an object as it maneuvers," states Harvard University astrophysicist Avi Loeb, the earlier-introduced current head of the Galileo Project. In fact, in December 2022, Dr. Loeb's research team began collecting high-quality scientific data "with a custom-built observatory that was temporarily located on the roof of the Harvard college observatory."[31]

The observatory, according to Dr. Loeb, will "capture continuous video of the sky at infrared, optical, and radio bands and can record ambient sound as well." Then he plans to analyze the data before providing the results to the scientific community via peer-reviewed journals. He hopes to eventually station one hundred such systems at locations across the world to best capture data.[32]

Of course, high-quality equipment is quite expensive. This is something our government must consider in the nation's annual budget process.

Standards must be set. A lot of individuals, organizations, and governments are collecting UAP data, and most use their own standards and methods of collection. That's a problem. We need to standardize the data system; without one common criterion, collaboration is almost meaningless.

UAPx is a Florida nonprofit organization manned by physicists and engineers who study UAPs. It deploys sensor-laden equipment such as infrared, visible, and ultraviolent cameras and spectrographs to collect reliable data much like the Galileo Project. However, it has its own reporting methods and standards.[33]

"All organizations, be they governmental, military, scientist, [or] civilian, have their own reporting methods and standards, and those taking their own data all use different technologies," explained UAPx's Matthew Szydagis, an associate professor in physics at the University at Albany, State University of New York. In the UAPx case, they only look at their own data, which means comparing results with other UAP-collecting groups is quite problematic because of the lack of a common standard.[34]

The New York City-based Enigma Labs is another private company that uses a data-driven approach. Their method is to engage a mobile platform for crowdsourcing UAP reports. Specifically, their smartphone app has a repository of reports of 270,000-plus sightings across the past century; new accounts are accepted by any user. Each observation is given an "Enigma Score," a number between 1 and 100 that is based on a variety of factors, including the "notional quality of the collected data."[35]

The lack of a common standard, whether government or private, creates a nightmare that prevents the scientific community from drawing any meaningful comparisons—much less crunching the data and then coming up with useful conclusions.

People who know government secrets about UAPs must come forward. Congress is forcing the US government to come clean about its UAP programs and records. In fact, the National Defense Authorization Act for fiscal year 2023 (Public Law 117–263—DEC. 23, 2022) includes a provision for UAP whistleblowers to reveal the government's secrets. Leslie Kean, a reporter who has covered the UFO/UAP topic for decades, said: "Those who have signed secrecy agreements [US Government's Standard Form 312—Classified Information Nondisclosure Agreement] related to UAP are now free to reveal that previously protected information to AARO [the Pentagon's All-domain Anomaly Resolution Office] and to Congress, without fear of retribution or prosecution."[36]

Assuming more whistleblowers come forward, Congress might have an opportunity to validate past reports or identify others as hoaxes. Of course, some of that information might yet remain too sensitive to release because of national security implications.

Professional divisions are needed. I began this chapter by explaining that the scientific community has its own peculiarities. One of those, not necessarily unlike other professional forums, is that it suffers from divisions attributable to professional jealousy, access to resources, and more. This could well be the Achilles' heel for future science-based UFO/UAP investigations.

One of the most controversial scientists in the astrophysics realm is Avi Loeb. Some of his peers accuse Loeb of being fixated on finding evidence of extraterrestrial life, which evidently undermines other legitimate investigations.

Dr. Loeb's most recent adventure along those lines was a project that took him to a location off the northeastern coast of Papua New Guinea, the site where a fireball allegedly splashed into the sea in 2014. Evidently, US government sensors at the time recorded the event, but nothing was done until 2019, when a Harvard undergraduate student came across the information and alerted Dr. Loeb of his find.[37]

In June 2023, Dr. Loeb led an expedition to retrieve fragments of the fireball from the Pacific Ocean seafloor. He explained that pieces of the object may in fact provide evidence of extraterrestrial life. No, it won't be like some "biological creatures, the way you see in science fiction movies," Dr. Loeb explained, but he's looking for something like "a technological gadget with artificial intelligence."[38]

Some of Dr. Loeb's colleagues aren't especially fond of Loeb's alleged outlandish projects and declarations, which are arguably evidence of his ongoing success. One critic, Steve Desch, an astrophysicist at Arizona State University, said:

> People are sick of hearing about Avi Loeb's wild claims. It's polluting good science—conflating the good science we do with this ridiculous sensationalism and sucking all the oxygen out of the room.[39]

As a result, according to Dr. Desch, several of his colleagues are refusing to engage with Dr. Loeb's work via peer review, the process that scholars use to evaluate each other's studies before they are published. "It's a real breakdown of the peer review process and the scientific method," he said. "And it's so demoralizing and tiring."[40]

Another Loeb effort raised eyebrows among his peers as well. Evidently, Dr. Loeb took note of an interstellar object—the Oumuamua—that passed planet Earth in 2017. At the time, Dr. Loeb argued that the object could be an artifact of intelligent life, not an asteroid or comet like his peers argued. Then Loeb studied the "fireball catalog" from the Center for Near Earth Object Studies at NASA. Evidently, Loeb concluded the Oumuamua fireball was "moving too fast for something gravitationally bound to our sun," which evidently meant "it must also have been interstellar."[41]

Based on that conclusion, Dr. Loeb wrote a paper that was initially rejected by the *Astrophysical Journal*. Yet, months later, the same journal accepted the piece for publication after the US Space Command announced that measurements of the Oumuamua fireball's velocity were accurate enough to infer an interstellar origin, a confirmation of Dr. Loeb's conclusion.[42]

Not everyone was pleased by the US Space Command's announcement, however. Dr. Peter Brown, a meteor physicist at Western University in Ontario, Canada, critically argued, "it's unknown how precise the US Defense Department [Space Command] data is, which affects how likely it is that the object came from beyond." Further, Dr. Brown and other astrophysicists are evidently troubled by Dr. Loeb's lack of engagement with them before announcing his conclusions.[43]

Dr. Loeb isn't the source of all division within the astrophysics community, therefore he won't doom that community's future efforts to produce critical UAP research. However, the well-publicized differences among these scientists expose the Achilles' heel within that sector of the scientific community, something that must be taken into account and overcome for the good of the entire scientific world.

Conclusion

The scientific community must play a major role in our efforts to find answers about UAPs. That will require resources, collaboration, sound methods, solid standards, and improved collaboration. We must avoid another few decades of no progress by heeding Dr. McDonald's 1969 "Default" conclusion: There "still exists no general scientific recognition of the scope and nature of the UFO problem." After all, the stakes are high, because we don't know whether UAPs are the result of harmless natural occurrences, the products of advanced enemy weapon systems, or invading aliens intent on taking the Earth and its inhabitants captive.[44]

8

RELIGION, ET FAITH GROUPS, AND ALIENS

*Space exploration leads directly to religious
and philosophical questions.*[1]

—CARL SAGAN (1934–1996), American astronomer,
cosmologist, author, and professor

This chapter makes the case that the growing interest in extraterrestrial (ET) beings is as much about science as religion. We begin this review of the issue by establishing not only the popularity of ETs, but the reason for that interest, which in some quarters is an abiding, deep, religious interest. We then examine the basis for UFO religions and their characteristics and profile some beliefs associated with the possibility that ET beings have or might visit planet Earth. Finally, we consider a Christian perspective about the theological challenges raised by the prospect that ETs are perhaps already here...or might soon visit. What might that mean for the Bible-believing Christian?

Setting the Stage for "Discovery" of ETs

Humanity is vulnerable to believe ETs exist, which has its origins in humankind's early times. Our ancient ancestors were affected by astronomical events and thoughts of more intelligent beings visiting from other worlds. Further, juxtapose that anticipation with religious beliefs that have deep biological roots. After all, humans are predisposed to seek order amid chaos, which explains why our ancestors embraced

112

animism and spirits, mythology based on observations of events seen in Earth's sky. Eventually, they were drawn to false gods of many mostly polytheistic religions and others to the one true God of the Bible.

What's the draw to ET religions? Understand that most modern people want to believe there is some form of alien intelligence, especially beings more advanced than us that can then come to Earth to provide guidance and wisdom to help us avoid wars and diseases that plague all humanity. Besides, many of us don't like it when contemporary science tells us we live in a chaotic universe, which might explain the hope that other advanced civilizations exist beyond our Earth and thus could provide us with a measure of reassurance and guidance to save humankind from self-destruction.

The hope of an advanced, wiser civilization is supported by polling. Specifically, the Pew Research Center consistently documents that a considerable percentage of Americans believe we have already been visited by aliens. In 2021, two-thirds of Americans (65 percent) said they believe intelligent life exists on other planets, and half (51 percent) said the UFOs reported by people in the military are likely evidence of intelligent life outside Earth. Further, more than a third (40 percent) say military-reported UFOs are "probably" evidence of ET life that has already visited our planet.[2]

The nexus for this widely held view—that highly intelligent beings exist beyond this world, and some have already paid us a visit—is built inside our very soul, the unseen, spiritual part of the human being. After all, it appears that humans are primed "to believe in a higher order or purpose, be that gods, intelligent design, or extraterrestrials," writes Klaus Brasch, an emeritus professor of biology at California State University, San Bernardino.[3]

Professor Brasch's assertion that we are "primed to believe" reminds me of a quote attributed to a seventeenth-century Christian thinker, Blaise Pascal, who famously said, "There is a god-shaped vacuum in the heart of each man which cannot be satisfied by any created thing but only by God the creator, made known through Jesus Christ."[4]

Arguably, Pascal's quote is a restatement of what King Solomon wrote 2,500 years earlier. Specifically, the ancient king wrote in Ecclesiastes 3:11 (NIV) that God "has also set eternity in the human heart; yet no one can fathom what God has done from beginning to end." In other words, every human soul is aware there is something more than what this world offers. Some humans look for alien beings to fill that vacuum, others turn to religion, and yet others look to the true God of the Bible.

The recent awakening to the possibility of aliens beyond our world and whether they might have visited Earth, explains what Walter Staggs, a religious studies professor at George Mason University, argues is evidence of a paradigm shift now seizing the world—a renewed interest and a serious reconsideration of ET-like beings, and arguably evidence of a hunger to fill the vacuum in our hearts. After all, we humans want to fill the vacuum Pascal and Solomon spoke of, and for some, that's a faith in unconfirmed ETs. They want a reason to believe ETs came to Earth with great technology and intelligence to help us overcome our differences and enjoy a promised blissful future.[5]

There are numerous UFO religions and cults,
most claiming some connection with alien beings.[6]

114

This view is supported by contemporary culture and a rather outlandish theory about the history of this world. Specifically, Professor Staggs writes about a History Channel television series, *Ancient Aliens*, which is based on the much-criticized work of Swiss writer Erich von Däniken, the author of the 1960 book titled *Chariots of the Gods?* In that book, Mr. von Däniken claims, "Our forefathers received visits from the universe in the remote part...these 'strangers' annihilated part of mankind existing at the time and produced a new, perhaps the first, homo sapiens.[7]

Mr. von Däniken's theory introduced what has come to be known as the "ancient astronaut theory," which, according to Professor Staggs, is "a new working hypothesis and place it at the very center of our research into the past [which]...claims that deities of most religions, including Jesus, were actually extraterrestrials."[8]

I need to create a sidebar about author Erich von Däniken. I call your attention to a 1974 interview of the writer published in the *New York Times*. That interview is not flattering and should be a giant red flag to anyone who grants von Däniken any credibility.[9]

The interview portrays von Däniken as a true charlatan who was convicted of embezzlement, fraud, and forgery by a Swiss court. A court psychiatrist who examined von Däniken said he was "a prestige-seeker, a liar and an unstable and criminal psychopath with a hysterical character, yet fully accountable for his acts."[10]

Mr. von Däniken was asked by the *Times* reporter about charges that he has a "credibility problem," especially vis-à-vis his "theory that has astronauts landing on earth 10,000 years ago and procreating homo sapiens." According to the reporter, "much of what von Däniken purveys depends upon ancient religious myths—specifically, the recurring references to sky-borne gods."[11]

Evidently, von Däniken had a deep "disenchantment with the Catholic faith in which he was raised." The *Times* reporter continued:

For the literal and symbolic fatherhood of God, he has now substituted the artificial insemination of visiting astronauts on shore leave. His gospel is a strange, almost visionary amalgam of the latest Scifi stuff with the most ancient myths—a marriage rather like that of his astronauts from a higher civilization with the beast-men who inhabited the earth when they arrived and whom they lifted by cross-breeding to manhood.[12]

Regarding von Däniken's book, the *Times* writer stated:

I think we are seeing a quasi-religious appeal at work here. Von Däniken's books provoke the childish question "Where did I come from?" Just as children sometimes fantasize that the man and woman they have been stuck with could not possibly be their real father and mother, so in a nonreligious age in which technology is god, von Däniken packs God the father off to the senior citizen's home and substitutes shiny, new-minted astronaut father-figures.[13]

Mr. von Däniken's bizarre views that ET beings are real and came to Earth long ago has now become a more acceptable view to a certain extent thanks to the US government's admission that UFOs are genuine (but not necessarily extraterrestrials), which gives the issue of potential ET visitations a new social legitimacy. Professor Staggs also fuels that view by citing the July 2023 congressional testimony of David Grusch, a veteran of the National Geospatial-Intelligence Agency and the National Reconnaissance Office, who claims the government is hiding classified evidence of "intact and partially intact craft of non-human origin."[14]

As further evidence ETs might be among us, Leslie Kean, a reporter of UFO-related issues over many decades, wrote:

The [US] Air Force carried out a disinformation campaign to discredit reported sightings of unexplained objects [an issue addressed in previous chapters of this book]. Now, with two public hearings and many classified briefings under its belt, Congress is pressing for answers [about what the US government actually knows regarding UFOs and especially ETs].[15]

Another expert, Jonathan Grey, who works for the National Air and Space Intelligence Center, a unit of the US Air Force, concludes about ETs: "The non-human intelligence phenomenon is real. We are not alone." Then he claims "retrievals of this kind [alien craft] are not limited to the United States. This is a global phenomenon, and yet a global solution continues to elude us."[16]

Contributing to the view that we are "not alone" is US Air Force veteran Sean Illing, a writer for Vox Media and the host of *The Gray Area* podcast. Mr. Illing said the growing anticipation about ETs visiting Earth is a full-blown paradigm shift: "It's a great time to believe in aliens."[17]

This paradigm shift toward wider acceptance of what used to be mostly a verboten, stigmatized issue—belief in the possibility of alien beings—blows a hole in previous theories of scientific interpretation. No longer is the growing number of UFO sightings only labeled as the product of natural phenomena, albeit unknown, but now a large segment of humanity embraces the view that some of these UFO incidents are evidence of real ET travelers.

The growing perspective that aliens may in fact exist doesn't necessarily destroy the basis for most religions, however. After all, religion offers answers to tough questions about the nature of humanity, the origin of the Earth, and the world beyond our understanding. In fact, nonreligious belief systems based on the existence of ETs ask many of the same questions addressed by contemporary religions.

Therefore, many people who believe ETs have visited Earth from distant galaxies believe those visitors are in fact superhuman, some are good (angelic) and others bad (demonic), and the cosmos beyond Earth is filled with forces impossible for us to understand. Such beliefs combine faith systems about ETs into a familiar religious framework, the topic addressed below.

UFO Religions: Origins and Beliefs in ET

What is the significance of UFO religions in the United States? Charles A. Ziegler, the coauthor of *UFO Crash at Roswell*, concludes that "tens of millions of adults in the United States believe that some UFOs are manifestations of an un-earthly intelligence." Further, John A. Saliba, a Jesuit priest, professor of religious studies at the University of Detroit Mercy, and author of the journal article, "The Study of UFO Religions," agrees with Ziegler. He wrote that belief in ETs has burgeoned in the "last half of the twentieth century," a view supported by recent polling and ample justification for considering UFO religions and their beliefs.[18]

We begin this brief exposé about UFO religions by first defining the term "religion." Roderick N. Smart (1927–2001), a Scottish writer and university educator, was a pioneer in the field of secular religious studies. He proposed seven dimensions of a religion, and most of these criteria appear to apply to UFO religious groups as well: "(1) the ritual or practical; (2) the doctrinal or philosophical; (3) the mythic or narrative; (4) the experiential or emotional; (5) the ethical or legal; (6) the organizational or social; and (7) the material or artistic."[19]

Now that we've defined "religion" in a broad sense, we consider what Father Saliba writes about the peculiar UFO religions. In his paper, the Jesuit priest states there "are many differences among UFO religions," such as some have elaborate ritual and/or mythology; several have regular communal worship services; some have core membership that might live communally; some have membership across several continents; and the level of organization varies widely.[20]

Characteristics of UFO Religions

There are "six main characteristics that set UFO religions apart as a unique phenomenon," according to Saliba. They are listed below:[21]

(1) A belief in extraterrestrial beings, who reside mainly, but not exclusively, in our solar system. God (in the Judeo-Christian

sense) often does not have a central role, is not present at all, or his existence is at times denied.

(2) An emphasis on the relationship between aliens and human beings. Some groups have a myth of human origin and stories of visits by aliens throughout human history. Some UFO religions have adopted Erich von Däniken's theory of the origins of the human race, which rejects the current theory of evolution. [Of course, given von Däniken's criminal history and troubled psychological past, one should view his work with great skepticism.]

(3) A strong belief that that there have been a series of encounters and communications between human beings and aliens. Select individuals are believed to be channels, messengers, or prophets chosen to relay messages to the human race, to have met personally with alien beings, and even to have been transported to other planets. Some, such as the leaders of the Extraterrestrial Earth Mission, claim to be "walk-ins," that is, individual alien beings have inhabited the bodies of humans. Though, usually, there is only one leader of a UFO group who is accepted as the contact with aliens, there are a few examples, such as the Lightside UFO Study Group, where the leading members are all contactees and/or walk-ins. In cases where the contactee is deceased, as in Unarius and the Aetherius Society, there is evidence that the movements have gone through an organizational period which Max Weber called the "routinization of charisma."

(4) A conviction that aliens are visiting Earth to offer help for human beings. They warn of impending disasters, such as nuclear war and environmental crisis. While there are trends in some Christian circles to demonize aliens, 12 UFO religions

are inclined to look on extraterrestrials as beneficent, even though the existence of evil aliens is not ruled out.

(5) A belief that a millennial age will begin with the public advent of the aliens. Human beings will receive more advanced technology and make great evolutionary strides in both the physical and spiritual realms. Some apocalyptic scenarios, if the human race is not ready to receive or welcome the aliens, are also present.

(6) A stress on the need for human beings to prepare for the public arrival of the aliens. These preparations are usually of a spiritual nature, but physical plans may also be proposed, as in the case of the Raëlian Movement, whose members have already designed an embassy to house the aliens when they arrive.

History of UFO Religions

When and where did UFO religions begin? Evidently, the First Industrial Revolution era (approximately AD 1760–1840) fostered a hotbed of speculation about astronomical developments and the "plurality of worlds," as well as the evident theological implications of those topics among both scientists and theologians.

Ronald L. Numbers (1942–2023), an American historian of science, argued that seventeenth- and eighteenth-century scientific debates were "suffused with religious overtones," which included speculation about ET beings and questions about salvation, heaven, and hell. That speculation fueled division between scientists and clergy, which arguably laid the groundwork for the emergence of UFO religions.[22]

Emanuel Swedenborg (1688–1772), a Swedish pluralistic-Christian theologian, scientist, and mystic, is identified with one of the first religious movements that addressed ET life and its theological identity. In Swedenborg's treatise, *De Telluribus in Mundo Nostro Solari*, translated *Earths in the Universe* (1758), he detailed his alleged visits to the planets Mercury, Jupiter, Mars, Saturn, and Venus. He wrote in *Earths* that during those visits (likely psychic trips), he interacted with the planets' inhabitants and learned religious messages they offered earthlings. Specifically, Swedenborg described the ETs as having utopian social, scientific, and religious systems; he encouraged earthlings to embrace those alien systems.[23]

Swedenborg's writings inverted the twentieth-century pattern—he allegedly traveled away from Earth (psychically) to visit ETs. Subsequently, his work became the forerunner for some of today's UFO religious thought and influenced current views about ET religious, social, and scientific harmony.[24]

UFO religion saw a surge in popularity thanks to the cultural climate of the 1950s in the shadow of World War II and especially the advent of the new atomic age, as well as the much-publicized UFO incidents at Roswell and Mount Rainer (1947). A significant advocate for ET in the 1950s was George Adamski (1891–1965), introduced in chapter 5 of this book. He, along with statements by his critics, evidently took a page out Swedenborg's playbook when he coauthored with Desmond Leslie *The Flying Saucers Have Landed*. That text recounts Adamski's alleged encounter with "Space Brothers," supposedly ETs from Venus who came to Earth using "flying saucers" with the aim of dispensing a message of occult wisdom. Also, according to Adamski, the "Space Brothers" lived "by a higher spiritual law of self-development, and through repeated reincarnations, all beings could evolve into a higher consciousness."[25]

Adamski's "Space Brothers" operated "using spiritual machinery, and only such a fusion of religion and science allowed them to visit other planets." Mr. Adamski's popularity vis-à-vis his book attracted readers across many countries and seeded several quasi-religious movements "dedicated to studying and promulgating the Venusian wisdom."[26]

One group that embraced Adamski's writings was the Aetherius Society, founded in 1954 by English spiritual seeker George King

(1919–1997), who claimed to have a message from advanced Venusians and Martians. King, not that different from Swedenborg, claimed he visited with ETs using psychic means. Further, King brought to earthlings the ETs' messages of peace and spiritual awareness, and called on them "to learn the divine law" and "the framework of its lasting truth."[27]

On the heels of the Aetherius Society was the founding of the Unarius Academy of Science, which claimed to represent the "interest of benevolent space aliens as psychically transmitted to humanity." This group claimed that "UFO[s] had physically visited [their] founders, but it did insist that such crafts would visit the earth in the near future." That view led to the group purchasing land in California "to build a landing strip for such extraterrestrial visitors."[28]

Many scholars who track UFO religions agree these groups "respond to modernity, and with it its foci on science, technology, and rationalism." However, Benjamin E. Zeller from Brevard College, Brevard, North Carolina, states in his article, "At the Nexus of Science and Religion: UFO Religions":

> But all UFO religions play with the innate sympathies between religious and ufological beliefs, namely the ideas of interacting with nonhuman and superhuman entities, answering questions about the nature of human life and what is beyond our planet, and ritualizing this worldview through religious practice. Clearly the topic of UFO religions continues to fascinate scholars as well as the public.[29]

Beginning in the 1970s, UFO religions have gone beyond concerns about atomic weapons as they were in the 1950s to more contemporary cultural developments. These groups tend to fuse Christianity and theosophical (teaching about God and the world based on mystical insight) approaches to UFOs, such as the group Heaven's Gate, which ended its existence in 1997 with the mass suicide of its thirty-nine members.[30]

There are currently a number of active UFO-related religious groups. My purpose below is to expose the reader to one group, perhaps the best-known today: the Raëlian movement, which boasts branches in fifty-two countries.[31]

The Raëlian movement, aka Raëlians, traces its origin to a French sports journalist, Claude Vorilhon, now known as Raël. He founded the Raëlians after what he described as an encounter in 1973 in Clermont-Ferrand, France, with aliens called the Elohim, followed by "his visit to the extraterrestrial planet of the Elohim 3 years later." It is likely not coincidental that the word *Elohim* is the Hebrew name for God in the Bible, such as in Genesis 1:1 (NIV), "In the beginning God (*Elohim*) created the heavens and the earth."[32]

The Raëlian movement describes itself as an atheist, spiritual, nonprofit organization and claims extraterrestrial scientists created life on Earth from their own genetic material. The Raëlians also claim to have cloned a human being and say they are working to build an embassy in Jerusalem "to [the] great people from space."[33]

Susan Palmer, a Canadian sociologist of religion and former professor of religious studies at Dawson College in Westmount, Quebec, who is now with Concordia University, Montreal, became interested in the Raëlian movement in 1987 when she attended a psychic fair in Montreal.

Palmer described the typical profile of a Raëlian member:

> I would say that, in Quebec at least, the movement attracts young, attractive adults, from a Catholic background that they have already rejected, who are upwardly mobile in society, ambitious in their education and careers, and individualistic and fun loving. Like many Quebecois youth, they reject conventional middle class and Christian family values, live alone or with a partner outside wedlock, and postpone or veto reproduction. They tend to revere science and despise religious institutions, particularly the Catholic Church.[34]

George Chryssides, a British academic and researcher on new religious movements and cults, writes that the Raëlian movement "has a coherent worldview which is scientific, hedonistic, materialistic, and atheistic." He attributes the group's so-called success to "efforts to deal with secularization and modern science, both of which are contemporary and unresolved challenges to traditional religions."[35]

Chryssides states that discussions with "Raëlian[s] is impossible, because they take literally Raël's encounters with the Elohim and accept uncritically his unique interpretations of the Bible, particularly his exegesis of the rather strange story in Genesis 6:1–4 [account of the Nephilim]." Chryssides concludes about the Raëlians:

The movement experiences an intellectual introversion which can only hamper its progress, since it fails to subject [itself] to critical discussion beliefs that the dominant culture finds problematic. Such beliefs are principally its belief that extraterrestrials are in contact with humanity, Raël's idiosyncratic biblical exegesis, its undemocratic elitism, and its failure to address ethical issues associated with politics and genetics.[36]

The Significance of UFO Religions

It is true that membership in UFO religions is quite small, but their impact is much larger than one might think, given the popularity of the issue even among mainstream religious people. Therefore, as Saliba asks, "How does one incorporate our expanding scientific view of the cosmos into a religious world view that has been rather earthbound?"[37]

That effort comes about with the meshing of science and theology on the topic of ET beings, which is tracked by two relatively new disciplines, "exobiology" and "exotheology." These "disciplines" attempt to answer, according to Saliba, "the scientific and theological questions that are asked about extraterrestrial intelligence or beings." These disciplines, states Saliba, "are indicative of the human quest for knowledge of the universe as a whole and the rejection of the provincial attitude that limits research to the planet earth."[38]

Exobiology, better known as "astrobiology," is the study of the prospect of life outside our planet, a discipline recognized by NASA. Specifically, the Space Science and Astrobiology Division at NASA's Ames Research Center "provides unique interdisciplinary scientific expertise and capabilities that advance human understanding of the Molecular Evolution of Galaxies, the Evolution and Formation of Planetary Systems and our Understanding of the Origin and Evolution of Life in the Universe." Evidently, NASA is using this discipline to "speculate on the conditions that might give rise to life, on the type of lifeforms that might have developed in different and yet unknown environments, and on the possibility of communicating with extraterrestrial beings, if they exist."[39]

The other term, "exotheology" or "astrotheology," is a branch of theology that considers what humankind might do if we ever make contact with ET intelligences. It asks questions about coping with different worldviews, supernatural beings, and more. This discipline addresses for Christians the issue of whether "God could have created worlds different from ours and whether intelligent aliens would have a religious and/or spiritual condition that is sinful and in need for salvation." And the logical question for the Christian is: What is the role of Christ in this broader view of the cosmos?[40]

Christians' Response

The final portion of this chapter addresses how Christians might respond to the deep theological questions should ETs actually arise.

What's the impact for religions, and especially Christianity, if there actually are aliens?

The most religious among us tend to reject the notion that intelligent life exists elsewhere, according to Pew Research Center. Specifically, "Americans who attend religious services at least weekly are less likely than those who seldom or never attend services to say that intelligent life exists elsewhere (44 percent vs. 75 percent)." Further, "adults who pray daily (54 percent) are also less likely than those who seldom or never pray (80 percent) to say intelligent life exists on other planets."[41]

Put the skepticism of the most religious among us to the side for the moment to consider the possible existence of alien life and the challenges it might create, especially for Christians. For example, the Christian theologian needs to consider tough questions such as: Did Jesus die for aliens, not just for human earthlings? What's the alien's relationship with the God of the Bible? Do aliens sin like human earthlings? How do ETs attain salvation, if that's even possible?

First, consider the theological argument that ETs actually exist.

"If we are the products of creation," said Duilia de Mello, an astronomer and physics professor at Catholic University, "why couldn't we have life evolving in other planets as well? There's nothing that says otherwise."[42]

In fact, many religious traditions teach that ET life is possible, according to David Weintraub, professor of astronomy at Vanderbilt University and author of *Religions and Extraterrestrial Life: How Will We Deal with It?*[43]

"Our knowledge about the likelihood of this [topic] is going to explode," warns Weintraub. "If we suddenly have that information, if that's a threat theologically, then maybe now is the right time to be talking about it so you're ready for the answer."[44]

David Wilkinson, an astrophysicist-turned-theologian who teaches at Durham University in the United Kingdom, cited many reasons some Christians would find extraterrestrial life threatening or confusing. Many Christians believe in a literal, six-day creation as described in the Bible, states Wilkinson, where aliens are not mentioned. Some of those people are worried that if there are other, albeit alien, beings, God would not have a special relationship with human beings.[45]

After all, Wilkinson said, theologians in the early centuries were open to speculation about other worlds, and authors such as British

Christian C. S. Lewis used science fiction to explore theology, such as in his work *The Chronicles of Narnia*.[46]

Many scientists today, as we learned in the previous chapter, believe we will inevitably detect ET life. They have reasons for this confidence, and their argument goes something like the following paragraph taken from a BBC article, "If We Made Contact with Aliens, How Would Religions React?"[47]

In 2000, astronomers knew of about 50 of these "exoplanets" [planets outside our solar system]. By 2013, they had found almost 850, located in over 800 planetary systems. That number may reach one million by the year 2045, says David Weintraub.... "We can quite reasonably expect that the number of known exoplanets will soon become, like the stars, almost uncountable," he writes. Of those discovered so far, more than 20 are Earth-size exoplanets that occupy a "habitable" zone around their star, including the most recently discovered Proxima b, which orbits Proxima Centauri.[48]

The search for ET intelligence may begin with the hard sciences, but it quickly engulfs the humanities and even theology. After all, Carl Sagan, the famous cosmologist and author, is correct in his book *The Cosmic Question* when he states, "Space exploration leads directly to religious and philosophical questions." Therefore, that leads us back to questions that challenge exotheology, the discipline introduced earlier that refers to "speculation on the theological significance of extraterrestrial life."[49]

Paul C. W. Davies, an English physicist and professor at Arizona State University, identifies three principles that address the exotheological question of humanity's uniqueness in his book *Are We Alone?* His first is the principle of nature's "uniformity."[50]

That principle, according to Davies, claims "the physical processes seen on earth can be found throughout the universe." In other words, as Davies explains, "the same processes that produce life here produce life everywhere." Like so many scientists, Davies is evidently a Darwinian evolutionist, believing life can come from nonliving matter.[51]

The second principle is called "plenitude," "which affirms that everything that is possible will be realized." This principle, according to Davies, claims "as long as there are no impediments to life forming, then life will form" or, as Arthur Lovejoy, the American philosopher who coined the expression, puts it, "No genuine possibility of being can remain unfulfilled."[52]

Finally, Davies' third principle is "mediocrity," which "claims that there is nothing special about Earth's status or position in the universe." Of course, for the Christian, this directly challenges a core belief shared by all Abrahamic religions (Judaism, Christianity, and Islam), which is that "human beings are purposefully created by God and occupy a privileged position in relation to other creatures."[53]

So, we return to the question: Might the discovery of ETs end all religions, including Christianity? Likely not, but there would be changes to our understanding of this world and our God as a result.

A study by Ted Peters, a Lutheran theologian with the Center for Theology and the Natural Science, in Berkeley, California, found that twice as many nonreligious people than those of faith believe the discovery of ETs will spell trouble for all religions (69 percent vs. 34 percent, respectively). But that's not necessarily true.[54]

The fact is religion has always been quite adaptable. Most faiths would survive the revelation that aliens exist. Catholic priest and theologian Thomas O'Meara, the author of *Vast Universe: Extraterrestrials and Christian Revelation*, writes, "If being and revelation and grace come to worlds other than Earth, that modifies in a modest way Christian self-understanding"—and, we might add, all religious self-understanding. However, he writes, "It is not a question of adding or subtracting but of seeing what is basic in a new way."[55]

"Many religions have always believed God names the stars. Is it really a stretch to believe God names the stars' inhabitants, too? And that they might possibly each have their own names for God?" asks

Brandon Ambrosino, the author of the BBC article, "If We Made Contact with Aliens, How Would Religions React?"[56]

Christianity Will Survive the Discovery of ETs

Later in this volume, I will address the issue of whether what we are seeing in our skies is evidence of ETs or something else, albeit from a biblical perspective, spiritual beings in the unseen realm. However, if in fact intelligent aliens are discovered in the future or there is evidence they have already been to Earth, I believe Christianity is quite firm in its foundation and will clearly survive that revelation for a variety of reasons, some of which are outlined below. But not everyone is confident that Christianity can handle the emergence of ETs.

Professor Paul Davies, introduced earlier, claims, "Whether or not we are alone is one of the great existential questions that confront[s] us today." He poses the question in his *Atlantic Monthly* article, "E.T. and God: Could Earthly Religions Survive the Discovery of Life Elsewhere in the Universe?" Then he argues that Christianity is especially vulnerable to what he claims is the inevitable appearance of ET beings.[57]

Professor Davies argues that, in the past, Christianity accommodated "new scientific facts" at the expense of doctrine. However, unlike in the past, says Davies, once ET inevitably is found to be real, "the impact [for Christianity] will be instant"—and, by inference, there won't be time for reflection and accommodation as in the past.[58]

The necessity for change at that "instant" could shake Christianity's foundations, according to Davies, especially if ETs are "far ahead of us not only scientifically and technologically but spiritually." After all, Davies asks, "Where does that leave mankind's presumed special relationship with God?" Of course, this conundrum challenges the Christian's view of incarnation because, according to the Bible, Jesus Christ is humanity's Savior and Redeemer. "But what of deeply spiritual aliens," asks Davies. "Are they not to be saved?" Then he adds, "Can we contemplate a universe that contains perhaps a trillion worlds of saintly beings, but in which the only beings eligible for salvation inhabit a planet where murder, rape, and other evils remain rife [a not-so-subtle reference to planet Earth]?"[59]

Davies also argues, "In the Christian view of the world, Jesus was God's only son. Would God have the same person born, killed, and resurrected in endless succession on planet after planet?" Davies cites as historical support for that view American founding father and political philosopher Thomas Paine (1737–1809), who subscribed to a similar perspective. Paine wrote in *The Age of Reason* that "the son of God and sometimes God himself, would have nothing else to do than to travel from world to world, in an endless succession of death, with scarcely a momentary interval of life." Then Paine evidently concluded that Christianity is simply incompatible with the existence of ETs, according to Davies.[60]

Professor Davies' "E.T. and God" article drew some rather strong rebuttals about his views regarding Christianity's resilience to the discovery of ETs. I've summarized a couple of those responses below.

Gerald E. Nora, an attorney of Vernon Hills, Illinois, responded to Davies in a letter to the editor of the *Atlantic Monthly*. Mr. Nora rightly argued that "Paul Davies' 'E.T. and God' was thoughtful but completely wrong when arguing that the discovery of extraterrestrial life would undermine Christianity's conception of God's special relationship with man."[61]

Christians learn from the first book of the Bible, Genesis, that God gave humankind stewardship over this Earth, not over the broader cosmos, argued Mr. Nora. Yes, we are the highest creation on planet Earth, but God Himself is the highest of all creation, and His angels are, for now, higher than even humans.[62]

Secondly, Mr. Nora argues that "Christianity recognizes Jesus as God, man, and savior." However, the "special relationship" between people and God doesn't negate the possible existence of ETs, nor would it, as Davies wrote, require "the existence of 'saviors' for other species of intelligent life." He continued, "Christians understand that God gave Jesus to humanity because humanity was a fallen species, not a successful species."[63]

"For Christians and Jews, the natural, incarnate world is the first revelation of God's existence," Mr. Nora wrote. "This revelation is more persuasive when the universe is encountered as generously made, with laws that continue to confound and amaze us as they are discovered."

Then Mr. Nora called out Davies' reference to the "God of the gaps," which alleges that God is "squeezed out by man's growing [scientific] knowledge." Nora called foul here to argue that "Christians worship a God who grants man a widening light of understanding—and a growing circle of darkness, wonder, and mystery."[64]

Therefore, Mr. Nora stated, "The discovery of an intelligent alien race would be an opportunity for enlightenment and error." Then he posed a question for humankind if ETs come on the scene: "The first question would be whether this race had escaped the same fall from grace that mankind had experienced.... What could mankind learn of creation and the Creator from the aliens, and what might man share in turn?" Mr. Nora offered that "aliens would also pose new opportunities for error and sin, but nothing would change Christian doctrine on man's relationship with God."[65]

Mr. Nora concluded his letter to the editor by stating: "The discovery of extraterrestrials will undermine pride, not faith." After all, he said:

Christianity has coped with many events that dismayed its adherents, including the discoveries of evolution and orbital mechanics, the invention of the printing press, the postponement of the Second Coming, the fall of imperial Rome, and the Resurrection. It is the secular humanists, I submit, who will be most challenged and overawed by extraterrestrial life.[66]

Another response to Davies' "E.T. and God" article came from the Reverend Nils Blatz, of the Church of the Redeemer in Mattituck, New York. He argued that "Davies fails utterly to fathom the cosmic inclusiveness of Christianity," and continued:

For Christians, the central religious metaphor is a crucifixion. God is decisively "personified" for us in the narrative of a human being bleeding and dying on a cross for the sake of both friend and enemy. The greatest of Christian theologians have long recognized that the Crucifixion requires neither recurrence nor reinterpretation for its significance and consequence to be manifested in other cultures, other worlds, and other creatures we may encounter. A love that bleeds for us, the Bible affirms, bleeds for all creation, and never ceases such self-oblation. As Pascal wrote, "Christ will be in agony until the end of the world."[67]

"The Crucifixion is thus not some mechanical salvific transaction," wrote Reverend Blatz. Rather, "the Anglican Bishop John Robinson rightly maintained, 'The New Testament does not affirm that in Christ our salvation "becomes possible." It affirms, rather, that in him what has always been possible now "becomes manifest," in the sense of being decisively presented in a human [life].'"[68]

"Davies distorts Christianity by insisting, too, that by its lights God's saving love is limited to human beings," wrote Blatz. He then quoted Davies to make a point:

Jesus Christ was humanity's savior and redeemer. He did not die for the dolphins or the gorillas, and certainly not for the proverbial little green men.

Reverend Blatz labeled that assertion "misguided," then quoted Cardinal Pierre de Bérulle, a French Catholic priest and seventeenth-century statesman, who wrote:

Incarnation is the manner and mode of all of God's work in His world.... The incarnation is the condition, the work, and the mystery wherein God reigns and whereby he reigns in His creatures.[69]

"Davies reveals, finally, a surprising ignorance that these comprehensive, cosmic themes are not simply the development of later theology but are often quite explicit in the New Testament," according to Reverend Blatz. Then Blatz called out the Apostle Paul in Colossians 1:16–17 (NIV) to affirm that in and through "God's self-offering love:"

For in him all things were created: things in heaven and on earth, visible and invisible, whether thrones or powers or rulers or authorities; all things have been created through him and for him. He is before all things, and in him all things hold together.[70]

"In Him all things (all creatures) cohere," the reverend pointed out. After all, "Christianity may not always live up to this utterly inclusive theology, but if it is faithful to the biblical witness, it should expect to encounter the same loving, 'bleeding' Creator deeply incarnate in alien cultures and extraterrestrial intelligence."[71]

No one, neither Professor Davies nor his critics, has a good handle on how Christians and the balance of religious humankind will handle the possible announcement that ET beings are among us. The issues debated, though, as evidenced above, are worthy of our further discussion and prayer.

Conclusion

This chapter demonstrates that there is considerable anxiety and speculation among the general population about ETs and what their appearance might mean for religion. Here, we explored, albeit briefly, UFO religions and their beliefs, and we completed this short trek by considering what the discovery of ETs might mean for age-old faith groups—especially Christianity.

9

UFOLOGISTS
AND OTHER BELIEVERS

One of the main goals of what we're trying to do here today is to move conjecture and conspiracy towards science and sanity.[1]

—DANIEL EVANS, assistant deputy associate administrator for research,
NASA's Science Mission Directorate
NASA news conference, September 14, 2023

The first two chapters of this section in *Out of This World* considered what the scientific and religious communities believe about UFOs and the possibility that there are extraterrestrial beings. Those chapters provide evidence that significant pluralities of some of our best experts in those fields either believe in ET life-forms or are open to the possibility. This chapter turns to the balance of the population. According to polling, four in ten Americans believe some UFOs have been alien spacecraft visiting Earth from other planets and galaxies, while overall, as cited earlier, two-thirds (65 percent) believe there is intelligent alien life on other planets. However, almost nine in ten (87 percent) don't think UFOs pose a security threat to the United States, according to Pew Research.[2,3]

We begin this chapter with a demographic profile of citizens who tend to believe UFOs are evidence of alien life. Then I provide some insights about the motivation that led them to that conclusion. We also consider a cohort of UFO experts (ufologists) such as members of UFO organizations across the world, their belief profiles, and where they are engaged on the issue.

Finally, there is an element of the UFO-believing public that most scientists, religious leaders, and even government officials tend to dismiss: those who are part of UFO cults, to be distinguished from religious groups discussed in the previous chapter, and others who claim to be victims of ETs—so-called abductees who are more often than not marginalized and categorized as mentally challenged or who are accused of perpetrating a hoax.

Who Believes in ETs, and Why?

There is good reason much of the world's population tends to think there might be something to reports about extraterrestrials. After all, governments across the world fuel that perception, and, as a result, our citizenry is concerned and confused; many who are skeptical about their government's reliability end up actually believing.

United States congressional hearings on the topic over the past few years (2021, 2022, and 2023) suggest some of the UFO/UAP sightings aren't a hoax. US House of Representatives' member Andre Carson, a Democrat from Indiana, said at a House intelligence subcommittee hearing in 2021 that those reporting UFO incidents should be treated "as witnesses, not as kooks."[4]

He continued, "The American people expect and deserve their leaders in government and intelligence to seriously evaluate and respond to any potential national security risks—especially those we do not fully understand."[5]

That message is getting attention inside the US government. On September 14, 2023, NASA hired an independent group of scientists to create a road map for aiding research into UFOs/UAPs. That group released a statement indicating NASA should play a crucial role in collecting more data on UFOs. Those experts sifted through mountains of UFO/UAP data to determine whether and how the mysterious phenomenon can be scientifically studied. However, they found no hard data that the unexplained incidents are evidence of intelligent extraterrestrial life.[6]

It might surprise the reader that "this is the first time that NASA has taken concrete action to seriously look into UAP[s]," NASA administrator Bill Nelson said. "We start this [investigation] without any preconceived notions but understanding that we're in a world of discovery."[7]

Adding to the sudden interest in the phenomenon was a third marker coming from Mexico that is truly bizarre, but part of the conversation about ETs and the UFO news. In September of 2023, alleged "nonhuman," alien "corpses" were displayed to the Mexican congress. Allegedly, the two small "corpses" that look amazingly like "E.T." in the 1982 science fiction film by Steven Spielberg were allegedly retrieved from Cusco, Peru. A journalist who spearheaded the event in Mexico City claimed under oath that the mummified, E.T.-like specimens are not part of "our terrestrial evolution." Meanwhile, Antigona Segura, one of Mexico's top astrobiologists, dismissed the claim, saying: "These conclusions are simply not backed up by evidence. The whole thing is very shameful."[8]

Worldwide Belief in UFOs and the Possibility of ETs

I previously cited polling among Americans that indicates a broad-based receptivity to the possibility that UFOs might be evidence of ET life. The relatively recent survey demonstrates a growing interest in the topic, even when compared to a 2019 Gallup survey that provides insights about which Americans tend to embrace UFOs as evidence of alien life.

Overall, according to that national survey, most (68 percent) Americans believe their government is withholding information about UFOs/ETs, a statistic that's comparable to the 71 percent found in a similar poll in 1996. That poll also found that a third (33 percent) of US adults believe some UFO sightings have in fact been alien spacecraft visiting Earth, which is significantly less than a more recent poll that found 40 percent hold that belief; meanwhile, 16 percent of Americans say they have personally witnessed something they thought was a UFO. Further, about half (49 percent) think people like us (humans) exist elsewhere in the cosmos, and a whopping 75 percent believe some form of life exists on other planets.[9]

Even though most Americans remain skeptical that aliens have already visited Earth, most (56 percent) believe those—such as military pilots—who report UFOs are seeing something real; it's not a hoax. This figure is up from 47 percent in 1996, and likely the increase is attributable to the growing interest in the issue.[10]

The demographics regarding UFO/ET belief are interesting, especially for those who live in America's western states. Forty percent of those residents believe some UFOs can be attributed to alien visitors. Further, more generally, the poll found significant differences in UFO sightings based on individual education and income levels. Specifically, lower socioeconomic Americans are more likely than their counterparts to report UFO/ET belief. Also, Americans with no religious affiliation are more likely to believe in UFOs than others who identify with a religious group, and 40 percent of nonaffiliated people say some UFOs have been alien visitors.[11]

Four in ten Americans believe some UFOs have been alien spacecraft visiting Earth from other planets and galaxies; two-thirds (65 percent) believe intelligent alien life exists on other planets.[12]

It is noteworthy that American views such as those above are not unique and, in fact, are shared by others across the world. For example, a 2008 article in the *Journal of Social Psychology* found that most Austrian and British citizens share similar opinions about UFOs and ETs.

Those views are evidently influenced by the constant flow of information that keeps the issue in front of our consciences: waves of UFO sightings, the discovery of alleged alien "corpses," the announcement of a road map to guide NASA's first-ever serious study of the phenomenon, and multiple US congressional testimonies about government secrets regarding alien craft and discovered "biologics."

Although ET life remains hypothetical and the scientific community has no real evidence either way (at least available to the public), large sections of Western society (up to 50 percent) believe ET life exists and the inexplicable UFOs dotting our skies are evidence of that life. In fact, as stated earlier, belief in ET life has grown dramatically since the early1960s, especially in the West.[13]

Why have such beliefs grown despite the lack of empirical evidence? Some research indicates the mass and entertainment media have played a role. After all, the promotion of paranormal experiences in television shows such as a *The X-Files* and *Unsolved Mysteries* and the uncritical acceptance of many UFO reports in the news have led to widespread public belief in the paranormal as well as suspicion about what government actually knows about the phenomenon.[14]

Another explanation of the extensive acceptance of the existence of ET beings is that it likely has a psychological root. Specifically, there are studies that show "a negative relation between paranormal beliefs and cognitive factors, such as analytical thinking style, reasoning skills, and intelligence." In fact, certain studies found "an association between schizotypal personality [disorder characterized by paranoia and social anxiety] and UFO-related beliefs," although that is not an exceptionally strong correlation.[15]

Further research reported in the *Journal of Social Psychology* associates beliefs in ET with a variety of demographic variables such as sex, age, and education level. For example, some investigations found that "men are more likely than women to believe that ET[s] exist and that aliens have visited earth." One explanation of this view stems from "the fact that men are socialized to take an interest in science, whereas women are better informed about religious issues and tend to have a richer fantasy life."[16]

Education level, according to research, appears to be a predictor of belief in paranormal events, including the existence of ETs. Those studies report "better educated people are less likely to believe in ghosts, astrology, and reincarnation and are more likely to believe in telepathy ['the supposed communication of thoughts or ideas by means other than the known senses']."[17]

Other research finds that the strength of religious views is related to extraterrestrial beliefs as well. Specifically, there appears to be a "negative association between individuals' religiosity and their extraterrestrial beliefs."[18]

The research about ET life using a multi-item scale carried out with Austrian and British citizens resulted in some interesting findings. For example:

> Overall, participants likely believed in the hypothesis that life could exist elsewhere in the universe and disagreed with the idea that life exists only on Earth. However, participants were skeptical of the idea that extraterrestrial life has visited Earth and that humans have had encounters with aliens.[19]

That study also confirmed that "higher levels of education were significantly associated with stronger general extraterrestrial beliefs, which is consistent with the suggestion that increasing education leads to more critical belief systems." Further, some evidence suggests ET beliefs are "related to participants' religiosity and political orientation. In general, higher religiosity and more right-wing political orientation were associated with decreased belief in extraterrestrial life."[20]

What's the Motivation for UFO/ET Belief?

The public's growing belief in the existence of ETs fuels "increased [government] funding for astrobiology" and suggests "the idea that the search for extraterrestrial life is a worthwhile scientific endeavor." Further, another contributor to the public's favorable views that ETs exist is the announcement of new scientific discoveries such as "extrasolar planets that could be conducive to life; the discussion of the possibility of organic life on Jupiter's moon, Europa; [and] or the dispute over microbial formations on a Mars meteorite—have filtered down into public consciousness."[21]

For some "believers," there is a financial benefit to belief in ETs. Think about UFO museums and gift shops like the one at Devils Tower, Wyoming, that sell trinkets with E.T.'s picture, and television programs/movies that address the issue. These efforts do return a profit for their sponsors because of the widespread interest. However, for the vast majority, there is no tangible benefit to holding to such beliefs.

Yet, there remains a stubborn and ethereal benefit for most people. They are legitimately interested in the truth, because the existence of ETs—especially should those beings come to Earth—potentially impacts all our lives in very perceptible ways. Therefore, we legitimately want to know whether UFOs are an indicator of ET life. That understandable hunger is fed by the constant drumbeat about UFOs, as well as enough opacity to keep even our now-engaged government guessing. Of course, to a certain extent, we can blame the "constant drumbeat" about UFOs/ETs on our public media, which does have a financial motivation in that genre.

Journalistic Malpractice Partly to Blame for UFO Hype

The modern hype about UFOs began in 1947 with the incidents at Roswell, New Mexico, and Mount Rainer in Washington State. That storyline became the most expansive and arguably enduring news topic of the twentieth century. Why? Blame America's news organizations, which became "deeply implicated in hyping and often obfuscating the UFO phenomenon," according to a study in the *Journal of American Journalism* titled "Journalism Versus the Flying Saucers: Assessing the First Generation of UFO Reportage, 1947–1967."[22]

"Journalists not only created and perpetuated the label 'flying saucers,' but news organizations also thrived on a synergistic relationship with the entertainment industry," wrote Phillip Hutchison, an associate professor at the University of Kentucky, and Herbert Strentz, a professor emeritus at Drake University, in their *American Journalism* article.[23]

Specifically, the 1947 sighting by Kenneth Arnold near Mount Rainier sparked a figurative gold rush in media reports about UFOs. "Archives indicate that hundreds of thousands—perhaps millions—of news items have covered UFOs since the Arnold sighting," wrote Hutchison and Strentz. In fact, it was journalists who perpetuated the now-famous label "flying saucers," and, to the present, the phenomenon has flourished at the intersection of journalism and pop culture.[24]

We can't place all the fault on journalism for the postwar relationship between journalists and Hollywood movie makers, however. Rather, as Hutchison and Strentz argued, "the inquiry [into UFOs] reveals a complex mélange of technological, social, and political circumstances that converged in the years following World War II."[25]

The "complex mélange" includes, as the writers explained, "the growth of civilian and military aviation, the Cold War, a science fiction craze, widespread fascination with the supernatural, changes in media technology and audiences, and evolving journalism institutions and practices." Evidently, those early (late 1940s and 1950s) journalists couldn't distinguish the facts from fiction in their UFO reporting, perhaps because much of it was "superficial, redundant, often silly, lacking in relevance, and poorly coordinated."[26]

Philip Morrison, a physicist at the Massachusetts Institute of Technology, was among those scientists and government officials who were quick to point fingers at journalists for fueling the UFO phenomenon. In 1967, Dr. Morrison told ABC News:

[The UFO craze] is a social phenomenon of journalism and television. If you look in the newspapers and journals of a hundred years ago, you'll see the same thing...they're much more frequent now.

Yet Hutchison and Strentz argued that the issue is more complex today because the phenomenon is dynamic and reflects "the interconnectedness of media, culture and society in time."[27]

The widespread interest in UFOs isn't an example of counterfeit journalism such as the Orson Welles' faux-journalistic *War of the Worlds* hoax in 1938. (That issue is addressed in appendix C.) Although UFO news coverage has included a few phony stories like the one Welles' launched, the vast majority of it "reflected genuine, significant journalistic concerns," according to Hutchison and Strentz. They stated:

Most notably, post-1947 UFO waves were not animated by fear of extraterrestrial invasions, even as popular culture exploited this perspective. Instead, much of the public's concern originally traced to fear of communism, Soviet invasion, and nuclear attack.[28]

That mix of issues explains why the UFO issue "commanded interest at the highest levels of the US government, and UFO sightings became a legitimate issue of public affairs reporting and science journalism." Further, in fact, interest in UFO sightings is an enduring phenomenon dating back thousands of years, as illustrated in the second chapter of this book.[29]

Hutchison and Strentz alleged that journalistic malpractice, however, is associated with the craze. "Journalists effectively named the phenomenon, and the attendant news coverage legitimized otherwise ambiguous and problematic situations and views," they pointed out. Evidently, James E. McDonald, a physicist at the University of Arizona, complained as well that "news organizations not only failed to adequately investigate these reports," but also demonstrated a "propensity to poke fun and to twist into feature-story humor the seriously reported sightings that many citizens have made."[30]

Researchers Hutchison and Strentz concluded that irresponsible journalists established and facilitated:

> ...one of the most compelling social-scientific issues of the era, but they often failed to follow up on many relevant news angles. In general, news organizations did not address the issue strategically, and assimilative "big picture" coverage was rare. Consequently, most UFO coverage was tactical, poorly coordinated, and reactive. Moreover, journalists evidenced little ethical or professional reflexivity in these contexts.[31]

UFO Experts and What They Do

"Ufology," a term introduced in chapter 1 of this book, is the investigation of UFOs by mostly those who believe they possibly indicate the existence of alien life. Although some UFO investigations are government-sponsored, ufology is not considered by much of academia as a legitimate scientific field of study. Rather, it falls into the category of pseudoscience, accused of not adhering to scientific method and lacking evidence, plausibility, and scientific status.

Although ufology isn't broadly recognized as legitimate, some credentialed scientists have associated themselves with the field. In fact, self-identified ufologists have been at work in at least thirteen countries today, many either in academia or government. For example, J. Allen Hynek (1910–1986) was an American astronomer and professor who advised the US Air Force on three UFO studies: Project Sign (1947–1949), Project Grudge (1949–1952), and Project Blue Book (1952–1969); James E. McDonald (1920–1971), introduced earlier in this book, was an American physicist at the Institute for Atmospheric Physics and a professor at the University of Arizona. He advocated for expanding UFO studies. Jacques Vallée, another ufologist, is a French computer scientist who began his professional life as an astronomer and co-developed the first computerized map of Mars for NASA.

These and many other ufologists typically associate with UFO groups that are found in many countries, such as the Mutual UFO Network (MUFON), a US-based, nonprofit organization that studies UFO sightings. It claims more than four thousand members worldwide, representing more than forty-three countries and all fifty US states.[32]

What Do Ufologists Believe?

Ufologists typically haven't been well received or respected by the broader scientific community, but that may be changing. What often separates this group from other scientists is they're not quick to dismiss unexplained cases as unimportant. In fact, a study of 2,611 members of the American Astronomical Society (AAS)—not all necessarily self-identified ufologists—found that "80 percent of astronomers believed that UFOs, certainly, probably, or possibly merited further scientific study."[33]

The survey confirms that among AAS members is found "the most frequent primary belief about the origin of UFOs was the extraterrestrial hypothesis." In fact:

Over a third (39 %) of the ufologists believed that UFOs were extraterrestrial in nature. Nearly a third (30%) of the population affirmed the belief that the UFO phenomenon was real, but they were unwilling or unable to cite a primary belief about the origin of UFOs.[34]

"A few ufologists (7%)," according to the survey, "conclude that the UFO phenomenon consists of a variety of misinterpretations and is 'bunk.' They insist that the small residual of unexplained UFO cases could eventually be identified if enough facts were available."[35] However, 5 percent of ufologists embrace multidimensional theories about UFOs, such as:

It was suggested that UFOs are interdimensional time travelers from other worlds. UFO theories based on religion made up four percent of the primary beliefs. Included was the belief that UFOs are angels or demons.[36]

How Does One Become a Ufologist?

Consider the case of Chris Rutkowski, a Canadian in the public relations department of the University of Manitoba. For decades, Mr. Rutkowski has been investigating and collecting reports of UFO encounters through the institute he founded in 1975, Ufology Research of Manitoba. "I suppose I'm the closest thing to Fox Mulder right now," he said, a reference to the main character on the science fiction drama television series *The X-Files*, which aired from 1993 to 2002.[37]

Mr. Rutkowski's fascination with UFOs began while he was studying astronomy at the University of Manitoba. Evidently, the Manitoba "flap" of 1975—"flap" is a ufology term for a group of UFO sightings in the same area—sparked many citizens to call the university's astronomy department. At the time, Rutkowski was working on his master's in astronomy, and he was the only person in his department willing to take those calls seriously.[38]

The frustration related to the lack of taking those reports seriously led Rutkowski and a colleague to start their own annual survey of UFO sightings across Canada. Today, a dozen dedicated UFO trackers across that country feed a database and network their reports.

Mr. Rutkowski demonstrates a sense of humor about his "hobby," in part because many people don't take his effort seriously. "My two younger kids, who are my natural kids, have grown up with it, so they just think [D]ad's on the radio again talking about UFOs," Rutkowski explains, "whereas my step kids just think I'm weird." His wife, he says, is "bemused" by his UFO hobby. Yet he continues his pursuit much like police work, in that it is "drudge work, walking the beat, talking to people."[39]

Rutkowski tolerates the criticism. He says:

I think that for the most part, the ridicule curtain has lifted, however there is still a stigma attached to some of the phenomenon—you can point to the tabloids as really damaging credibility. My own approach is probably why I'm taken seriously. I'm not running around with pyramids on my head, I'm not saying the aliens are definitely here or warning that the sky is falling. I'm simply studying the phenomenon in a scientific manner using methodology that is accepted in any other branch of science.[40]

"My astronomy background and education and training," said Rutkowski, "have shown me that there likely is life somewhere out there, but whether they're coming to Earth is a great matter of debate, and we simply don't have incontrovertible evidence that this is so."[41]

Another pathway to becoming a ufologist is to be assigned the task by your government. Nick Pope was a career civil servant with Britain's Ministry of Defence. In 1991, Pope was assigned the task of investigating every UFO sighting reported to the British government, vis-à-vis the Secretariat (Air Staff) Department 2A—"The UFO Desk." After many years, Mr. Pope became known as one of the world's leading UFO experts thanks to his government work.[42]

"I really started from a baseline of zero," Pope explained. His job of four years required him to call up UFO witnesses, "gather as much information as possible about the appearance of the mystery objects, as well as the precise locations and times of the sightings, and then get to work checking those facts against 'the usual suspects.'"[43]

Mr. Pope admits 95 percent of the UFO sightings had simple explanations, such as aircraft or weather balloons. However, he admits there were rare cases that couldn't be explained. His job was "to downplay [the sighting's] significance to the public, the media and British lawmakers." His message was simple: "Move along, folks. Nothing to see here."[44]

Later, Mr. Pope coauthored a book, *Open Skies, Closed Minds*, with witnesses of the Rendlesham Forest incident (see chapter 5), popularly known as "England's Roswell." In that book, Pope claims to have become persuaded that "extraterrestrial spacecraft really are routinely breaching the United Kingdom's air defense and are a major threat to national security.[45]

Evidently, the success of Pope's book earned him notoriety and the title "UFO investigator." By 2012, he moved to the United States to become a full-time UFO expert and a regular on television shows.[46]

Pope eschews the title "ufologist"; instead, he prefers "UFO investigator." However, he is a regular on the UFO circuit and admits that, given his background, "some people, I suspect, think that I'm the bad guy, and I've heard a lot of people in the conspiracy theory community say that I'm still secretly working for the government, that I'm part of some disinformation campaign or whatever the theory is."[47]

Degrees in Ufology?

No traditional colleges or universities offer degrees in ufology, but there are some programs online. One, presented by the International Metaphysical University, is taught by Richard Dolan, a UFO expert with a history degree. That program of instruction includes a course entitled Introduction to Ufology.[48]

In September of 2023, the IMHS Metaphysics Institute offered online ufology degrees. The institute's website states, "The ufology metaphysics degree covers all aspects of ufology and abduction research giving students a broad base of knowledge." Twelve courses "are required for a bachelor's and master's degree. For a doctoral degree, the doctoral degree assignment is required." The required courses include ones such as the Nature of Metaphysics, Metaphysical Psychology, Paranormal Science Course, and Forensic Anomalous Evidence Analysis and Collection Course 1 & 2.[49]

Thomas Francis University (TFU) offers ufology degrees, identified as "accelerated metaphysics bachelor's, master's, and PhD degrees." TFU, an educational program of the International Church of Metaphysical Humanism, Inc., is a "global, online metaphysical ministry based in North Port, Florida."[50]

TFU indicates its "degree program is excellent for students who desire to conduct paranormal and/or UFO investigations and research, conduct alien abduction research, start and lead a paranormal investigation team, write books on paranormal topics, present lectures and talks in the paranormal field, and more."[51]

Making a Living as a Taxpayer-funded Ufologist

Few ufologists have a government job like Nick Pope that pays them to research UFOs. Rather, most ufologists either are self-funded or write books, write for media outlets, speak at conferences, and the like. Still, others are funded through government grants—and that category appears to be growing.

One of the first government grant programs goes back a few years to the relationship between former US Senator Harry Reid (D-NV) and the National Institute for Discovery Science (NIDS). That organization was established in 1995 by Nevada businessman Robert Bigelow to study UFO sightings. Soon, the Federal Aviation Administration directed pilots interested in reporting UFO incidents to pass their sightings directly to NIDS.[52]

Evidently, Senator Reid was already interested in UFOs when a journalist told him about Bigelow's NIDS. Reid had previously represented Bigelow as an attorney. Soon, the senator reached out to the businessman and was invited to a NIDS board meeting. Eventually, Bigelow introduced Reid to James Lacatski, a Defense Intelligence Agency rocket scientist who shared their mutual interest in UFOs. That was the beginning of the path to a government grant to study UFOs.[53]

Evidently, Mr. Lacatski read *Hunt for the Skinwalker*, a book by Colm A. Kelleher about the strange incidents at Skinwalker Ranch, located southeast of Salt Lake City in Uintah County, Utah—where there were reports of UFO sightings, dead cows, mysterious spirit-like orbs, and more. Evidently, Lacatski became convinced these incidents were worth investigating; therefore, with the help of others, he created a Pentagon contract mechanism, the Advanced Aerospace Weapons Systems Application Program (AAWSAP), to look into the UFO matter for the US government.[54]

Senator Reid recruited two other US senators, Ted Stevens (R-AK) and Daniel Inouye (D-HI) to support the Senate Appropriations Committee for Defense subcommittee to fund the contract for the AAWSAP, a research program on UFOs. Years later, Mr. Reid told the *New York Times* that the meeting with the two senators in a secure facility "was one of the easiest meetings I ever had."[55]

At that meeting, Senator Reid told his fellow senators, "I had talked to John Glenn a number of years before," a reference to the former US senator from Ohio and former NASA astronaut. Mr. Reid said Glenn told him "he thought that the federal government should be looking seriously into U.F.O.s, and should be talking to military service members, particularly pilots, who had reported seeing aircraft they could not identify or explain."[56]

The three senators agreed at that meeting to avoid public debate about the AAWSAP. "This was so-called black money," Reid said. "Stevens knows about it [black money for researching UFOs], Inouye knows about it. But that was it, and that's how we wanted it." Mr. Reid explained that a "black money" project referred to the Pentagon budget for classified programs, which eluded public scrutiny.[57]

Thus, the AAWSAP became a funded black program allegedly on the surface to consider developments in aerospace weaponry: propulsion, power generation, and human effects. However, only one proposal was received for the secret government contract; it came from a new organization, BAASS—Bigelow Aerospace Advanced Space Studies, a firm created by Lacatski, Bigelow, and Reid. The contract proposal said the researchers would study UFOs "at BAASS headquarters in Las Vegas and at Skinwalker Ranch [which Bigelow purchased in 1996]." That $22 million contract was passed by BAASS to the Mutual UFO Network, a volunteer-based organization that kept a UFO database. "Its researchers did extensive investigations at [the 480-acre] Skinwalker Ranch [named for a shape-shifting Navajo witch], attempting to observe both supernatural activity and the UFOs they felt were related." The prior owners of Skinwalker Ranch claimed they were "driven away by coruscating [flashing] spheres, exsanguinated [drained of blood] cattle, and wolflike creatures impervious to gunshots."[58]

The AAWSAP story was virtually unknown until the *New York Times* reported about it in 2017 with the headline "Glowing Auras and 'Black Money.'" That piece was the first public identification of Luis Elizondo, who was introduced much earlier in this book. He was the point person for the AAWSAP contract at the Pentagon and the director of the Advanced Aerospace Threat Identification Program (AATIP), mentioned earlier as well. Elizondo resigned in 2017 with a letter to the Secretary of Defense, citing frustration with the slow pace of UFO-related investigations.[59]

Going forward, expect more government grants to investigate UFO/UAP incidents, especially now the US Congress is interested in the issue. Already, two commercial firms, UAPx and Enigma Labs (introduced in chapter 7) are aiming at setting up sophisticated databases to track UFO sightings and likely at taxpayer expense, assuming they can win government grants or contracts. Also, expect these and other firms to try to link such efforts to future military technologies, such as quantum computers and artificial intelligence, issues the Pentagon is already pursuing with contracts larded with taxpayer funds.

UFO Cults and Alien Abductions

Now we turn to the fringe of the UFO movement, the cults and the abductee believers. Both groups are typically marginalized even by many ufologists, the US government, and especially the skeptical scientific and religious communities. However, because they are part of the broader community of UFO believers, they warrant consideration.

UFO Cults

I make a distinction between a UFO "religion" addressed in the previous chapter and a UFO "cult," whose members tend to be semi-religious and might claim to communicate with alien beings using telepathy and astral projection. The difference, though narrow, is that a cult tends to be led by a single charismatic and self-appointed leader who excessively controls the group's members, requiring unwavering devotion to a set of beliefs and practices. Perhaps the first UFO cult was "I AM Religious Activity" founded by Guy Ballard in 1930. This group was allegedly the theosophical forerunner to UFO religions like the Aetherius Society. Each of the three cult examples below are classic illustrations typified by self-appointed leader(s), strict control of members, and a clear UFO/ET nexus.

Unified Family and the Children of God: This cult captured national attention in the fall of 1975, when more than thirty people disappeared in Oregon after attending the cult's lecture about "flying saucers." Evidently, those missing people joined the cult and went off the grid, separating themselves from their previous contacts—including their families.[60]

At the Oregon meeting, the audience heard from a man and woman who called themselves "Bo" and "Peep," who offered eternal life in the "literal heavens." Bo and Peep claimed to be members of the kingdom of heaven who had assumed human bodies to help humankind. Shortly after the Oregon lecture on "flying saucers," the authors of the study, University of Montana professors Robert W. Balch and David Taylor, joined the cult for seven weeks, traveling with different "families, observing, and taking part in every aspect of their daily lives."[61]

Bo and Peep traveled across America promising that, to enter the "next evolutionary kingdom," followers had "to abandon their friends, families, jobs, and material possessions." Then they would travel as small "families," camping and leading a spartan life until they would be taken to heaven in UFOs via a process called "Human Individual

Metamorphosis," a "chemical and biological change" that made the followers new creatures with indestructible bodies.[62]

"Bo and Peep's UFO cult was one of the remarkable religious success stories of the mid-seventies," according to an *American Behavioral Scientist* article by Balch and Taylor. They argue that Bo and Peep didn't necessarily "brainwash" their members. Rather, "Bo and Peep's UFO cult can only be understood in terms of the unique point of view of the metaphysical seeker, whose outlook is shaped by a religious underworld variously known as the cult milieu, the occult social world, or the metaphysical subculture."[63]

Heaven's Gate: This cult was founded in the 1970s by Marshall Applewhite and Bonnie Nettles, who claimed to have traveled to Earth in a spacecraft. They developed a following by telling recruits "they were aliens inside bodies, which would transform into their higher alien beings when they were picked up by an incoming ET spaceship."[64]

Meanwhile, as they waited for that spaceship, the leaders insisted their followers abandon all possessions, families, and sex. They were also expected to live only with the other members of the group.[65]

In 1997, Applewhite and Nettles became convinced a spaceship was following the famed Hale-Bopp comet, one of the most widely observed and "brightest" comets in history. The comet was to come closest to Earth on March 22, 1997, which became the very day the thirty-nine members of the Heaven's Gate cult committed suicide at "The Monastery," their rented mansion near San Diego. The group came to believe the close passage to Earth by the Hale-Bopp comet represented the "closure to heaven's gate," and, as a result, they killed themselves, believing the spaceship trailing the comet would pick them up as it passed close to Earth and then carry their souls to heaven.[66]

Superior Universal Alignment: In the 1980s, Valentina de Andrade was the leader of this Brazil-based UFO cult. De Andrade claimed ETs told her the world was coming to an end, and only those "who followed her precepts could be saved." Further, ETs allegedly told her God didn't exist, and Jesus was an alien messiah on Earth to instruct humanity about enlightenment. Additionally, she said, ETs were sending a spacecraft to save true believers from the "end times." Bizarrely, she also taught that all boys born after 1981 were evil and had to be killed.[67]

By 1993, the cult sexually assaulted, mutilated, or killed at least nineteen boys. It took the Brazilian police eleven years to bring de Andrade to trial along with four male cult members. The men were sentenced for the murder of the boys, but de Andrade was acquitted because she wasn't near the crime site at the time. Superior Universal Alignment is still an active cult, at least online.[68]

Alien Abduction

Alien abduction is a real phenomenon for 3.7 million Americans, according to an extrapolation based on the results of a poll by the Roper Center for Public Opinion Research, which randomly sampled 5,947 American adults in the early 1990s. The authors of a 2002 study published in *Neuropsychology and Neuropsychiatry* did the extrapolation and explained that those incidents of alien abduction were likely related to frightening experiences associated with the condition known as "awareness during sleep paralysis [ASP]." Evidently, the ASP was all that remained of an "alien encounter"; "once their memories had been wiped (almost) clean [that] at least allowed them to begin to make sense of the episode. It also reassured them that they were not 'going crazy.'"[69]

Those reported alien abduction experiences have common features, including "capture by the aliens and subsequent examination (physical, mental, and/or spiritual)," according to the 2002 study's authors Katharine J. Holden and Christopher C. French at the University of London, Great Britain. The encounter may also include communication with the aliens "telepathically," a tour of the UFO craft, trips to other worlds, and a message for humanity upon their return. Another study cited by Holden and French found that abduction accounts included "various reproductive procedures such as collection of sperm or ova, implantation of alien-human hybrid embryos, removal of fetuses, sexual activity, and presentation of hybrid babies."[70]

The most famous case of alien abduction dates to the 1961 incident reported by Betty and Barney Hill, mentioned in chapter 1 of this book. Recall that the Hills alleged they were driving through New Hampshire when they were abducted by aliens and taken to a distant star. Upon their return to Earth, they shared details of their journey with the press.[71]

Understandably, skeptics argue that encounters like the one detailed by the Hills are really hoaxes, much like the Roswell "flying saucer" episode. Psychologists and psychiatrists have developed a number of explanations for people's supposed ET abductions like the Hills'.

One possible reason is that people have misinterpreted, distorted, and/or conflated real and or imagined events. In fact, multiple studies report that accounts of alien abductions do not typically differ from other objective psychopathological measures. Further, "one characteristic that is associated with abduction experiences is a proclivity for fantasy."[72]

Evidently, "fantasy-prone people engage in elaborate imaginings and often confuse fantasy with reality." There is also the issue of dissociation, a psychological explanation that the so-called abductee's "mental processes detach from each other and from reality," sometimes as a "response to extreme or stressful life events."[73]

Yet other studies claim reports of alien abduction indicate sleep paralysis and temporal lobe sensitivity might explain the episode. Evidently, sleep paralysis is like being conscious and unable to move, which "occurs when a person passes between stages of wakefulness and sleep." Those who experience sleep paralysis report "a sense of being awake, not dreaming, and realistic perceptions of the environment." Such feelings are evidently accompanied by fear, dread, and the sense of an evil or malevolent presence, and they're associated with pressure on the chest as well as difficulty breathing.[74]

Another explanation is temporal lobe sensitivity, the result of the brain being especially vulnerable to low-level magnetic frequencies. Neuroscientist Michael Persinger with Laurentian University in Canada states, "Increased temporal lobe activity can explain paranormal experiences such as alien abduction." He argues that magnetic fields stimulate the temporal lobes, which result in hallucinatory experiences, e.g., alien abduction.[75]

Yet another perspective is offered by Anne Skomorowsky, a medical doctor and assistant professor of psychiatry at Columbia University who considered the Hills' abduction account for *Scientific American*. Dr. Skomorowsky contends that the Hills' alleged experience inside a "flying saucer" may actually be evidence of a syndrome known as "accidental awareness under general anesthesia." This occurs when a patient wakes up while on the surgical bed. After all, to a groggy patient looking up at bright lights from the operating table, the surgeons dressed in their gowns, masks, and other gear could appear to be alien-like.[76]

Mr. Hill, according to Dr. Skomorowsky, described his abduction experience as being much like his prior tonsillectomy:

[It is] like that, but my eyes are closed, and I only have mental pictures. And I am not in pain. And I can feel a slight feeling. My groin feels cold.

Further, to suggest there is a deep-seated psychological issue here, Dr. Skomorowsky states Barney Hill told his psychiatrist, "I don't want to be operated on."[77]

"Alien abduction has been considered a fantasy, a hoax [see appendix C: Notable UFO Hoaxes], and even to some, a fact," writes Dr. Skomorowsky, "but it is now clear that it may also represent a recovered memory." She states, "Recovered memories are frequently astounding and implausible—if they were orderly and digestible, we would not have forgotten them." Evidently, recovered memory is at the heart of controversial claims such as childhood sexual abuse, satanic cults, and other disturbing actions of one family member against another.[78]

Arguably, according to the above medical authorities, many of the reported "alien abduction" stories can be explained scientifically. However, there remains a small fraction of all abductions, much like UFO sightings, that simply can't be easily discounted. Those perplexing stories warrant further investigation, not outright dismissal.

Conclusion

This chapter profiled the citizen who tends to believe UFOs are evidence of alien life, which appears to account for a significant portion of all people. That vast slice of humanity is joined by a cohort of UFO experts, ufologists who came by their expertise either out of curiosity, thanks to a personal UFO sighting, or—like Nick Pope—a government job. We concluded the chapter with the hardest issues to understand and accept: UFO cults and UFO abductees, the most marginalized of all believers.

Although much of the scientific, medical, and academic world reject UFO and ET believers, so much doubt remains about the phenomenon that the intrigue continues and is likely to remain an issue of interest until, if ever, there is definitive evidence of their existence one way or the other.

SECTION FOUR

GOVERNMENT SECRETS ABOUT UAPS, UFOS, AND ET THREATS

In July of 2023, David Grusch, a former US intelligence officer, told a US House of Representatives panel he is "absolutely" certain the federal government is in possession of UAPs, "citing interviews he said he conducted with 40 witnesses over a four-year period.[1]

Official US government spokespersons to this day deny that they possess UFOs/UAPs associated with extraterrestrial life. Unfortunately, that is contrary to some accounts, such as the one presented by Mr. Grusch and others over the years suggesting otherwise. Who is the citizenry to believe?

This section considers in two chapters the publicly available information about what our government officials in the US and other nations, as well as international government-related organizations, may know about the UFO/UAP issue—especially the ET matter—but have not told the public. The cloak of secrecy continues to create doubt and feed the widespread conclusion that governments are conspiring against their citizens by withholding significant information about the true nature of UFOs and whether ET beings are real and perhaps a serious threat.

Chapter 10 relies on circumstantial evidence to suggest the US government—somewhere in likely classified "black programs" deep inside the Pentagon—has information about UFOs and possibly ET beings. The officials who know that information, if true, evidently believe it is in our collective best interest to withhold the facts from the public—that is, except for the whistleblowers who are calling for full disclosure and now have Congress on their side demanding answers.

Chapter 11 surveys what foreign national governments might know about UFOs and ET beings. Are those foreign governments also withholding information about a threat similar to what many believe to be the case with the US government?

10

US GOVERNMENT AND
ALIEN TALES

The U.S. government hasn't maintained secrecy regarding UFOs.
It's been leaking out all over the place. But the way it's been handled
is by denial, by denying the truth of the documents that have leaked.
By attempting to show them as fraudulent, as bogus of some sort.[1]

—GORDON COOPER (1927–2004),
original astronaut in US Project Mercury

Two-thirds of Americans don't believe the US government's account on UFOs/UAPs. They believe our government is hiding the truth from the public, according to Gallup polling, and that view has remained consistent over the last few decades.[2]

This chapter doesn't reveal government secrets. After all, even if I knew classified information about UFOs/UAPs, which I don't, revealing such would be illegal. However, in this chapter I reference publicly available material, personal insights about government functioning, and the results of interviews (on and off the record) with key players to address three issues: government foot-dragging on the UFO/UAP issue; government promises to better inform the public about UFO/UAP findings; and speculation about what the government might know about UFOs/UAPs that's currently not public knowledge.

Unfortunately, suspicion about the UFO issue has been cooked into American pop culture for decades. As a result, the Internet is full of misinformation, plenty of conspiracy theories, and many hoaxes related to UFOs. Further, as previously explained, our news and entertainment media have totally distorted the subject to the point that not only do most Americans doubt the US government's accounts, but they have a very distorted opinion about UFOs. In fact, much of the public tends to share views about interplanetary aliens and their craft more akin to Steven Spielberg's *Star Wars* aliens like Yoda than anything related to the actual facts.

Therefore, it is an almost insurmountable challenge to cut through the flood of misinformation to provide a definitive explanation of the phenomenon. However, that's my task here—sorting out fact from fiction regarding a popular and arguably mysterious matter.

There are many conflicting opinions about UFOs. On one hand is a camp that will never believe aliens and/or their spacecraft exist, full stop. On the other hand, another cohort believes aliens walk among us in our local grocery stores and have been on Earth for thousands of years. In the middle of these beliefs are most of us who don't totally dismiss the possibility of ET life, but are skeptical enough not to fall for wild speculation at the extremes. We would like to see proof that ETs exist and be given the time to consider related facts.

Area 51 is a top-secret US government facility north of Las Vegas, Nevada, suspected by many Americans of housing alien aircraft.[3]

160

Consider the views advanced by examples of two polar opposite cohorts. One extreme opinion is represented by the Center for the Study of Extraterrestrial Intelligence, which states on its website it is "an international nonprofit scientific research and education organization founded by Dr. Steven M. Greer and dedicated to the furtherance of our understanding of extraterrestrial intelligence."[4]

Dr. Greer, an American ufologist and retired medical doctor, also founded The Disclosure Project, an organization that claims the US government has first-hand knowledge of ET aliens, which it alleges is the greatest secret in human history.

The Disclosure Project advertises itself as "a research project working to fully disclose the facts about UFOs, extraterrestrial intelligence, and classified advanced energy and propulsion systems." The project is said to have "collected over 500 government, military, and intelligence community witnesses testifying to their direct, personal, first-hand experience with UFOs, ETs, ET technology, and the cover-up that keeps this information secret."[5]

In 2001, Dr. Greer hosted a briefing at the National Press Club in Washington, DC. That briefing was intended "to establish the reality of UFOs or extraterrestrial vehicles, extraterrestrial life forms, and resulting advanced energy and propulsion technologies." In that briefing, Dr. Greer claimed "untold numbers of alien craft have been observed in earth's airspace," and, in fact, some extraterrestrial spaceships have been "downed, retrieved and studied since at least the 1940s and possibly as early as the 1930s." Also, the US government supposedly, according to Greer, has reverse engineered those craft, leading to "significant technological breakthroughs in energy generation." Of course, such information, Greer says, remains highly classified and is kept from the public to protect the "social, economic and geo-political order of the world."[6]

On the other end of the UFO and ET credibility spectrum is Mick West, a British-American science writer and true skeptic who routinely tries to debunk claims about aliens. Mr. West, author of *Escaping the*

Rabbit Hole: How to Debunk Conspiracy Theories Using Facts, Logic, and Respect, runs an online forum called Metabunk, which seeks to explain away UFO-related conspiracies with the help of like-minded contributors.

Mr. West writes at Metabunk.org:

[Metabunk] is dedicated to the art and pastime of honest, polite, scientific investigating of unusual claims. It is primarily a discussion forum; however, the focus is on providing concise useful resources, attempting to avoid repetitive debate and arguments.[7]

He rightly targets what appears to be some pseudoscientists, such as the infamous ufologist Jamie Maussan, who presented two alleged mummified "alien bodies" at a public hearing in the Mexican Chamber of Deputies, Mexico City, Mexico, in early September 2023 (previously mentioned in chapter 9). Mr. West writes at his website an article, "Alien Bodies at a Mexican UAP Hearing," to declare:

Maussan has a poor reputation, even amongst UFO fans, he's been parading these and similar [mummified] bodies around for years. They are generally considered to be fakes, made, in part, from human remains.[8]

Mr. West points out there is "some academic debunking" of Maussan's alleged mummified alien display. Specifically, he quotes from the authors of *Fake and Alien Mummies*, a study by Guido Lombardi and Conrado Rodriguez Martin, who wrote:

Recent on-line and television appearance of purportedly extra-terrestrial remains excavated in unknown circumstances in the Southern Peruvian coast has revealed itself as the end product of a long process which joins grave looting, yellow press, and some disoriented professionals. Organizers and attendees to the IX World Congress on Mummy Studies held in Lima, Peru, faced a disinformation campaign by presenting a declaration preventing the public and the media [from] this hoax. Since then, the producers of this scam program have kept, unfortunately, trying to validate their claims by using fallacious strategies, fueled by the revenue of selling the show.[9]

I've found many UFO hoaxes that feed the anxiety about UFOs, which stigmatize anyone who shows an interest in the issue. See examples at appendix C.

The wild differences in opinions about the UFO issue as evidenced by Greer and West do in fact affect the US government, though indirectly. For example, government officials acknowledge being bewildered by the phenomenon and the significant differences of opinion across the citizenry. But the conflicted cultural situation hasn't confused some leaders, like US Senator Marco Rubio (R-FL), the former chairman of the Select Committee on Intelligence who still speaks out about the phenomenon.

Senator Rubio called out the UFO issue and our lack of understanding. "We have things flying over military installations, over military exercises, and other places, and we don't know what it is," he said. Yet, he confirmed his beliefs about UFOs/UAPs in an interview with Fox Business, "It isn't ours. It isn't anything that's registered to the FAA [Federal Aviation Administration], and in many cases exhibits attributes of things we've never seen."[10]

Even former Central Intelligence Agency director John Brennan admitted much the same in an interview. "It's a bit presumptuous and arrogant for us to believe that there's no other form of life anywhere in the entire universe," he said, continuing:

I think some of the phenomena we're going to be seeing continues to be unexplained and might, in fact, be some type of phenomenon that is the result of something that we don't yet understand and that could involve some type of activity that some might say constitutes a different form of life.[11]

Evidently, these and other current and former government officials agree there is something out there, and "it isn't ours," as Rubio said. That leaves the government in a difficult position. It must act responsibility for the benefit of the citizenry without appearing to jump to unsubstantiated conclusions advanced by the likes of the Greers and the Wests of this world.

Until recently, the government resisted the UFO matter to a fault and has been rightly accused of dragging its feet—or worse, of covering up the issue. The evidence of bureaucratic foot-dragging is well documented.

US Government: Dragging Its Feet or Covering Up?

Conspiracy theories about US government programs tend to be resilient, like the one known as Majestic 12, or MJ-12 and Majic. The existence of Majestic 12, which dates back to the 1950s, represented an alleged group of top military personnel assigned the task to investigate UFO sightings and crashes. Evidently, the program may have been a total hoax, according to a host of personnel representing UFO experts, former Air Force special agents, and even the FBI.[12]

A search of the FBI's Vault (the FBI's electronic Freedom of Information Act library) finds a file titled "Majestic 12," which states:

In 1988, two FBI offices received similar versions of a memo titled 'Operation Majestic-12'…claiming to be highly classified government document. The memo appeared to be a briefing for [then] newly-elected President Eisenhower on a secret committee created to exploit a recovery of an extra-terrestrial aircraft and cover-up this work from public examination. An Air Force investigation determined the document to be a fake.

Of course, that's exactly what you would expect government to say/do: deny everything, admit nothing, and make counteraccusations.[13]

It is understandable why conspiracy theories, which might include Majestic 12, tend to have extended lives. After all, the US government for a long time has been openly dismissive of UFO sightings and often took steps to obfuscate the issue. However, the post-World War II surge in reports led the government, especially the authorities in the Pentagon, to respond to those upticks in alarm by hosting programs—mostly known as public relations efforts—that might be considered knee-jerk reactions to tamp down the near hysteria about the matter.

Consider how the Pentagon's response has waxed and waned bureaucratically over the last few decades.

Pentagon Bureaucracy: Never Seriously Considered the UFO Subject

Although I previously addressed some of the following material, it is necessary to now review a bit more in order to weave together the broader picture of just how insidious and perhaps even deceptive the federal bureaucracy can be regarding the UFO issue.

A series of Pentagon UFO projects begins and ends. The first Pentagon UFO-related effort was in 1948, Project Sign, following the much-publicized incidents at Roswell and Mount Rainer. However, Pentagon authorities quickly decided to slow roll and bureaucratize the investigation of those sightings. In 1952, Major General John Samford, the Air Force director of intelligence who oversaw the issue at the Pentagon, called a press conference to report that, in most cases, there was no evidence the UFO sightings were related to aliens or spaceships. "However," General Samford explained, some of the reports "have been made by credible observers of relatively incredible things. It is this group of observations that we now are attempting to resolve."[14]

Project Sign was soon replaced by other programs spanning the years 1947–1969, ending with Project Blue Book. That combined effort catalogued 12,618 sightings of UFOs and concluded after Dr.

Edward U. Condon, a physicist with the University of Colorado who is mentioned as debunking the Tulli papyrus in chapter 2, led a congressionally mandated study initiated at the time by then Michigan Congressman Gerald Ford, the future president. The final report from that study states: "Our general conclusion is that nothing has come from the study of UFOs in the past 21 years that has added to scientific knowledge." Therefore, Condon recommended that further investigation "cannot be justified."[15]

Although the Pentagon's official effort—Project Blue Book—ended in 1969 based on Dr. Condon's recommendation, UFO sightings and rumors of inexplicable objects in the skies persisted. In 1985, the US Air Force tried to tamp down the continued public alarm about UFOs, especially the media-fed public curiosity for locations like Hangar 18 at Wright-Patterson Air Force Base near Dayton, Ohio, a government facility some ufologists at the time and others in the press claimed were used to house top-secret alien aircraft. However, the Air Force released a fact sheet about the allegation of a cover-up that was unequivocal on the issue: "There are not now nor ever have been, any extraterrestrial visitors or equipment on Wright-Patterson Air Force Base."[16]

Of course, Dr. Condon's report and the US Air Force's subsequent denial memorandum didn't end speculation about UFOs; in fact, they did just the opposite. Although the government vigorously denied it was hiding information about ETs, the nongovernment ufologists doubled down on their efforts to compile and study UFO sighting reports and then, as mentioned earlier, interested citizens like millionaire Robert Bigelow stepped up efforts to expose the perceived threat. Mr. Bigelow convened a group in Las Vegas, Nevada, in 1995, which he called the National Institute for Discovery Science. Participants in that institute included two former astronauts, Ed Mitchell and Harrison Schmitt, and most notable was the US Senate leader, Harry Reid of Nevada. Eventually, Reid drove the government back into the UFO investigation business.[17]

Facts and politics force Pentagon officials to pick up the issue once again. Pentagon interest in UFOs was once again piqued by incidents reported in 2004 by US Navy pilots operating off the coast of San Diego, California. During a routine carrier operation, US Navy pilots videotaped a mysterious, oval-shaped craft as it hovered over the Pacific Ocean. As cited earlier in this book, F/A-18F pilot Commander David Fravor described the object as having "no plumes, wings or rotors and outran our F/A-18Fs." Evidently, although the reaction was somewhat delayed, the Pentagon, with the encouragement of Senator Reid, finally launched yet another UFO program.[18]

The Pentagon's new program was known as the Advanced Aerospace Threat Identification Program (AATIP), a "black program"—classified effort—physically located on the fifth floor of the Pentagon's C Ring. That twelve-man team was run by the earlier-mentioned Luis Elizondo, a former counterintelligence officer who worked closely with Bigelow's aerospace research company in Las Vegas.[19]

Evidently, Elizondo quickly came to believe UFOs were not a hoax. He said:

> I realized within a couple of [AATIP] meetings that there was something to this, that this was real, and there were things coming into our controlled airspace affecting our military pilots, and we had no understanding of what it was.[20]

More time passed and the number of UFO sightings surged. For example, in 2014, this time off the East Coast, US Navy pilots video recorded an extended series of encounters with unidentified craft near Florida and Virginia that traveled at high altitudes and hypersonic speeds. Later, a former US Navy pilot, Lieutenant Ryan Graves, tried to describe the unidentified craft on CBS' *60 Minutes*: "You have rotation, you have high altitudes," he said. "You have propulsion, right? I don't know. I don't know what it is, frankly."[21]

Mr. Elizondo said that, during his tenure with AATIP, he "saw hard evidence that entities unknown to the Pentagon are using technology the United States cannot match or reproduce to have their way with the nation's restricted airspace and sensitive nuclear sites." He considered this an existential threat, yet the US government refused to officially acknowledge it.[22]

In a *Popular Mechanics* interview, Mr. Elizondo said that, in 2023, the stakes were high:

We know they [ET beings] are conducting some sort of ISR— intelligence, surveillance, and reconnaissance—on our military weapons systems and our nuclear technology, globally. That's not up for debate, because we have declassified reporting to prove it.[23]

Unfortunately, Mr. Elizondo couldn't persuade Pentagon leadership to embrace the threat even though AATIP documented encounters with alarming frequency around nuclear facilities and other sensitive locations. For example, there was a record of one instance in 1967, when a UFO appeared to have actually shut down nuclear-armed missiles at the Malmstrom Air Force Base in Montana, an incident mentioned earlier in this book. How many still-classified incidents are in the Pentagon records?[24]

Many expertly documented UFO-related events kept flowing into AATIP. "We've had military exercises canceled because there were unidentified aircraft on the training range, and they were afraid of midair collisions," said Chris Mellon, a former deputy assistant defense secretary for intelligence. "These are aircraft that don't have transponders, and haven't filed flight plans, and nobody knows what they are."[25]

Unfortunately, as shocking as the evidence suggests, AATIP couldn't get the attention of the Pentagon's top brass. In 2017, Elizondo became so disgruntled by the Pentagon's lack of interest that he submitted his resignation to then defense secretary Jim Mattis. In that letter, Elizondo wrote, "Why aren't we spending more time and effort on this issue?" He continued, "There remains a vital need to ascertain capability and intent of these phenomena for the benefit of the armed forces and the nation."[26]

Mr. Elizondo's letter was leaked to the press, exposing the AATIP program, which Pentagon officials grudgingly acknowledged to the press. That public acknowledgment of the previously classified program stated the AATIP was created "to assess far-term, foreign advanced aerospace threats to the United States," but was discontinued in 2012 for "other higher priority issues."[27]

On the day of Elizondo's resignation from AATIP, he met with Leslie Kean, a long-time UFO reporter, to participate in his first of many media interviews. Soon Kean joined Ralph Blumenthal and Helen Cooper to write about AATIP for the *New York Times* in an article titled "Glowing Auras and 'Black Money': The Pentagon's Mysterious UFO Program." The report, published on the front page of the *Times* on Saturday, December 16, 2017, stated AATIP was official from 2007 to 2012, and was initially funded by the former senate majority leader (Harry Reid) along with Senators Ted Stevens (Alaska) and Daniel Inouye (Hawaii). In the piece, Senator Reid was quoted as saying, "I'm not embarrassed or ashamed or sorry I got this going."[28]

Even though the funding for AATIP dried up by 2012, the program kept going. Elizondo said the program was never formally disestablished and kept running by funds siphoned from other programs until 2017.[29]

It is noteworthy that the explosive *New York Times* article came embedded with two videos showing UFOs without visible means of propulsion and making physics-defying maneuvers. That prompted former US Navy pilots to come out of the shadows to provide their eyewitness perspectives on those sightings.

Once Elizondo submitted his resignation, the threats poured in. His Pentagon boss told Elizondo he would "tell people you are crazy, and it might impact your security clearance." The message was clear: Keep quiet.[30]

Then Elizondo's office computer was confiscated to determine whether he'd taken unauthorized material. Also, the Air Force Office of Special Investigations looked into the release of the UFO videos embedded in the *New York Times* article. Obviously, the implication was that Elizondo had violated his security oath and could be subject to criminal charges.[31]

After Elizondo left the Pentagon for good, and while still addressing the issue in the media, he was stalked by the government's bureaucracy. "I think they were literally watching his appearances, his social media, his press, his show, looking for any nugget they could use to go after him," an intelligence official told the author of the article about Elizondo published by *Popular Mechanics*.[32]

Evidently, the Pentagon's misinformation agents tried to discredit Elizondo's story by denying he was ever part of AATIP. The Intercept, an online American nonprofit news organization, quoted a Pentagon official as claiming that Elizondo "had no responsibilities with regard to the AATIP program."[33] Fortunately for him, Senator Reid rebutted that statement in a letter affirming "as a matter of record Luis Elizondo's involvement and leadership role in this program."[34]

NASA pushes for more action: Before long, another spark of official interest in UFOs was created by a couple of NASA scientists who wrote in *Scientific American* that it was past time to revisit the conclusions of the 1969 Condon report that had doomed Project Blue Book. In July 2020, Ravi Kopparapu and Jacob Haqq Misra wrote: "Perhaps some, or even most, UAP events are simply classified military aircraft, or strange weather formations, or other misidentified mundane phenomena." The NASA scientists said further, "However, there are still a number of truly puzzling cases that might be worth investigating."[35]

On the heels of the NASA scientists' piece in the *Scientific American*, in August 2020, Deputy Secretary of Defense David L. Norquist directed the Department of the Navy, overseen by the Office of the Under Secretary of Defense for Intelligence and Security, to create yet another UFO program—the Unidentified Aerial Phenomena (UAP)

Task Force (UAPTF), allegedly to "detect, analyze, and catalog UAPs that could potentially pose a threat to U.S. national security."[36]

Intelligence leader categorizes UFOs: Less than a year after the stand-up of the UAPTF, the Navy, in April 2021, confirmed the existence of a video of unidentified objects harassing US warships off the California coast.[37]

A couple of months later, the Office of the Director of National Intelligence issued its assessment of UFO sightings. The report, which covered the years 2004 to 2021, indicated that UFOs, renamed as "unidentified aerial phenomena" by the time of the report, could be categorized into five groups: airborne clutter, natural phenomena, public and private aerospace development programs, foreign adversary systems, and other. The report called for more funding to conduct further research.[38]

Yet another Pentagon UFO project is established as pressure builds: In July 2022, the Pentagon announced the UAPTF would be succeeded by a new organization, the All-domain Anomaly Resolution Office (AARO), which was given the task to investigate objects "that might pose a threat to national security." At nearly the same time, NASA announced it intended to create its own effort to address the issue from a scientific perspective, NASA's UAP independent study team.

"We will be identifying what data—from civilians, government, nonprofits, companies—exists, what else we should try to collect, and how to best analyze it," said team lead David Spergel, the Princeton physicist introduced earlier in this book.[39]

The drumbeat about UFOs/UAPs continued through 2023. In June, the Office of the Director of National Intelligence (DNI) released another report indicating there were an additional 510 UFO/UAP sightings, and 171 remained inexplicable. That report indicated those UAPs often "appear to have demonstrated unusual flight characteristics or performance capabilities."[40]

Whistleblowers shock nation with allegations about government cover-up: Less than a month after the release of the report by the DNI, whistleblowers testified before a congressional committee about an alleged Pentagon cover-up. Specifically, David Grusch, a former US Air Force major and intelligence officer, alleged the US government possessed "intact and partially intact vehicles" from UFO crash sites. Further, he claimed there were "non-human" biologics in the government's possession.[41]

In the wake of decades of trying to ignore the issue, the US government's bureaucracy, with a fresh congressional mandate, seems to be taking steps to get serious about the issue once again.

US Government Promises to Get Better

A host of people doggedly forced our government to get serious about the UFO issue. In that universe, there is Leslie Kean, who encouraged action through her 2010 book, *UFOs: Generals, Pilots and Government Officials Go on the Record*, in which she states:

> The US Government routinely ignores UFOs and, when pressed, issues false explanations. Its indifference and/or dismissals are irresponsible, disrespectful to credible, often expert witnesses, and potentially dangerous.[42]

By 2017 the publication of the *New York Times* article about AATIP, which Leslie Kean co-wrote, brought about a surge in national attention, putting the government's newest UFO program in an uncomfortable spotlight.

Of course, Luis Elizondo was especially uneasy at the time because he took a big risk to expose the AATIP program with Kean's article, especially given the Pentagon's previous foot-dragging to avoid getting serious about the issue. As we learned from the *Times* piece, Elizondo is a true patriot for pushing his Pentagon bosses to take action and then risking his future by going public about what he believed could be an existential threat to our country and the world.

Others took risks as well. A number of Navy pilots like retired

Commander Fravor and former intelligence officers like David Grusch put their reputations on the line. These and many others created a firestorm of public interest that eventually compelled the Pentagon and Congress to show renewed interest and grudgingly take action.

Others earned honorable mention as well for turning the Pentagon around. John Ratcliffe, the former DNI, is also someone who pushed for action. "When we talk about sightings," he said, "we are talking about objects that have been seen by Navy or Air Force pilots, or have been picked up by satellite imagery, that frankly engage in actions that are difficult to explain, movements that are hard to replicate, that we don't have the technology for, or are travelling at speeds that exceed the sound barrier without a sonic boom."[43]

The best news for Elizondo, Kean, and others came when Congress inserted into the 2019 National Defense Authorization Act a provision that obligated the Pentagon to continue investigations of UAPs. "The UAP issue is being taken very seriously now, even compared to where it was two or three years ago," a former Pentagon official said.[44]

Soon the US Navy revised its official guidelines for pilots, encouraging them to report UAPs without fear of retribution or stigma. Then in 2020, Senator Marco Rubio added text to the 2021 Intelligence Authorization Act requesting the DNI to produce "a detailed analysis of unidentified aerial phenomena data and intelligence reporting." This appears to have taken hold at the DNI, given its recent reports on UAP.[45]

Of course, congressional authorizations, new directives, and promises of no more stigma aren't enough. It is past time the Pentagon and, more broadly, the US government come clean on what, if anything, they may know about UFOs and extraterrestrials.

What, If Anything, Is the US Government Hiding?

This is a hard question to answer if the government continues to be mute on the issue. Perhaps only a few people inside the Pentagon or at the Nevada secret facility, Area 51, really can provide a comprehensive answer. Maybe we have been lied to for many years, there really *is* significant evidence of alien life, and the US has both craft and alien biologics, as some claim. I don't know, but the public record states the following about the issue:

Area 51 is a highly classified US Air Force facility inside the Nevada Test and Training Range at Nellis Air Force Base, eighty-three miles north of Las Vegas. It is thought to support the development and testing of experimental aircraft. Area 51's secrecy inspires conspiracy theories and is a key focus of UFO folklore. Official claims the US government has neither alien spacecraft nor ET biologics at Area 51 or elsewhere is contradicted by a number of whistleblowers.

Who should we believe?

I asked Nick Pope, the former United Kingdom Ministry of Defence UFO investigator, that question. He answered:

Yes, but—unless the rumors are true and there really is some sort of extraterrestrial "smoking gun"—this secrecy often has to do with not wanting to disclose methods and sources by which intelligence is obtained, or not wanting to disclose the capabilities of our own systems.[46]

Alien Spacecraft Materials

Mr. Elizondo worked with contractor Bigelow Aerospace from 2007 to 2011. Although he won't discuss the particulars of that relationship, according to the *New York Times*:

Under Mr. Bigelow's direction, the company modified buildings in Las Vegas for the storage of metal alloys and other materials that Mr. Elizondo and program contractors said had been recovered from unidentified aerial phenomena. Researchers also studied people who said they had experienced physical effects from encounters with the objects and examined them for any physiological changes.[47]

These claims are misleading, according to Elizondo, who said they are wrongly identified. Evidently, the substances at those Las Vegas facilities were not metal alloys, but "metamaterials," synthetic materials with composite structures that exhibit properties not found in nature. "To engineer these materials with that degree of precision is something that we, so far, do not believe we have the technical capability to reproduce," according to Mr. Elizondo, who then said he wouldn't say where the materials came from.[48]

Part of UFO folklore includes alleged efforts by the US government to reengineer alien materials. Perhaps the best-known account of such efforts is the bizarre story of Robert "Bob" Lazar, who participated in an interview with a Las Vegas television station to claim he once worked at a super-secret, unconfirmed section of Area 51 called "S4," where the government purportedly kept recovered extra-terrestrial spacecraft. In that 1989 interview, Lazar said his job was to "reverse-engineer an alien material called 'element 115,'" which he claims is the fuel used to power alien spacecraft.[49]

On January 20, 2019, Lazar said on *Larry King Now*:

[Element 115 is] a superheavy element. When it's exposed to radiation, it produces its own gravitational field—its own antigravitational field, and it's what's used to lift and propel the craft.[50]

Evidently, according to an interview with Vice.com, Lazar "has repeatedly hinted that he took a piece of element 115 from Area 51, and that this element is of great interest to the federal government." However, when asked by the Vice.com reporter whether he had a piece of element 115, Lazar said, "If I had some, would I reveal it to confirm my accounts? Absolutely not."[51]

Years after supposedly leaving Area 51, Mr. Lazar formed a private firm, United Nuclear Scientific, which was raided by the FBI and local police. The Vice.com article indicates that Lazar and his followers theorized the "FBI was attempting to recover samples of element 115 that Lazar [allegedly] took from Area 51."[52]

"To date," according to Vice.com, "there's never been any tangible evidence proving Lazar ever set foot inside Area 51, much less worked on alien spaceships or obtained any mysterious elements." For some ufologists, Lazar "is a black eye on a field they desperately hope to see achieve mainstream legitimacy," states Vice.com. "Others see him as a truth teller."[53]

More recently, in July 2023, a House of Representatives' sub-committee heard some rather sobering allegations from a former intelligence officer whistleblower, an account previously mentioned. Specifically, David Grusch, a US Air Force veteran who worked at the National Reconnaissance Office until early 2023, testified America has possession of "intact and partially intact" alien vehicles. Then he said the US government has conducted a multi-decade program to collect and attempt to reverse engineer crashed UFOs. Further, he claimed to know "the exact location" of UAPs in the government's possession.[54]

Mr. Grusch also said the government possessed a "very large, like a football-field kind of size" alien craft. Further, he asserted that the government had a "bell-like craft," which the Benito Mussolini government recovered in northern Italy prior to the Second World War.[55]

Jonathan Grey works for the National Air and Space Intelligence Center, a unit of the US Air Force, where he analyzes UAP events. His statements tend to back up what Elizondo and Grusch said. "The non-human intelligence phenomenon is real. We are not alone," Grey said. "Retrievals of this kind are not limited to the United States. This is a global phenomenon, and yet a global solution continues to elude us."[56]

Finally, there is the disturbing Pentagon decision to deny access to supposed evidence of alien craft in the government's possession. Then Senate majority leader, Harry Reid, asked but was denied clearance to see what he understood were crashed UFOs in the possession of Lockheed Martin Corporation, a leading Pentagon aerospace contract company. Senator Reid said at the time:

And I tried to get, as I recall, a classified approval by the Pentagon to have me go look at the stuff. They would not approve that. I don't know what the numbers were, what kind of classification it was, but they would not give that to me.

Evidently, the Pentagon never provided Reid an explanation for denying him access to what the senator believed was irrefutable evidence of alien craft.[57]

Non-human Biologics Allegedly Found

Mr. Grusch testified that the US government has been recovering nonhuman bodies of "pilots" for many years. "That was the assessment of people with direct knowledge on the [UAP] program I talked to, that are currently still on the program," said Grusch, the retired Air Force major. He also stated he has not personally seen any alien craft or alien bodies, and his statements were based on accounts of more than forty witnesses he interviewed over four years in his role with the UAP task force.[58]

Much fact-checking must be performed regarding Mr. Grusch's claim. No doubt this information is "interesting, if true." What appears to be true at this point is that Mr. Grusch is who he says he is, in that he worked on the UAP Task Force. However, as Nick Pope, the former British civil servant investigating UFOs for the UK's Ministry of Defence, said, "We've really only heard [Grusch's] testimony, and not [seen] any evidence in terms of documents, photographs, videos, materials etc." Hopefully, the federal agencies are evaluating the allegations.[59]

Years earlier, in 2001, retired US Army Sergeant Clifford Stone, now deceased, stated he had been part of a military group assigned to recover crashed UFO or ET parts, alien bodies, and artifacts. He explained that, while assigned to a nuclear, biological, and chemical retrieval and abatement detail at Fort McClellan in Anniston, Alabama, he had participated in regular UFO retrieval duties.[60]

Sergeant Stone revealed what he labeled classified projects known as "Moon Dust and Blue Fly." Evidently, according to him, these projects were created to hide the UFOs' debris. Stone said, as a member of the recovery team, he was allowed to read a notebook containing information on fifty-seven types of extraterrestrial biological entities known to the military.[61]

Freedom of Information Act requests regarding projects Moon Dust and Blue Fly revealed their previous existence, but nothing more. The 1986 FOIA response from the government states: "The programs (UFO, Blue Fly, Moon Dust) no longer exist, and records were destroyed."[62]

Mr. Stone, speaking at a 2001 press conference about his experiences, said:

> UFO crashes are not events that take place every day. They're rare. I know we're not alone in the universe. I know that the absence of evidence is not evidence of absence, it's evidence that has been denied to the American people. I stand before you today and my Almighty God, and I tell you this: if the Congress calls me in and says: "Will you testify in detail what you know?" I stand here today prepared and ready to do just that, governments must never lie to the people for no reason. Thank you.[63]

Evidence of UFOs with Extraordinary Capabilities

The AATIP maintained files of UAPs that include numerous descriptions by military aircrews detailing unrecognizable craft. Elizondo said that meant "images captured by radar or gun-sight cameras that didn't resemble any known craft or projectile, friendly or hostile." Also, according to Elizondo:

> There were times we were able to very quickly rule out that this was something extraterrestrial. But there are, absolutely, some

cases that defy anything we can definitively look at and say, that is an aircraft, that is a drone, that is a missile, because the performance parameters are so way off the charts.

He continued, saying the existence of UFOs using technology far more advanced than human capabilities, in his opinion, has been proved "beyond reasonable doubt."[64]

Some of the UAPs, explained Elizondo, were craft traveling at extreme speeds without any obvious signs of propulsion such as contrails. He said further:

It was enough where we began to see trends and similarities in incidents. There were very distinct observables. Extreme maneuverability, hypersonic velocity without a sonic boom, speeds of 7,000 mph to 8,000 mph, no flight surfaces on the objects. A lot of this is backed with radar signal data, gun camera footage from aircraft, multiple witnesses.[65]

Witnesses at the 2023 House committee hearing included retired Command David Fravor, the former US Navy F/A-18 pilot mentioned earlier. He testified he saw a strange object—a "white Tic Tac shaped object"—in the sky during a 2004 training mission over the Pacific Ocean. The object had "no rotors, no rotor wash, or any visible flight control surfaces like wings." He continued, "The technology that we faced is far superior to anything we had."[66]

Another witness, Ryan Graves, also a former US Navy lieutenant and F-18 pilot, now the founder of Americans for Safe Aerospace, a nonprofit organization, claimed he saw UAPs off the Atlantic Coast "every day for at least a couple years." Further, he indicated the sightings were "not rare or isolated," and other military aircrew members and even commercial pilots witnessed the UAPs. He described the objects as "dark grey or black cubes inside of clear sphere" and "the apex or tips of the cube were touching the inside of the sphere." Finally,

Mr. Graves urged the government to stop hiding such reports through "excessive classification."[67]

US Government Retaliation

Mr. Grusch led analysis of UAPs within a US Department of Defense agency until 2023. Further, he said he was denied access to secret government UFO programs, and then asserted he has faced "very brutal" retaliation for his allegations. Also, he told the House subcommittee he knew of "people who have been harmed or injured" while trying to conceal UFO information.[68]

Ufology Community Agrees, Pentagon and Allies Deny

Predictably, the ufology community agrees with the above assertions and the US government's alleged cover-up. Bob Spearing, the director of international investigations for MUFON, the Mutual UFO Network, said "the UFO 'street' has understood that material and bodies have been in U.S. custody since 1947." He continued, "This is nothing new except this [congressional testimony] was allegedly told under oath. That's telling." Spears surmised that Mr. Grusch's testimony is "a slow turn towards disclosure" or part of an effort to mislead the public. Then he warned, "Until [the US government] show[s] the physical evidence, caution dictates it is a misinformation campaign. I think it is all orchestrated."[69]

In April 2022, Sean Kirkpatrick, the director of the AARO, said his office had found no evidence of ET beings. He testified:

> I should state clearly for the record that in our research AARO has found no credible evidence thus far of extraterrestrial activity, off-world technology, or objects that defy the known laws of physics.

However, Dr. Kirkpatrick's assurances changed just prior to his late 2023 retirement from federal service.[70]

On November 7, 2023, physicist Kirkpatrick confirmed in an interview there is evidence of UFO activity "in our backyard," which he attributes to either a foreign power or "aliens." Of course, he fails to define "aliens," which presumably might include beings in the spiritual realm and not just entities from other planets or galaxies. Further, Mr. Kirkpatrick said "none" of the UFO reports reviewed by the AARO to date "have been positively attributed to foreign activities."[71]

Mr. Kirkpatrick's acknowledgment that UFO activity in America's backyard could be of an "alien" origin makes him just the latest US government official to express that possibility. It is also noteworthy that Kirkpatrick, earlier in 2023, coauthored a paper with Harvard astrophysicist Avi Loeb of Harvard and the director of the Galileo Project that hypothesized extraterrestrial "parent craft" might have released "many small probes" to explore Earth-like planets.[72]

Kirkpatrick and Loeb suggest in their March 2023 unpublished paper, entitled "Physical Constraints on Unidentified Aerial Phenomena," that such "extraterrestrial technological probes…would necessarily be looking for water" to refuel.[73] After all, according to Kirkpatrick, government sensors and personnel have observed "metallic orbs" that are "making very interesting apparent maneuvers" across the globe, such as "suddenly bolt[ing] off the screen" in "dozens" of unreleased videos recorded by surveillance drones.[74]

It is indeed refreshing that Dr. Kirkpatrick has become rather open about the UFO issue. Still, his openness comes just as he exited the Pentagon, and there's no evidence the department's bureaucracy is going to follow his lead. Just the opposite is the case.

AARO and Pentagon officials have nongovernment allies who defend official opacity. Specifically, a spokesman for the RAND Corporation, a US government contractor, warned that increased government transparency regarding UAPs "could take a dark turn if policymakers aren't careful."[75]

Marek N. Posard and Caitlin McCulloch issued that warning in an article on RAND's website, "UFO Research Is Only Harmed by

Antigovernment Rhetoric." They noted the Pentagon's AARO and NASA's UAP Independent Study Team are evidence of an effort to afford the public more transparency on the issue. However, they cautioned:

> If the information release is haphazard, with a focus on one-off reports of sightings, that could backfire. U.S. national security agencies could suffer damage to their reputation. Those who work on or report, such phenomena could be stigmatized.[76]

RAND earns millions of taxpayer dollars annually to conduct research for the American government. Recently, Dr. Posard, a sociologist at the organization, was the lead researcher for a 2023 RAND government-funded study on UAP sightings, "Not the X-Files, Mapping Public Reports of UAP Across America." Likely, RAND and especially Dr. Posard will continue to conduct research for the Pentagon, especially now that he is defending Pentagon officials on the issue.[77]

Here's a case in point: Dr. Posard's article defends the Pentagon hierarchy against "claims of a vast conspiracy by the U.S. Department of Defense, U.S. intelligence agencies, and their contractors [which includes RAND] to conceal evidence of extraterrestrials." Posard points out some government officials claim they were insulted by the allegations made by people who testified to Congress about a government cover-up.[78]

The RAND spokesman then warned that "antigovernment rhetoric can also sow public distrust." Dr. Posard reminded the reader that confidence in both Congress and the White House are already at rock bottom, and even public confidence in the military is now at 60 percent, a recent low.[79]

Conclusion

It is difficult to dismiss all of this bureaucratic foot-dragging. Clearly, strange things are happening in our skies, and such events have a very long and well-documented history. It is too easy to dismiss many unidentified object sightings as natural or man-made phenomena. However, there is so much more data that's inexplicable, and a growing list of eyewitnesses and government whistleblowers are calling foul. As a result of the above material and decades of misinformation by the US government and the media, it's quite understandable why most Americans believe our government has more information about the UFO phenomenon, but for some reason it remains mum.

FOREIGN GOVERNMENT UFO PROGRAMS AND HISTORIES

11

*If you ask me, do I believe there's life in a universe that
is so vast that it's hard for me to comprehend how
big it is, my personal answer is yes.*[1]

—CLARENCE WILLIAM "BILL" NELSON
NASA Administrator and former astronaut

The US government isn't alone among world administrations regarding
ongoing efforts to better understand the UAP issue. At least ten countries around the world have in the past or presently track UFOs/UAPs.
In fact, it is encouraging that the world community might be waking up
to the issue and taking appropriate action for our collective good.

At least ten countries around the
world have in the past or presently track UFOs/UAPs.[2]

This chapter highlights the new dawn of interest across the world on the UFO issue, in part thanks to America's renewed efforts. Further, to put the issue in context, in this chapter, I review some of the history on the topic of other countries, especially in the former Soviet Union and its satellite states—the former Warsaw Pact—as well as a couple of countries in Western Europe.

It's important to understand at the outset of this chapter that what other countries know about the UAP issue is significant for our future investigations. It is noteworthy that Mr. Elizondo refused to tell the British *Sunday Telegraph* whether his former organization, AATIP, considered UFO sightings recorded by other countries, including the United Kingdom, our best ally, in their analysis. However, he soberly acknowledged to the *Telegraph*:

> But we took a very comprehensive approach. Nothing was too small to investigate. In my opinion, if this was a court of law, we have reached the point of "beyond reasonable doubt."[3]

The inference from Mr. Elizondo's response is that AATIP and likely the Pentagon's current UAP watchdog group, AARO, regularly consults with allies and foreign partners on the issue. That makes sense and, in fact, Mark Esper, a former secretary of defense under President Trump, was asked at a Senate Select Committee on Intelligence hearing whether Pentagon officials consult with allies and foreign partners about UAPs. Although Esper hesitated at first, he eventually testified, "We would not have moved forward without briefing close allies. This was bigger than the U.S. Government."[4]

Collaborating on sensitive issues with allies and foreign partners is important, as in any significant national security issue. Arguably, the possibility that aliens are real and visiting Earth is of paramount importance and warrants intelligence sharing, especially with foreign governments.

Foreign Nations Getting Serious about UFOs Thanks to US

UFO researcher Ian Dubin, who is based in Hong Kong, explained the growing global interest in the UFO issue. "It is a commonly held belief amongst UFO researchers that other countries are waiting for the USA to take the lead on this investigation," he said. Evidently, now with US congressional hearings and new programs at the Pentagon and NASA, other governments may begin to come out of the shadows regarding UFOs.[5]

European nations like Sweden appear to be on board with the new search for explanations about UFOs. "Lots of people in UFO societies and the public in general are now feeling that they can discuss this [issue] without being put under ridicule," said Clas Svahn, the chairman for the Sweden-based Archives for the Unexplained, which is host to a large digital library of UFO sightings and investigations. Svahn explained that Washington's new openness to the issue is "having very much a tangible impact…when it comes to society and how we are dealing with the subject."[6]

The consequences of America's new openness to UFOs will be significant, according to Svahn. He said military pilots are now more likely to report sightings because the stigma is lifted. Further, other governments like China and Russia may move to declassify information about UFOs that remain secret.[7]

The governments of the "Five Eyes"—USA, Canada, New Zealand, Australia, and Great Britain—have historically been the least interested in the UAP issue, according to Robert Spearing, the director of international investigations for the Mutual UFO Network (MUFON). In fact, according to Spearing, those nations have "at times…mocked the idea something was going on." Now, he says, "the abrupt turnaround in attitude [by the US government] and release of information now has been startling."[8]

Mr. Spearing said there is already considerable information on the issue across the world. Specifically, he stated, "I personally know there are thousands of military cases they could analyze from Korea, Vietnam, Afghanistan, et cetera, submitted to MUFON and other entities by reliable soldiers and sailors and pilots over the decades."[9]

Unfortunately, many government reviews of the UFO issue remain classified, such as those in Brazil, Britian, France, and Spain. Hopefully, the new openness on the issue might spur those governments to open their files and encourage others, like communist China, to share their records with the world as well.[10]

It might surprise the reader that on September 20, 1979, the Peoples' Republic of China (PRC) permitted the formation of a UFO investigative office, the China UFO Enthusiasts' Liaison Office, at Wuhan University, which came about in response to thousands of inexplicable object sightings across that country. Soon the effort was rebranded as the China UFO Research Association, a division of that government's Academy of Social Sciences. In February 1980 it began publishing the *Journal of UFO Research*, which reported on "alleged sightings of UAPs in China." At a conference in Beijing, the association's chairman explained his organization was "searching for creatures that might be living in other solar systems."[11]

In 1981, the All-China Qigong Science Research Association (QSRA) was established with the blessing of the Chinese Communist Party. It was "established as a national-level umbrella organization for all qigong practice ("a system of coordinated body-posture and movement, breathing, and meditation used for the purposes of health, spirituality, and martial arts training"[12]) and research; everything from extrasensory perception to telekinesis and ghosts." That group became the hub for all paranormal research and in 1988, the China UFO Research Association formally affiliated with the QSRA as a "second level study society," meaning it had legal standing in the PRC. Yet, in 1997, the association lost its status under the QRSA and disbanded.[13]

The Shanghai Research Center is an organization that studies UAPs in China. Lou Zhongrong, the Center's founder, recalls that, in 1971, while serving in China's National Air Force, he saw a "spiral-shaped shiny object moving across the sky." He said the object wasn't a plane, and "it was not an illusion because many of my comrades-in-arms saw it too."[14]

Lou retired from the air force and established the Shanghai Aircraft Design and Research Institute, focused on UAP research. He socialized his UAP-related views and soon formed the Shanghai UFO Research Center.[15]

Lou's colleague, Wu Jialu, became the organization's director. In 1999, Wu witnessed a "strange object moving in a 'V' formation" and "determined humanity has something to learn from UAPs." Mr. Wu wrote:[16]

> We discussed the issue of whether the Earth rotates around the Sun or vice versa from 1,600 years. We human beings have to walk on the endless road of scientific discovery. So, there must be aliens. There are ten billion planets in the universe. I don't think Earth is the only planet with life—creatures live in cold, oxygen-free conditions at the bottom of the sea.

Today, the Shanghai organization monitors and assesses UAP sightings across China. According to Lou, most objects (90 percent) are explained as optical phenomena "such as light reflecting off a plane, or an aberration in a photograph."[17]

Some of the organization's UAP records are inexplicable, however. There are examples of objects like a spinning "oval plate and a comet with a tail like an umbrella." In 1990, thousands of residents of Shanghai reported a UAP with "a white head and orange edge, brighter than stars, flying at around 2,000 meters (6,500 feet), and shaped like a 'U', 'fish' or 'shuttle.'" Meanwhile, an airliner crew witnessed the same UAP, which "reportedly changed direction, height and speed several times, and split into two parts before merging together again and disappearing."[18]

The PRC does not appear to have a formal UAP monitoring and research organization like the Pentagon's AARO. However, given the presence of UFO groups around that country and the apparent ongoing incidents, it is likely the Beijing government does monitor sightings and, in time, might collaborate with other governments.

Meanwhile, elsewhere across much of the world, there is growing government endorsement of scientific research on UFOs, according to Peter Whitley, a researcher in Japan. "The public may be surprised to find out just how much research is being conducted by public organizations such as MUFON into uncovering the mysteries behind these sightings," Whitley said. He continued, "Certain aspects of these sightings are so consistent on a global scale…[that] it is indisputable that this is a physically real phenomenon worldwide and not simply the result of media influence or cultural bias."[19]

Europe's Craze over UFOs in Review

After World War II, the UFO phenomenon hit Western Europe and the Soviet Union much like the craze that enveloped America, arguably prompted by all the media attention given to incidents in Roswell and near Mount Rainer. That media-driven drama resulted in a clamoring for more information, and local citizen groups jumped to action. Even governments took cautious steps to investigate the phenomenon.

A 2014 article in the *Journal of Transatlantic Studies*, "'A Transatlantic Buzz': Flying Saucers, Extraterrestrials and America in Postwar Germany," argues that "both Cold War geopolitics and the occult were used to explain [UFO] sightings, but…suspected American influences and anti-American sentiments figured heavily in how most reports were interpreted."[20]

Arguably, the Europeans were ahead of America in terms of the first major UFO incident to spark widespread interest and fear. Between May and November 1946, thousands of Swedes and other citizens of Norway, Finland, and northern Germany reported seeing brightly lit cigar-shaped or circular wingless missiles moving at incredible speeds across their skies. These images came to be known as the "Ghost Rocket Scare of 1946" and seized the attention of much of the

European lay public, garnering interest even among both the British and American intelligence agencies as well.[21]

As a result, there was a surge in UFO reports across Europe, eliciting fear as well as distrust in government. Evidently, at the time, leading German space researchers concluded that some of those "flying saucers" were really reconnaissance aircraft "sent by inhabitants from another planet." This "only added to the battling nature of things," according to one report.[22]

At the time, there were bizarre stories from German and Italian engineers and scientists who claimed knowledge that "both Hitler and Mussolini had sponsored the development of flying saucer technology during the Second World War." It wasn't clear at the time whether those vehicles survived to haunt post-war Europeans.[23]

During the 1950s, the West German press openly discussed the reality and meaning of flying saucers. No one, not even government officials at the time, seemed to know what to make of the phenomenon. People from all walks of life expressed a range of viewpoints about the mystery.[24]

That curiosity didn't wane among many Europeans who were quite fascinated by the subject. Since 1989, UFO clubs and societies appeared across the continent to include in the east, Russia and much of Central Europe. For example, Hungary and Poland became important centers for ufology, and in Western European countries like Germany, 20 percent of citizens came to believe ETs have visited Earth and 40 percent of Czechs said they believed there is life on other planets. In fact, the level of concern about ETs was evidenced by the fact that, in 1995, a Sofia, Bulgaria, insurance company offered coverage to compensate for "physical and psychic damage" associated with a presumed "alien abduction."[25]

The rage about aliens led to international UFO conferences in a variety of European countries. And meanwhile, the pop-culture press devoted considerable space to ETs, such as Croatia's "Dossier UFO"; filmmakers also tapped the interest with ET-related productions.[26]

Perhaps more interesting is how the phenomenon played out in the former Soviet Union. Beginning in the late 1940s, the UFO craze hit Russia and Eastern Europe much like it did in Western Europe and the United States. Decades later, another surge of UFO activity happened in Russian skies about the time of the fall of communism (1991), especially given the publicity associated with a major incident in the Russian city of Voronezh, addressed a couple pages below.[27]

Nonetheless, it is noteworthy that the communist governments of the former Soviet bloc countries, once known as the Warsaw Pact, were mostly ambivalent to the public's fear associated with the UFO phenomenon. The governing class publicly treated the sightings as "bourgeois propaganda," such as the Hungarian government's 1954 claim that "all reports concerning UFOs had originated in capitalist countries." However, some key communist officials tended to look past such internal propaganda and seek reliable information.[28]

In 1948, Soviet dictator Josef Stalin invited Valery Burdakov, a Russian scientist, to review secret materials regarding the Roswell, New Mexico, incident. A few years later, in 1955, Dr. Felix Zigel, a professor at the Moscow Aviation Institute, began collecting data on UFO sightings, and by 1967, he helped form a group of top Soviet scientists and cosmonauts (Russian astronauts) to research the topic.[29]

Meanwhile, in 1959, there was a report from a Soviet tactical missile command in Sverdlovsk, on the eastern slopes of the Ural Mountains, where UFOs allegedly hovered and circled over the command's headquarters for more than a day. The base commander was said to have ordered his fighter jet pilots to attack the UFO, but there are no reported results from that encounter.[30]

Another UFO incident with the Soviet military took place on August 26, 1983, when Russian radar detected the presence of an undeclared aircraft near the top-secret submarine base at Ventspills on the Latvian, Baltic Sea coast. The local command launched six fighter jets carrying heat-seeking missiles with orders to destroy the intruder. Evidently, upon reaching the altitude of nine thousand feet, the fighters fired their missiles at the UFO. However, mysteriously, the missiles exploded instantly, destroying five of the Russian aircraft, which had just launched their ordnance. Only one Soviet pilot returned alive, Second Lieutenant Mikhail Anisimov. Interestingly, the official report of the incident blamed the loss of five pilots and their aircraft on "ball lightning," not on an unidentified (alien) aircraft as originally reported.[31]

The Soviet Union became the first nation to put a man in space, which introduced an entirely new set of UFO sightings. It was reported that an early Soviet spacecraft incident was blamed on UFOs. Specifically, on October 12, 1964, the Soviet spacecraft Voskhod 1 returned to Earth quite prematurely. Although the flight was billed as "a prolonged flight," S. R. Olinger, who wrote for a German newspaper at the time, cited Moscow sources as stating the mission was aborted because of "extremely fast-flying discs, which struck the [Soviet space] craft [with] violent, shattering blows with their powerful magnetic fields."[32]

Not all UFO sightings in the former Soviet Union and its satellite states, though, were attributed to government and military officials. One UFO incident evidently involved a young Polish girl, who claimed in July 1954 she encountered an alien while on holiday at Węgierska Górka, which is in southern Poland. Reportedly, the girl was invited on board an alien craft by human-like creatures identified as having "humps" on their backs.[33]

In 1978, another Pole, a farmer, Jan Wolski, claimed he was stopped by "entities" with slanted eyes and was taken aboard their spaceship, where he was stripped naked and given a medical exam.[34]

Perhaps the most bizarre UFO-related incident during the Soviet era was what Russian scientists claimed happened during the 1969 American moon mission. Three Russian scientists (Dr. Vladimir Azhazha, Dr. Sergei Bozhich, and Aleksandr Kazantsev [pioneer of Soviet ufology]) claimed Soviet intelligence monitoring America's moon landing observed two extraterrestrial craft near the Apollo lunar module on the moon's surface. Allegedly, Soviet intelligence claimed astronaut Neil Armstrong had informed mission control in Houston at the time about the alien craft in the vicinity, and his companion Buzz Aldrin had taken pictures of the object. The three Russian scientists said NASA censored Armstrong's report about the UFOs, however. It is noteworthy that Dr. Bozhich at the time asserted that the ET craft were at the site as a "backup" in the event the Apollo ran into difficulties.[35]

By 1989, ufology got a boast thanks to *glasnost*, the new openness popularized by Russian leader Mikhail Gorbachev. The regime became momentarily receptive to public interests and concerns. Evidently, at that time in the city of Voronezh, in the heart of European Russia, many children reported seeing a spaceship and a headless alien that exited his craft and walked around. That story seized the attention of the 860,000 residents of Voronezh. TASS, the Russian state-owned news service, reported on the sightings:

> Voronezh, October 9: Scientists have confirmed that an unidentified flying object recently landed in a park in the Russian city of Voronezh. They have also identified the landing site and found traces of aliens who made a short promenade about the park.[36]

The article about the Voronezh incident stated the aliens visited the city at least three times aboard their large shining ball or disc. Once the craft landed, according to the report, a hatch opened and several human-like creatures and a small robot emerged. Small-headed aliens stood three or four meters tall, according to eyewitnesses. Another report by TASS said one alien "had three eyes, was clad in silvery overalls and 'boots' the color of bronze, and had a disk on its chest."[37]

Review of Other World Governments' UFO Programs

Previously in this book I provided an overview of a few foreign government UFO programs—i.e., Peru, Australia, and France. The following will not repeat those summaries, but will introduce other countries' efforts and conclude with a report concerning our best ally, the United Kingdom, which at present no longer has a formal UFO program.

We begin by looking at three South American countries with documented histories of tracking UFOs: Uruguay, Chile, and Brazil.

Uruguay: In 1979, the Uruguayan air force created the *Comision Receptora e Investigadora de Denuncias sobre Objetos Voladores no Identificados* (CRIDOVNI), that is Reception and Investigation Commission of Unidentified Flying Objects Denunciations, the first South American government program to officially track UFOs. The group's researchers are all paid government employees and operate independently from that country's air force.[38]

Researchers with CRIDOVNI admit that only 2 percent of sightings remain unexplained, including a variety of alleged abductions, cattle mutilations, and evidence of physical landings. In the case of an inexplicable incident, Colonel Ariel Sanchez, chairman of CRIDOVNI, had the soil tested at the suspected UFO landing site and found there had been chemical composition changes in the soil.[39]

CRIDOVNI works closely with its civilian counterparts, such as the Regional Center for Investigation of Aerospace and Terrestrial Phenomena and, more broadly, with members of the ufology community. Colonel Sanchez indicates his organization operates with objective methodology and a quick response to incidents. "We still have no answers regarding the UFO phenomenon, what these vehicles and their origin are, but we keep on researching with the utmost disposition," said Colonel Sanchez. "As men at the service of Uruguay we must be impartial. We don't encourage or discourage any particular point of view."[40]

Chile: In 1997, the government of the Republic of Chile established an official UFO program under the guidance of the ministerial Department of Civil Aeronautics and in collaboration with the Chilean air force. That program, the Committee for the Studies of Anomalous Aerial Phenomena (CEFAA), was formed after government officials observed aerial anomalies over two nights, which led to a surge in media interest. The commission's mission "is to collect information and investigate reports on unidentified aerial phenomena in order to determine any danger to Chilean aviation."[41]

The CEFAA is governed by a federal transparency law mandating that the government acts in an open manner. In fact, CEFAA must release hard physical evidence such as photographs, videos, and audio recordings of all UFO encounters to the public. For example, the CEFAA publicly released a video reviewed by journalist Leslie Kean in an article, "UFO Caught on Tape over Santiago Air Base." Kean described the object in the video as "a dome-shaped flat-bottomed object with no visible means of propulsion...flying at velocities too high to be man-made."[42]

When CEFAA is in doubt about a UFO sighting, it turns to top scientists to assess the material. A review in 2014 of a mysterious sighting concluded:

> If, as many witnesses have declared, the [UFO phenomenon] demonstrates "intelligent behavior," and if we admit this fact, then we must look for "the intention behind" that intelligence, whatever it may be—a form of energy, perhaps—it doesn't matter. Intelligence is what matters. If this is so, we must ask: has it shown hostility or carried out openly threatening maneuvers? Has it actually attacked our aircraft? To date, this doesn't seem to be the case. We cannot possibly call something a threat to something or someone if they have not shown any open intention to do harm. And even less, we do not even know their exact nature![43]

Brazil: The largest country in South America is governed by the Federative Republic of Brazil, which has the biggest UFO investigation program, *Operacao Prato*, or "Operation Plate." That program was prompted by a number of UFO sightings, specifically, military personnel who encountered disk-shaped UFOs hovering above them that sounded "like an air conditioner [and] like a bicycle sprocket when you pedal backwards."[44]

Captain Uyrange Hollande, who encountered the UFOs above, inherited the task of investigating the incident. He went about interviewing more than three hundred personnel and gathering photographs of the UFOs. The objects appeared as a variety of shapes: disks, pyramids, and a one hundred-meter-long "mother ship" shaped like a barrel. Local people from the UFO site referred to the objects as *chupa-chupas*, "a reference to blood-sucking, as there were multiple reports of the UFOs paralyzing people with a flash of green light and burning them with a flash of red light that left welts on the skin."[45] Another account of the incident, according to French ufologist Jacques Vallée, indicated some people were killed by the "lights" fired upon them by the UFOs, and the wounds on the deceased bodies were consistent with radiation effects from microwaves.[46]

In 2009, many documents related to Operation Plate were released to the public. By 2013, representatives from each of the Brazilian military services met with UFO researchers to combine their ongoing UFO studies.[47]

United Kingdom: The British government's interest in UFOs dates to the era of the "foo fighters" seen during the two world wars. "Foo fighters" is the name attributed to "spherical, circular, disc-like, or wedged shaped 'bogies'" that often glowed or shined and were seen by World War II pilots. Most often they followed British fighter aircraft. However, no foo fighter was known to have attempted any interaction with humans; they were known for their high rate of speed, agility, and extreme maneuverability.[48]

In 1950, Britain's Ministry of Defence (MoD) created the Flying Saucer Working Party (FSWP) to ascertain whether the foo fighters, or UFOs, were of ET origin, an effort shared with the American CIA. The FSWP was manned by experts from the technical intelligence branches of the air ministry, admiralty, and war office of the MoD. They spent eight months in 1950 rummaging through UFO reports to conclude most sightings were spurious. The final report recommended that the government debunk the sightings and suppress public knowledge about the inexplicable incidents.[49]

Between 1959 and 2007, the MoD recorded more than eleven thousand UFO sightings. However, it became the ministry's practice to have reports older than five years old routinely destroyed if "they weren't [evidence] of a possible security threat." In 2009, the MoD closed their UFO report hotline, which it labeled as a "waste of resources" because there "had been no indications of a security threat in 50 years of investigation."[50]

Nick Pope worked for the Secretariat (Air Staff) Department 2a—"The UFO Desk"—from 1991 to 1994. In 1997, he wrote a book, *Open Skies, Closed Minds*, about the "irrefutable evidence" that persuaded him "extraterrestrial spacecraft really are routinely breaching the United Kingdom's air defenses and are a major threat to national security."[51]

Mr. Pope wasn't convinced while serving in MoD, nor is he today, that the British government is engaged in a cover-up. Rather, he believes British authorities are ignorant even though their files include significant information about UFO technologies.[52]

Pope explained that, while he was at the MoD working on the UFO Project, his immediate bosses were not impressed with the evidence. Their attitudes, he said, ranged "from complete skepticism to a more open-minded position." In fact, in 2009, when the MoD disbanded the office, Pope labeled that decision as "outrageous," because the UK government ceased taking "meaningful action" to probe the UAP issue.[53]

Now, decades later, Mr. Pope believes the UK must follow the American example of getting serious about UAPs. "The MoD needs to restart UAP investigations, a task force of some sort needs to be set up, and the defence committee needs to start holding the MoD to account on UAP," wrote Mr. Pope in an email to this author. He alleged "the MoD is falling back on a lazy, closed-minded 'it can't be so it isn't mindset,' which is exactly how asymmetric threats get missed."[54]

Mr. Pope did explain in an email:

While a couple of well-placed sources have suggested to me that investigations continue—perhaps outside of any formally constituted program—it may be that there's nothing going on aside from drafting boilerplate responses to people who raise the issue. The MoD may genuinely have no meaningful corporate memory here.[55]

He wrote further:

The one glimmer of hope is that a recent [2023] Five Eyes panel on UAP was held. While the MoD hasn't confirmed their attendance, falling back on the policy of not commenting on intelligence matters, it's likely that someone in the defence intelligence staff attended…so perhaps things are starting to happen, at least behind closed doors. It's long overdue, because the UK can make a significant contribution to the wider search for the truth about UAP, by leveraging its world class intelligence community imagery analysis resources and capabilities.[56]

Conclusion

A few national governments are seized with the UFO issue. Still, it appears that the US is in the lead among all nations regarding the subject, and if it is going to be properly addressed, it will require a concerted and sustained effort by Washington to get to the bottom of this age-old phenomenon.

SECTION FIVE

WHAT HAVE WE LEARNED AND WHAT SHOULD WE DO?

There are two types of UFOs—the ones we build
and the ones they build.[1]
—BENJAMIN R. RICH (1925–1995), American engineer
and director of Lockheed's Skunk Works

We have much to learn about UFOs/UAPs. The pregnant question for all of us at this point is: What do we do with what we have learned in the previous eleven chapters of *Out of This World?*

Chapter 12 summarizes what the previous 11 chapters of *Out of This World* informed us about UFOs/UAPs. That information can be contradictory and confusing; it may make the phenomenon more mystical and seemingly more complex with each new revelation. However, what are the key take-aways that ought to inform our future efforts?

Chapter 13 answers the question: What should the US government do in conjunction with the international community with the information it has regarding UFOs/UAPs? It certainly appears the phenomenon is real, and therefore we need an honest broker to sort out fact from fiction to help chart a way ahead. Certainly, educating the public is a necessary step, especially given decades of media-fed misinformation and a host of conspiracy theories littering the Internet. Of course, the government needs to rebuild confidence among the citizenry and can do so with meaningful engagements with the public, a big dose of transparency, and evidence of true scientific investigation.

Chapter 14 addresses what the public sector, in collaboration with the government, ought to do about the phenomenon. That cohort includes communities of interest most affected by whether UFOs/UAPs are proven to be evidence of ET beings, a "new" physics, and/or spiritual beings. Specifically, how should our media respond to the bevy of often-conflicting information? How should the religious community at large attempt to answer the tough metaphysical questions raised if we find that humankind is not alone in this vast universe? Also, we desperately need our scientific community to respond in a pragmatic, arguably "scientific, empirically based" manner to our current understanding of UFOs/UAPs, especially as more information is discovered. What should the academy teach or research? Finally, how will the business community adjust to the challenges presented by the various possible causes?

12

UFO TAKE-AWAYS AND IMPLICATIONS

I happen to be privileged enough to be in on the fact that we have been visited on this planet, and the UFO phenomenon is real.[1]

—EDGAR D. MITCHELL (1930–2016)
NASA astronaut, Lunar Module pilot of Apollo 14

his chapter summarizes what the previous eleven chapters of *Out of This World* informed us about the UFO/UAP phenomenon. That information can be contradictory and confusing; it may make the phenomenon appear more mystical and seemingly more complex with each new revelation. However, there are take-aways that have significant implications for humanity, which ought to inform our future efforts.

We begin by identifying the primary points from the previous chapters and then propose the implications and what they might mean for the future of humankind.

Key Outcomes Regarding the UFO Phenomenon

The previous chapters of this book demonstrate at least five key take-aways regarding the UFO phenomenon. They are:

1. **Paranormal is becoming normal.** That is not an oxymoron, because as we enjoy more technological advances today, it seems as if we understand less about our world;

the unexplained becomes the norm. Specifically, the inexplicable are now categorized into three hard-to-understand groups: unknown aspects of physics (natural causes), alleged alien beings from a growing number of earth-like exoplanets in this and other galaxies, or spirits from a dimension beyond mankind's senses.

Paranormal is almost the new normal.[2]

2. **Inexplicable sightings have occurred throughout human history, as evidenced in this book—especially in chapters 2 and 4.** Perhaps surprisingly, most of those incidents have common characteristics across time (ancient to modern) and have been seen at every corner of the Earth.

3. **Modern religion avoids the UFO phenomenon.** The world religions once took these issues more seriously than today, as evidenced in ancient scriptures and art. Too often, the task of addressing the religious aspects of the so-called inexplicable is left to marginalized groups—e.g., UFO religions and cults.

4. **The scientific community keeps its distance from the UFO matter.** Most scientists have kept their distance from UFO investigations, mostly due to the stigma. As a

result, we have no standardized universal mechanism for recording those sightings, much less an empirically sound methodology for studying them.

5. **Governments try to avoid the subject.** Governments tend to give the phenomenon tepid attention, if any, which results in public distrust. After all, most citizens believe members of the US government are hiding something or lying about what they know regarding UFOs. Also, the rest of world governments expect the US government to take the lead on the issue, even though until recently, Washington had no appetite for such an effort.

With these key take-aways in mind, let us consider some of their implications. The next two chapters will address what we ought to do.

Take-away 1: Paranormal Is Becoming Normal

The implication of this take-away is that we need to consider the likelihood of at least three possible causes for UFOs: alien beings, unknown physics (natural causes), and the unseen realm, the spirit world.

Have Aliens Visited Earth?

The possibility that aliens are the source of some UFOs is very much in play. Regardless, for that to be true, extraterrestrial beings must exist and have visited our planet.

A 2020 study in *The Astrophysical Journal* estimates (speculates) that there are a minimum of thirty-six communicating intelligent civilizations in the Milky Way galaxy, Earth's home galaxy, which is a huge collection of stars and solar systems. That figure assumes there are intelligent life-forms on other planets, based on what is called the Astrobiological Copernican Limit.[3]

Of course, the researchers at the University of Nottingham who wrote the study assume Earth is not special among all planets. Rather, it was not created by God, and humans evolved over billions of years.

They also assume other Earth-like planets that orbit sun-like stars evolved from inorganic (non-living) material just like humans. Those beings like us would presumably send out signals from their planet attempting to find other life-forms in this massive universe.[4]

Researcher Christopher Conselicem, one of the authors of the 2020 study, explained, "There should be at least a few dozen active civilizations in our galaxy under the assumption that it takes 5 billion years for intelligent life to form on other planets, as on earth."[5] Further, whether these civilizations can find and visit our Earth is another issue entirely. After all, scientists indicate those civilizations would be thousands of light years away, and to visit this planet would require technology far beyond our understanding.[6]

The above would have to be possible to believe alien civilizations exist and are advanced enough to visit Earth. Arguably, the assumptions supporting this theory are pretty stunning and require considerable "faith" to make alien visits possible.

Is There a "New" Physics That Might Explain UFOs?

The possibility that unknown physics are the source of some UFOs must be considered. What is the likelihood there are laws of physics we do not yet know?

Physicists have found a potential flaw in the Standard Model, our best theory that explains the workings of our universe. Just perhaps subatomic particles called "quarks" can be further divided, according to experiments run on the 16.7-mile-long, circular tunnel built under the French-Swiss border. That tunnel, known as the Large Hadron Collider, smashes proton particles together to help researchers better understand the limits of physics.[7]

The new behavior by quarks is that there may be yet-to-be discovered subatomic particles, the presumed flaw in the Standard Model.

"We were actually shaking when we first looked at the results, we were that excited," said Dr. Mitesh Patel with the Imperial College London. "Our hearts did beat a bit faster."[8]

Further, "We may be on the road to a new era of physics," said Professor Chris Parkes from the University of Manchester, "but if we are, then we are still relatively early on that road at this point. We have seen results of this significance come and go before, so we should be cautious as well as excited.[9]

And, according to Dr Konstantinos Petridis, from the University of Bristol in the United Kingdom, "The discovery of a new force in nature is the holy grail of particle physics. Our current understanding of the constituents of the Universe falls remarkably short—we do not know what 95% of the Universe is made of or why there is such a large imbalance between matter and anti-matter.[10]

Yes, there may be a "new physics," subatomic particles that act in a way we do not understand. Could this explain UFOs? Likely, it will be years before we come to understand the implications of this discovery.

Are Unseen Spirits Real and a Source of UFOs?

The unseen spirit world might be the source of some UFOs, which is documented by many religions and even suggested in the material addressed in chapter 3 of this book. However, for that to be true, there must be a real spiritual realm, and those entities or their effects must be active and observable through human senses.

I cannot prove to the reader using empirical data the existence of a spiritual realm that is beyond our five senses. The best I can offer is testimony from the Bible, which is arguably based on a series of anecdotes (albeit, I believe, God-inspired) that provide insights into the spiritual realm of actors, both angels and demons.

There are a variety of views regarding the spiritual world beyond our senses.

For example, demons are evil spirits, "members of God's heavenly host who have chosen to rebel against His will," as defined by the late Dr. Michael Heiser (1963–2023), an American Old Testament scholar and Christian author. Dr. Heiser wrote in his book, *Demons: What the Bible Really Says about the Powers of Darkness*, that demons have their origin with the Nephilim (Genesis 6:4), those born to the sons of God (fallen angels) and the daughters of men. He suggested that, once the Nephilim died, their spirits became demons who then engaged in spiritual warfare.[11]

Today, demons live in a spiritual realm despite their rebellion against God. Dr. Heiser wrote that some demons are "associated with the realm of the dead and its inhabitants," and others are identified with specific geographical locations alienated from God." Still others are "preternatural creatures associated with idolatry and unholy ground."[12]

The other entities in the spiritual realm are angels, described in the Bible as strong and powerful beings. There are 273 references to angels in the entire Bible. Their purpose (Hebrews 1:7, 14) is to serve as God's messengers to humans. We saw that task carried out when the angel Gabriel told Mary (Luke 1:26–38) she would become the mother of Jesus. In other situations, two angels came as humans in appearance to save Lot from the impending disaster in Sodom (Genesis 19).[13]

Unfortunately, this possible explanation for UFOs is running into bureaucratic resistance at the Pentagon. Specifically, according to UFO researcher Ron James, who directs media relations for MUFON, claims there is a "very large contingent of people" at the Pentagon who oppose the ongoing UFO/UAP research because UAPs are "regularly reported by US military sources" as piloted by "creatures from Hell." Further, according to Luis Elizondo, the former AATIP director at the Pentagon, it "was not just a little voice in the Pentagon…but a huge group of people thought the phenomenon that was being witnessed was demons."[14]

I want to comment on why the official "Pentagon" is pushing back on the possible "spiritual" cause of UFOs. Many military members like the US Navy pilots who might report on unidentified objects come from mostly conservative, albeit religious, backgrounds that embrace a spiritual dimension to life. It is therefore logical for them to surmise that spirits, especially of the evil/demonic variety, are behind some UFOs. However, generally speaking and based on my multiple decades of experience at the Pentagon, many top officials (flag officers and political appointees) and public-relations professionals eschew anything that might be construed as religious. Therefore, they quickly dismiss any attempt to conclude there is a metaphysical cause to some UFO sightings.

The Pentagon's counterpart in the United Kingdom, the British Ministry of Defence (MoD), allegedly in the past, at some level, held the view that demons were the source of UFOs as well. Nick Pope, who, as noted earlier in this book, ran the UFO desk at the British MoD, said some officials at the ministry "felt the UFO phenomenon was real, but demonic in nature." He explained this view was based on the book of Ephesians, which describes Satan as "the prince of the power of the air [Ephesians 2:2, KJV]." Mr. Pope said a proponent of this view was Reverend Paul Inglesby, who circulated a pamphlet claiming key personnel within the MoD shared the same thinking, such as Admiral of the Fleet the Lord Peter John Hill-Norton, a retired five-star officer who had served as chief of the defense staff and chair of NATO's military committee.[15]

In August of 2023, I elaborated on the possibility that UFOs might be evidence of the spiritual, unseen realm in an article, "The Bible's Explainer on UFOs," which was published by Fox News. In that piece, I wrote, "Most religions address this spiritual reality," that is, history is rich with "evidence of spiritual engagements." I cited the example in 2 Kings 2:11, where we read about Elijah going up into heaven like a whirlwind aboard a chariot pulled by horses of fire. Was that a UFO? Then I asked, "Are the many references to angels [and demons] in the Bible old wives' tales?"[16]

I continued:

Years ago, evangelist Billy Graham wrote a book, *Angels: God's Secret Agents*, in which he chronicled many first-hand accounts of angels interacting with humans. A search of Amazon's website finds many books testifying to the reality of angelic beings.[17]

Certainly, people of many faiths understand God's nemesis, Satan, is very real and his army of demons are not to be dismissed. Jesus dealt with demons who understood His identity and obeyed His command. He cast the demons—"My name is Legion; for we are many"—into a herd of swine [pigs] that subsequently rushed over a steep bank into the Sea of Galilee (Mark 5:1–13, NKJV).[18]

Today, Satan's demonic army is very active. They manifest themselves through various practices such as divination, witchcraft, channeling, and wizardry (Deuteronomy 18:10–12). They deceive, attack the human mind with the intent of control, and they leverage power to take captive people, especially the prominent.[19]

Some readers will dismiss the possibility of spiritual beings—angels and demons—struggling for control. However, many of us accept that there is much we do not understand.[20]

Whether aliens are probing Earth or are already among us is yet to be officially confirmed. What is not in doubt for many of us is the spiritual battle between the forces of God and Satan, which is intensifying.[21]

Take-away 2: Inexplicable Sightings Have Occurred throughout History

It is fascinating when one compares ancient UFO sightings with those from the modern era. There are numerous conclusions about the enduring nature of UFO incidents. For example, perhaps the same natural phenomena that created the ancient UFOs are present today. Just maybe the lack of understanding about "new physics" has long played the devil with humankind's comprehension of nature, or the same spiritual activities in the unseen realm recorded thousands of years ago continue to manipulate our skies. Finally, it could be that alien beings have been visiting Earth for thousands of years. The big difference today versus in the past is a growing concern that modern UFOs may have a maligned interest.

Chapter 2 of this book profiled ancient UFO sightings. In that chapter, recall how Dr. Strothers applied a modern UFO template for ancient incidents. He found ancient UFO sightings were described as:

...disks or other extended objects, including vertical cylinders enveloped in "clouds" and associated with smaller disks. Depending on the viewing angles (perspective), their intrinsic shapes might be similar or even identical: a disk seen face-on looks circular, although edge-on it looks elliptical or oblong. Colors in the daytime are usually described as silvery or gray, and in the night as resembling red or multicolored lights. Estimated dimensions range from about one meter to hundreds of meters, with the scatter being probably intrinsic. UFOs are usually said to be noiseless. They are seen in the air or on the ground, hovering or stationary, or moving across the sky in a continuous fashion, even if erratically. Sometimes they suddenly appear or vanish.[22]

In chapter 4, I profiled modern UFOs. For example, I cited a study that used the "treemaps" method to capture the most frequently used words in UFO descriptions: terms describing speed ("fast," "rapid," "steady"); those depicting movement ("erratic," "strange," "rapid"; those noting shape ("cigar," "triangular," "oval," "disk," "saucer"); and words relating to color/light ("bright," "white," "orange").

Certainly, the ancient descriptions compare favorably with modern, "treemaps"-profiled sightings. Sometimes the language translation of the sightings is not exact, but they are similar enough to conclude that what ancient humans saw is very similar to what modern people are viewing. The bottom line: Our ancient forefathers did not understand some of the UFOs then, and we still do not understand a subset today.

The implication of this take-away is that, although ancient UFOs tended to be rather benign and their descriptions are quite similar to those of today, some modern UFOs appear to be more threatening. That should be a concern for all of us.

Back in April 2004, the US Navy video recorded UFOs buzzing the sky near F-18 fighter jets and under the water near our warships. US Representative Sean Patrick Maloney (D-NY) said of those incidents:

> We take the issue of unexplained aerial phenomena seriously to the extent that we're dealing with the safety and security of US military personnel or the national security interests of the United States, so we want to know what we're dealing with.[23]

Luis Elizondo, the former director of AATIP, said UAPs disrupt not just military training exercises. Specifically, he said, "In this country we've had incidents where these UAPs have interfered and brought offline our nuclear capabilities." Then he added, "We also have data suggesting that in other countries these things have interfered with their nuclear technology and actually turned them on, put them online."[24]

"We are quite convinced that we're dealing with a technology that is multigenerational, several generations ahead of what we consider next generation technology, so what we would consider beyond next generation technology," Elizondo told the *Washington Post*. "Something that could be anywhere between 50 to 1,000 years ahead of us."[25]

Take-away 3: Modern Religion Avoids the UFO Phenomenon

The historical record suggests ancient religions admitted there were forces, phenomena beyond their comprehension that, for the most part, they attributed to gods and/or spirits. However, in today's high-technology society, humanity tends to either ignore the inexplicable or allow marginalized religious groups, cults, and bizarre paranormal interest factions to provide explanations of the "unexplainable." It is especially noteworthy that there is little interest by mainline religions to wrestle with the theological difficulties/issues UFOs introduce for humankind and their faiths.

The theological implications of alien beings will impact every religious group in terms of doctrine, understanding their sacred text, and much more. Arguably, some religions reject the view that there is intelligent life in outer space, an idea seeded in the culture by self-identified agnostic and evolutionist Dr. Carl Sagan (1934–1996), an American astronomer, planetary scientist, cosmologist, astrophysicist, and author of the 1977 book *The Dragons of Eden: Speculations on the Evolution of Human Intelligence*. Yet Sagan's view that there is intelligent life beyond Earth is also based on an evolutionary perspective, as outlined in the explanation of the implications of the first take-away (above).[26]

Accepting the theory of evolution, which I do not, then one can argue that intelligent life must exist elsewhere other than on Earth, given the size of the universe and the millions of possible similar, Earth-like planets that might have conditions similar to the ones found on this planet. Therefore, one can further postulate about the possibilities of that life, which for our various religious traditions raises some interesting questions.

The Christian theologian, as an example, would argue that intelligent life elsewhere would necessarily be affected by the Fall of Adam, like humankind was on Earth, based on our understanding of the Bible. Therefore, those alien beings would, like humanity, be doomed to die because of their sin. In the future, their planet, like Earth, according to the Bible, will be destroyed by fire in God's final judgment. However, for the alien, that being cannot have Jesus' salvation, because the blessing is given exclusively to the people on Earth, according to John14:6 (NIV), which states: "Jesus answered, 'I am the way and the truth and the life. No one comes to the Father except through me.'"

Take-away 4: The Scientific Community Keeps Its Distance from the Matter

The scientific approach must be applied to complex issues, such as ascertaining whether aliens are the cause of UFOs. However, as seen earlier in this book, the scientific community tends to avoid UFO-related studies because of the stigma.

We need consistency of research, standardization of the collection of UFO sightings, and a sound methodology for investigating the phenomenon.

Avi Loeb, the former chair of the astronomy department at Harvard University, argues in the *Scientific American*, "Irrespective of whether the origin of UFOs is terrestrial or extraterrestrial, we will learn something new and exciting from studying them scientifically." Loeb's article, "What We Can Learn from Studying UFOs," continues:

And it is not just the hardware that will interest us. It is the meaning behind its existence—the intent of those who manufactured it. A single UFO of extraterrestrial origin will inspire fear among humans that the aliens could be malevolent, as Stephen Hawking believed—but they could be benevolent as well.[27]

Dr. Loeb points out that our technology evolves exponentially, such as global Wi-Fi connectivity, artificial intelligence, robotics, and genetic engineering. He writes:

It is conceivable that technological civilizations that emerged around them had more time to develop their science and technology than we did, and created equipment that represents our future and would appear magical to use now.[28]

"A fresh scientific study that offers reproducible evidence for UFO sightings and resolves their nature would demonstrate the power of science in answering a question that is clearly of great interest to the public," Loeb says. He continues:

> Finding a conclusive answer based on open data will enhance the public's confidence in evidence-based knowledge. Currently, the UFO mystery surrounding the expected inconclusive interpretation of the Pentagon report will fuel unsubstantiated speculations. A decisive scientific experiment holds the promise of clearing up the fog.[29]

Take-away 5: Governments Try to Avoid the Subject

Arguably, the world needs governments to play a significant role identifying the causes of the UFOs, then they should lead the efforts necessary to protect us if there is a security threat.

Most Americans and perhaps citizens in other countries doubt their government is being truthful about the causes of UFOs and whether it has compelling information about them. There must be transparency on the issue or those doubts will persist.

Unfortunately, government lucidity on the issue is suspect. Specifically, a 2023 poll of US voters found that 57 percent of respondents believe our government has more information about UFOs and alien life than "it has publicly revealed." Similarly, members of Congress call for more government openness on the issue.[30]

At a July 2023 congressional hearing, lawmakers and witnesses accused the federal government of failing to provide key UFO-related information to the public. For example, US Representative Tim Burchett (R-TN) said, "I just want transparency. I just want the truth," about the UFO phenomenon from the witnesses. Of course, at that hearing he got an earful, such as claims the Pentagon is allegedly hiding from the public alien spacecraft and alien "biologics."[31]

US Representative Robert Garcia (D-CA), released the following statement: "The American people deserve transparency about UAP's, and Congress should work in a bipartisan way to understand any potential national security implications."[32]

In 2023, in an effort to promote openness, Senate Majority Leader Chuck Schumer (D-NY) tapped into the widespread angst about UFOs to propose sweeping provisions in the law regarding transparency. Specifically, he proposed legislation that would codify such UFO-related terms as "non-human intelligence," a "legacy [UFO retrieval and reverse engineering] program," and "technologies of unknown origin" into federal law. Further, the proposed legislation would require government contractors that might possess recovered UFO materiel or "biological evidence of non-human intelligence" to turn over all such items to the government.[33]

Most of the world governments expect the United States to lead the effort to find the cause(s) of UFOs and to begin to mitigate any threats. They will participate in that effort, but the US government must lead.

Conclusion

This chapter identified five key points from our study of the UFO phenomenon and then considered their implications. Chapter 13 addresses what the US government ought to do given the information in this chapter, and chapter 14 is a call for action by the media; academia; and the scientific, religious, and commercial communities regarding these implications.

13

GOVERNMENT'S STRATEGY
FOR "PROJECT UFO"

UAPs, whatever they may be, may pose a serious threat to
our military or civilian aircraft. And that must be understood.[1]
—US Representative Robert Garcia (D-CA)
House Oversight subcommittee hearing on UFOs, July 26, 2023

t is crucial that the US government determine whether the growing number of UFOs/UAPs (terms used interchangeably below) pose a threat to national security. Further, the fact that these "craft" defy our current understanding of aerial flight is sufficient justification to make this a priority, if for no other reason than to lift the veil of secrecy that has historically undermined public trust in government and fueled conspiracy theories since the 1947 Roswell UFO incident, which exploded in the press and stirred fear across the world.

This chapter will propose a future role for the US government—a strategy—to address the matter. Based on the five take-aways outlined in chapter 12 and their derived implications, I will propose the skeleton of a national strategy going forward.

We need a plan that is a whole-of-government approach to tackle this complex issue, because historically the US government has treated it as a nuisance and has mostly dealt with it as a public-relations task to calm the nervous population by pretending there is nothing to be concerned about because these incidents are allegedly harmless. However, given the emergent and growing number of threatening and unexplained sightings, we no longer have the luxury of continuing our previous hapless approach.

The best whole-of-government tactic to address the subject is to draft a "UFO Strategy," a document promulgated by the White House—perhaps as part of the National Security Strategy or as a stand-alone document—that directs specific actions, fixes responsibilities, and has the necessary funding, much like our successful 1969 mission to put a man on the moon.

Man on Moon Project as Precedent

President John F. Kennedy traveled to Rice University on September 12, 1962, to address the nation's space effort. "We choose to go to the moon," President Kennedy said in his speech at Rice University's stadium in Houston, Texas. He said our mission was to land a man on the moon before 1970 and bring him safely back to Earth.[2]

The president's speech was intended to invoke America's tradition of the pioneer spirit and to encourage the nation to action, given the accelerating competition—and perhaps growing fear among Americans—we faced from the nuclear-armed and threatening Soviet Union. Before that speech, Kennedy, who became president in January 1961, properly perceived that the US was losing the space race to the Soviets, who had successfully launched the first artificial satellite, Sputnik 1, four years earlier. Our collective concern about the space race gained momentum on April 12, 1961, when Russian cosmonaut Yuri Gagarin became the first human in space. Meanwhile, on other fronts, American prestige was further damaged by the Bay of Pigs episode in Cuba, a failed attack orchestrated by our Central Intelligence Agency to push Cuban leader Fidel Castro from power, an effort coming just five days after the Soviet's manned launch and weeks before President Kennedy's speech at Rice University.

Prior to announcing the moon mission, President Kennedy turned to Vice President Lyndon B. Johnson to recommend how the United States could gain the upper hand in the space race. At the time, Mr.

Johnson was the chairman of the National Aeronautics and Space Council. After consulting with NASA officials and others associated with the council, Johnson told the president that our best option was to land a man on the moon. President Kennedy ran with that recommendation.

Weeks after his speech at Rice University, President Kennedy addressed Congress on May 25, 1961, to officially propose that the United States "should commit itself to achieving the goal, before this decade is out, of landing a man on the moon and returning him safely to the earth."[3]

The president's fresh vision for NASA's new Apollo Program, also known as "Project Apollo," was clear. That effort required a whole-of-government achievement with multiple federal agencies assigned specific roles, it required government-wide discipline, and, yes, more federal funding.

Project Apollo became a memorial to President Kennedy, which was fulfilled in July 1969 with the successful Apollo 11 moon landing. That accomplishment within the promised decade propelled the US into the front position in the global space race and arguably helped America acquire a technological edge over Russia that ultimately contributed to the demise of the Soviet Union by 1991.

Today, we need another project like the Apollo Program, a whole-of-government effort to address yet another daunting challenge, the mysterious and threatening UFO issue. "Project UFO" requires presidential leadership and a clear strategy that begins with our understanding of the problem, a clear mission, and a plan that charts the pathway to find answers regarding perhaps the most pressing problem humankind faces.

A Strategy for "Project UFO"

We begin this strategy-building effort by nesting the "take-aways" identified in chapter 12. Those represent the most daunting questions and issues related to the current UFO matter based on the survey of related topics in the first eleven chapters of this book. Then I identify a few implications that align with each take-away to provide direction—required action—for our "Project UFO."

Now, in a series of sections below, I will build the skeleton of a strategy for the US government that addresses the proposed Project UFO, which includes a mission statement, outlines a structure, and proposes a measurable approach supported by numerous federal efforts.

Having said that, permit me a brief caveat at this point. I am trained in writing strategies for the US military and have decades of experience. I have written military regulations, service-wide guidance documents, and strategies for complex campaigns, as well as worked with multiple federal government agencies to help produce plans that can be executed using our giant bureaucracies. Writing such documents is part science and part art. I fully expect this effort regarding UFOs to morph as the issue evolves and people smarter than I get involved. However, at this juncture, for this effort to be successful like the Project Apollo, I believe we must begin with the political will of our chief executive, the US president, be assured of the full support of the all-federal agencies, and enjoy the necessary funding. Until now all have been lacking.

Photo by NASA / We need a "Project UFO" that is a whole-of-government effort much like the 1960s Project Apollo that put a man on the moon.[4]

Project UFO's Mission

The project's mission is defined by the problem we face and the associated implications. Chapter 12 identified the five key take-aways that provide the elements of the problem from which our mission is built.

The elements of the problem are as follows.

Identify the cause(s) of UFOs. We do not know the cause(s) of a significant number (around 5 percent) of all UFOs. Are the causes natural (unknown physics), alien in origin, or manifestations of spirits from another dimension?

UFOs are an enduring problem. A portion of all UFOs share similar profiles across history. That leads us to conclude that perhaps the same causes for contemporary UFOs were evident in ancient times as well.

Past efforts to identify the causes of UFOs were underwhelming and inconclusive. Governments and most institutions tend to ignore the UFO phenomenon because of the social stigma. Therefore, much of the effort to understand this issue has been relegated to marginalized efforts lacking in scientific rigor and conducted by mostly underfunded entities.

Most scientists avoid UFO research. The scientific community often tries to avoid the UFO phenomenon, labeling any investigation as pseudoscientific, not legitimate. This has resulted in no standardized ways of recording UFO incidents and less than empirically sound methodologies for applying scientific rigor to investigations. No wonder, after decades of festering concern about the issue, we know next to nothing about the matter. Although the US government—and, in particular, the Pentagon's AARO—promises action, we will likely have to wait for years to see any meaningful results if any are ever proffered.

The government's lack of interest promotes public mistrust about the issue. The government's proclivity regarding UFOs has been to avoid the subject except to reassure the public there is no threat. Recent information seriously undermines the public's trust in the government's truthfulness.

Given these five elements of the problem, we need to define the mission for Project UFO. Simply put, much like President Kennedy's mission for Project Apollo to "land a man on the moon before 1970 and bring him safely back to earth," we need a simple mission statement for Project UFO. I recommend the following:

The United States will identify the cause(s) of the currently inexplicable UFO sightings and determine how to mitigate any threat they may pose to our national security.

A Strategy for Project UFO

Much like President Kennedy tapped the whole-of-government and national funding to accomplish his moon landing mission, Project UFO's mission requires a strategy with definable tasks and responsibilities to lead our government's effort.

That structure will be along three lines of effort (LOE), a military term that links multiple tasks using the logic of purpose (mission) to focus activity toward establishing desired outcomes.[5]

Those three LOEs are:

1. Identify the cause(s) of UFOs by using scientific investigations of at least three possible explanations: "new" physics, alien beings, and/or spiritual entities.
2. Institutionalize the federal government's approach to paranormal events and provide a mechanism to mitigate any security threat they might pose.
3. Make Project UFO mainstream by recruiting key public institutions—academia, the media, and the scientific and religious sectors—to recognize the threat and do their part at mitigation.

We operationalize these three LOEs by identifying measurable tasks that rely on the "implications" from chapter 12, and pinpoint specific metrics along the path to the final goal as outlined in our mission to "identify the causes and determine how to mitigate any threats."

I will now propose for each LOE some supporting outcomes, including specific assignments for the various federal agencies.

LOE 1: Identify UFO Causes

Outcome: Standardize and catalog the collection of UFO sightings, as well as launch comprehensive scientific efforts to identify the causes of UFOs by 2030.

The tasks along the path to this outcome include:

- Publish a standardized and scientifically useful UFO/UAP sighting collection program. The Director of National Intelligence, which already submits an annual report to Congress on UFOs/UAPs, is the appropriate agency to oversee this issue. Of course, the AARO would provide support.
- Direct NASA to be the principal agency to scientifically investigate the cause(s) of UFOs/UAPs and publish the results. The causes investigated as a minimum will include alien beings or their technological proxies (robotic entities); unknown physics; and the unseen realm, the spiritual world.
- Work collaboratively with foreign allies and partners regarding these investigations and share UFO sighting data.
- Promote standardization of UFO/UAP-related efforts— i.e., collection of data and methods of investigation—across international agencies and organizations like the United Nations, and especially with trusted foreign partners.

LOE 2: Institutionalize Federal UFO-related Authorities

Outcome: By 2030, create a permanent part of the US government to oversee all UFO-related efforts that is vested with the necessary authority and annually funded based on the perceived threat.

The tasks along the path to this outcome include:

- Create permanent responsible offices within key federal agencies to address the UFO/UAP "cause" issue.
- Each permanent office will include an outreach program and scientific collaboration branch that seeks to keep the public informed with the objective of removing the stigma associated with UFOs and rebuild trust in the government's policies and shared information about UFOs.
- Require each permanent office to plan for and man its UFO efforts with the necessary means to address UFO-related maligned activities.
- The Department of Defense will lead the US government's defense preparations by equipping a force to quickly respond to emergent UFO threats, if the use of force is possible and potentially effective. The Department of Homeland Security will provide a supporting role to the Department of Defense.

LOE 3: Recruit Public Institutions to the Response

Outcome: By 2030, all major US public institutions will actively collaborate with the US government to provide standardized UFO sightings, promote fact-based information about UFOs, and participate as appropriate in mitigating any UFO-based maligned activities.

The tasks along the path to this outcome include:

- The appropriate federal offices will promote collaboration with public institutions regarding the UFO issue. As a minimum, that collaboration will include the following institutions: media, academia, relevant commercial companies, and religious groups (for the sharing of information only).
- The appropriate federal offices will provide fact-based information about UFOs on at least an annual basis to the public.

- The appropriate federal offices will coordinate with the public entities regarding their legitimate role(s), if any, in helping to mitigate all UFO-based maligned activities.

Other Considerations and Guidance for Project UFO

Project UFO requires congressional oversight and funding. Lacking oversight, the federal agencies, no matter how prescriptive our strategy, might quickly abandon the mission, given the bureaucracies' other priorities. In fact, it may be necessary not only to hold the federal agencies responsible for frequent reports regarding the project's performance, but also to hold their budgets hostage to compliance with the strategy. Further, as necessary, legal mandates/statutes ought to be put in place to guide that effort, such as the intelligence oversight of the committees' current functions.

There is a particularly difficult issue for the US government if, in fact, LOE 1 finds through its investigations that UFOs are either in part or in whole evidence of spiritual beings, especially if they are "demonic" and carry out Satan's malevolent actions against humankind, which is what some people of faith sincerely believe. At that point, the government must admit it is powerless to exercise the levers of state against such spiritual beings. Rather, it must turn to humans who are spiritually discerning and ask them for assistance. Further, Congress may have to consider amending the Constitution to permit the government's involvement in what is considered a "religious" issue.

There are other points of consideration by those creating Project UFO. I have borrowed liberally from Nick Pope, the former British UFO expert at the Ministry of Defence (MoD), to raise four questions for government going forward.

How Should We Evaluate any UFO Threat?

When a country's defense establishment considers the UFO issue, it looks at the problem rather differently than might the public. Specifically, defense experts consider UFO incidents in terms of threats and opportunities. In fact, according to Nick Pope, there is within the intelligence world an equation that defines threat. "Threat is expressed as capability x [times] intent…when it comes to UFOs, we have some good data on capability," wrote Pope, which "suggests an impressive capability, with very high speeds, rapid acceleration and extreme maneuvers being frequently seen. In the context of our equation, this gives us a high value for capability."[6]

The "intent" part of the equation is quite different. Specifically, there is a "lack of definitive data in a situation where there [are] multiple, competing theories about the nature of the UFO phenomenon." Pope continued, saying:

> If we were dealing with technology from Russia or China, intelligence officers specializing in these countries could simply assess intent, drawing on their existing knowledge. But if we're dealing with something unknown—possibly even extraterrestrial—we can't even begin to make any assessment of intent. Thus, going back to our equation, no accurate value for intent can be given.[7]

"Not only can we not assess the extent of any threat," wrote Pope, "We can't say if one exists at all." For the government, the mindset on such issues tends to be "binary: either a threat exists or it doesn't." However, there is a default from a military perspective. It is, wrote Pope, "better to assume a threat exists and to be relieved when one doesn't materialize, as opposed to assuming there isn't a threat, and thus being unprepared if one suddenly emerges."[8]

Project UFO must embrace the view that these highly capable "craft" pose a significant threat and act accordingly.

What Is the Basis for Funding Project UFO?

"In government, an excellent way to get a program funded is to highlight an actual or potential threat, and then put forward your program as being the way to mitigate or eliminate that threat," wrote Pope. That is true, yet, "in relation to UFOs, the issue of threat is always going to be front and center. Indeed, it's almost an inevitable outcome, which highlights an interesting point about where one places a UFO program."[9]

Past US government UFO programs like Project Blue Book received minimal funding and then were scrubbed because interest waned or bad science concluded the effort was unproductive. This must not happen going forward, which is why, until proven otherwise as unnecessary after significant scientific investigation, the program must become a permanent fixture of government, free of bureaucratic manipulation and dismissal. Having said that, there must also be a mechanism in place to review whether the effort continues to be necessary.

Who Should Lead Project UFO?

What federal agency is the most appropriate to oversee Project UFO? "Most nations that have run UFO programs have embedded them in the military (usually the air force), or in the department [ministry] of defense," wrote Pope. However, "one exception to this rule is France, where their UFO program is embedded in the French National Space Agency. The other exception [at the time was] the Pentagon's AATIP... project which, while originally commissioned by the Defense Intelligence Agency, was largely conducted in the private sector [by Bigelow Aerospace, which reported to AATIP]." Therefore, Pope argues, "where you embed a UFO program has a discernable effect on not just mindset and methodology, but arguably on outcomes too."[10]

The UFO issue is as much about science as defense. Arguably, the Department of Defense has not shepherded this issue well since World War II. Therefore, although the Pentagon needs to be involved, the effort should be led by either NASA or another to-be-determined agency, like the Department of Energy, that can best balance the demands of the strategy's three LOEs.

What Should Be the Project's Classification?

The classification shrouding Project UFO will impact the public's perception of transparency, an age-old issue. However, as Nick Pope indicated, there is a concern regarding "the most sensitive part of UFO work," which "is related to technology acquisition." Specifically, as Pope noted by referencing a declassified British report, that document stated, "We could use this [UFO] technology, if it exists."[11]

The technological capabilities observed in UFO sightings, wrote Pope, are "likely to be significantly ahead of anything we have, simply because viable interstellar travel is suggestive of a technology, orders of magnitude beyond our current level. The nation on earth that first acquires that technology will likely be the dominant force on this planet for the foreseeable future: militarily, politically, and economically."[12]

This national level interest in UFO technology, wrote Pope, is therefore "the real reason for UFO secrecy. The US Government was thinking along exactly the same lines."[13]

Therefore, Project UFO's leadership must be honest with the public. Parts of the program may need to be kept classified for national security reasons. Given the US government's history on the issue, that statement will sound hollow, but it is a necessary part of the overall effort.

Conclusion

The United States must create Project UFO, backed by a suitable strategy with fixed responsibilities if we are going to become serious about this possible threat.

Project Apollo provided an outstanding template for how to move the entire federal government and the American people toward a significant and worthwhile goal—putting a man on the moon and safely returning him to Earth. We should do much the same for Project UFO or, as the mounting evidence suggests, we could come to reject not taking the issue as serious as it appears to be and potentially suffer grave consequences should the cause(s) of these inexplicable incidents be a force with a truly maligned intent.

HOW THE PUBLIC MIGHT RESPOND TO UFO CAUSES

Perhaps we need some outside, universal threat to make us recognize this common bond. I occasionally think how quickly our differences worldwide would vanish if we were facing an alien threat from outside this world.[1]

—President Ronald Reagan (1911–2004),
fortieth president of the United States

The public sector will respond in quite different ways regarding the determination of the actual cause(s) of unidentified flying objects than will the US government. Most importantly, though, the government will need to partner with key private institutions as it seeks to advance its findings about UFOs if it ever hopes to restore the public's confidence on this issue.

Not all alleged causes will earn the same response from private institutions, however. For example, if it is determined that "new" physics is the cause of UFOs, then the government and private sectors will collaborate to teach, inform, and adjust commercial technologies to adapt to those new realities. If UFOs are found to be the product of spiritual entities, there likely will be little for government to do, but across the private sector there will probably be a religious revival or at least worldwide curiosity about the spiritual realm spun in the press and academia. If aliens are found to be the cause of some UFOs, then government and the private sector are likely to work together on a multi-varied scientific and defense-related response, some of which is identified in the previous chapter. Finally, if all three causes and/or perhaps others are found to contribute to the UFO phenomenon—aliens, "new" physics, spiritual entities, et cetera—then humanity's response could be incredibly complex and daunting, by far the most challenging problem humanity has ever faced.

Government must partner with key private institutions to restore public confidence regarding UFOs.[2]

What follows is the enumeration of some of the implications associated with each of the three most likely possible causes across five key public sectors—media, education, religion, science and commerce—and suggestions as to how each might respond. A government-public sector franchise is necessary if citizens are ever to regain confidence in the government regarding the UFO issue and mitigate any potential emergent threats.

Media's Response to UFO Cause(s)

I fully anticipate that if, in fact, aliens are determined to be the cause of some UFOs in the future, there will be yet another rush to publish by the media, and, as a result inevitable distortions will once again fuel fear and perhaps hysteria. Of course, this time around, we have more alternative news outlets than we did in the late 1940s during the Roswell and Rainer incidents. And, of course, today we have the almost instantaneous global communication network provided by the Internet to spread both truth and lies at the speed of light to a greater cross section of humanity than ever before.

We previously saw how the public media responded to the possibility that aliens were invading Earth. Beginning in 1947, thanks to the incidents in Roswell and Mount Rainer, journalists consistently failed to sort out the complex mélange of technological, social, and political circumstances that became the UFO story. They distorted their reports because of a variety of factors: the explosive growth in civilian and military aviation, the tensions brought about by the Cold War, a popular thirst for science fiction, and a broad fascination with the paranormal. At the time, there were also radical changes in technology as well as the evolution of journalism institutions and practices.

Simply, journalists at the time failed to sort out these issues to report the facts without distortion. Factors related to the UFO phenomenon such as science, national security, and culture were confused by many reporters who were giving superficial, redundant, silly at times, irrelevant, and too often not properly sourced accountings.

This failed coverage created quite a stir across the world with its spread of half-truths (misinformation) that quickly got out of hand. After all, the whole "flying saucer" label was picked up and recklessly parroted by reporters who helped proliferate distortions across the world; the result was fear and almost hysteria among many people. However, as expected, those stories sold newspapers, the primary motivation for the rush to publish at the time.

Alternatively, what if spirits are determined to be the cause of UFOs? The result could be just as distorted as the reporting about invading aliens in the late 1940s. Why? The fact is many journalists, according to polling,[3] tend to be left of center politically, and, according to the Journalism Institute, "the field of journalism is notoriously secular and largely averse to including religious angles and storylines."[4] Yet, writing about the "spirit" world must address the paranormal, which includes religion, an issue that is completely out of the comfort zone for many journalists.

Finally, the best UFO "cause" for the public media to address is evidence of "new" physics. Reporters will explain our old understanding of the universe and the laws of nature dating back to Sir Isaac Newton (1642–1726), an English mathematician, physicist, and theologian who formulated the laws of motion and universal gravitation. Then, based on interviews with scientists, journalists will explain the new laws (physics) and their implications for everyday life.

The caution we get from these three possible explanations of the cause(s) of UFOs is that we must be discriminating about what is accepted as fact. We should question the source and should not rely upon any single news outlet or risk falling into the trap that captured the attention of Americans in the late 1940s who were tormented by the conflicting and often notoriously poor reporting.

Religious Communities' Response to UFO Cause(s)

Religious beliefs and traditions vary across the world. There are a variety of possible responses from this global community to the confirmed cause(s) of UFOs; perhaps polytheistic religions will differ on the issue compared to monotheistic faiths like Christianity.

The easiest cause of UFOs for the religious communities to address at large is to consider the discovery that "new" physics creates the UFO phenomenon. After all, religion has little to say about the laws of nature (physics) other than that God—or some unknown deity worshiped by pagan religions—established many principles, such as Newton's law of gravitation, his three laws of motion, the ideal gas laws, and Mendel's law ("a principle in genetics: hereditary units occur in pairs that separate during gamete formation so that every gamete receives but one member of a pairs").[5]

230

On another front, most religious communities will embrace news that spirits are the cause of UFOs. That potential reality fits well with many sacred scriptures and their understanding of the world, as explained in chapter 3 of this book. In fact, this news will likely spark a new religious renaissance of sorts, a period of global awakening as humankind seeks understanding of the unseen, spiritual realm.

The spiritual cause has plenty of support, even among those in the nonreligious world. French astronomer Jacques F. Vallée, the co-developer of the first computerized map of the planet Mars for NASA, an Internet pioneer, and ufologist, believes UFOs are not physical objects. He wrote:

> If UFOs are, indeed, somebody else's "nuts and bolts hardware," then we must still explain how such tangible hardware can change shape before our eyes, vanish in a Cheshire cat manner (not even leaving a grin), seemingly melt away in front of us, or apparently "materialize" mysteriously before us without apparent detection by persons nearby or in neighboring towns. We must wonder too, where UFOs are "hiding" when not manifesting themselves to human eyes.[6]

A special challenge here is separating the spirits, however. After all, the occult is quite active, and possibly demonic spirits, not God's angels, are the forces behind UFOs, according to some experts.

In the 1960s, the US government asked Lynn Catoe, a librarian at the US Library of Congress, to research the UFO phenomenon. In 1969, Ms. Catoe summarized her work based on eyewitness testimonies. Her report states:

> Many of the UFO reports now being published in the popular press recount alleged incidents that are strikingly similar to demonic possession and psychic phenomena which have long been known to theologians and parapsychologists. Therefore,

references to these subjects have been included as well as references to occult works which have similarities to the general tone and content of the UFO literature.[7]

Dr. Pierre Guerin, an astronomer and senior researcher at the French National Council for Scientific Research, shares Ms. Catoe's view. He wrote, "UFO behavior is more akin to magic than physics as we know it…the modern UFOnauts and the demons of past days are probably identical."[8]

Former high-ranking military leaders shared this view as well. In 1955, British Royal Air Force Marshall Lord Hugh Caswall Tremenheere Dowding discussed a UFO investigation in which he said UFOs were "paraphysical in nature," meaning "spiritual in substance." Then he said the UFOs were "immortal in nature" and "would manifest themselves in various forms, including human forms." Further, the Air Force Marshall indicated the UFOs "could render themselves invisible to the human eye" because "they have the ability to materialize and dematerialize as will."[9]

Perhaps the most difficult finding for the world's religious communities will be the determination that alien beings are the cause of UFOs. That will challenge these groups who in some instances are focused exclusively on a universe with the Earth as the center and their views of life. Discovering there are other beings that do not necessarily share our views, our physiology, and certainly not our histories will present many difficulties, such as regarding ontological views: relationship with an infinite God, the path to a post-mortal existence, purpose of life on Earth, and many other taxing questions religion seeks to answer.

I address the Christian view of the possibility of alien beings in the next section, including what this cause might mean for end-times prophecy.

The Scientific Community's Response to UFO Cause(s)

The scientific community will demonstrate radically different levels of enthusiasm based on the identification of the cause of UFOs.

Scientists will be beside themselves with glee if a "new" physics is determined to be the cause. This revelation will be quickly followed by all sorts of new research projects—a boon for serious laboratories, their scientific staffs, and most government contractors.

There will also be a burst of interest if spirits are identified as the cause. However, this scenario will be the most challenging for the scientists, because the application of the scientific method might not work when addressing the spirit world—which, frankly, is rejected by many scientists. After all, a large majority of all scientists (87 percent) "say that humans and other living things have evolved over time and that evolution is the result of natural processes such as natural selection," according to a 2009 Pew Research Center survey of 2,500 scientists. Therefore, many, if not most, scientists tend to dismiss things beyond our five senses that exist in the spiritual realm to blindly embrace the view that life can materialize from an inanimate, nonliving combination of substances.[10]

Of course, the idea of alien beings visiting Earth fits many scientists' worldview. They will jump at the opportunity to explore, to better understand aliens and their actions, and much more. However, that community needs to exercise caution going forward.

Some valuable insights about how the scientific community ought to address the UFO issue are recommended by two social scientists. Greg Eghigian, professor of history and bioethics at Penn State University, and Christian Peters, managing director of the Bremen International Graduate School of Social Sciences, co-wrote an article, "It's Time to Hear from Social Scientists about UFOs," for *Scientific American*. They admit the clamor for answers about UFOs "no longer seem[s] quite so far-fetched." Rather, they say we must now "all focus on the question of whether the phenomenon is something that exists in nature, whether worldly or other-worldly," a view consistent with mine.[11]

Eghigian and Peters argue that "UFOs are social facts" that transform politics and culture. Convincingly, they point out that social scientists offer effective techniques for conducting research relevant to

UFOs, such as topics like "human-technological systems, behavioral factors in manned space travel, public attitudes toward UFOs, and the psychophysical and cognitive aspects of sightings."[12]

Besides the logical area of astrophysics, the social scientists claim there are three pressing issues for the UFO social science researcher: intelligence, trust, and research ethics. Each ought to be pursued by the scientific community.[13]

The issue of intelligence vis-à-vis UFOs is complex, because it involves classification of military knowledge and the reliability of the information. Eghigian and Peters write that UFOs "represent a challenge to governmental and military authority. This is because the state is expected to have answers to all possible threats."[14]

The lack of trust is a major issue regarding UFO-related research as well. The writers point out that, today, "the sciences have increasingly assumed this role [judging the credibility of UFO witnesses]—one that is being contested." After all, public communication in the US "is characterized by a growing suspicion about established experts."[15]

On the research ethics issue, Search for Extraterrestrial Intelligence (SETI) researchers have already "mapped ways to responsibly search for, communicate with and reveal the existence of extraterrestrial civilizations." Still, those researchers caution "about built-in bias and failure to account for complexity also apply to computational methods working with large amounts of text and language data."[16]

Eghigian and Peters also caution us to be careful about putting UFO work into private hands, as we saw in the case of AATIP, the government program directed by Luis Elizondo:

> The UFO phenomenon long ago turned into a commercial enterprise, now hyped by streaming services, podcasts, social media and cable television. Its entertainment value has provided the hook for Enigma Labs [a private, commercial enterprise] to promote an app for mobile phone users to report sightings. This raises serious privacy concerns about what this

enigmatic company plans to do with the vast number of users' personal data it collects.[17]

The scientific community must become a key player in our efforts to understand the cause(s) of UFOs and how to address those findings. Evidently, there are differences of opinion and certainly multiple approaches that must be considered as we move forward to better understand the phenomenon.

Academia's Response to UFO Cause(s)

The government education establishment and much of our university/ collegiate community espouse the concept of openness to learning. Therefore, they should eagerly welcome "new" physics, and a growing minority of them favor aliens as the primary cause. However, they will be less prepared and even less willing to investigate should spirits be identified as the cause of UFOs.

"New" physics for the educational establishment means revamping various curricula from science courses to humanities. The implications of learning about new laws of nature means significant change and excitement for academia, top to bottom.

The government academy tends to be rather secular (primarily nonreligious), thus any indication that UFOs are caused by spiritual beings will be met with more skepticism than the alien cause. That is primarily because not only do most government schools eschew any reference to religion—allegedly for constitutional reasons of the separation of church and state—but a significant percentage of college professors tend to self-identify as agnostic or atheist.[18]

Confirmation that we are not alone in this universe will significantly impact the academy as well. Likely, alien studies programs will pop up across every college and university, and social studies books in elementary schools will include chapters about alien beings.

Law schools will wrestle with the legal implications of humans interacting with alien beings and will eagerly seek to discern how those civilizations regulate behavior. What does the addition of alien beings mean for our judicial system and civil liberties, property rights, and much more?

Medical schools will become most anxious about the physiology of aliens. Do their bodies function like humans? Volumes of new texts will be written as our learning curve embraces a new physiology and medicines. There will be important questions such as, "Will humans have sexual contact with aliens, or is that even possible?" There are so many questions to be explored if aliens are found to be the cause of UFOs.

It might surprise the reader that there is already at least one collegiate-level alien studies course. Thomas Bania, a professor of astronomy at the College of Arts and Sciences at Boston University, tells the students in his Life Beyond Earth course, which he has taught for more than thirty-five years, "It is a matter of the survival of the human species that we, as soon as possible, get a significant fraction of our population living in closed-cycle communities off-planet. 'Cause there are just too many ways to screw up our earth.'"[19]

In that course, Professor Bania points out that reputable scientists such as the late Carl Sagan and deep-pocketed space company CEOs like Elon Musk and Jeff Bezos believe "millions of us will have to move elsewhere in the galaxy someday."[20]

The final project in Life Beyond Earth requires the students to "imagine yourself part of a wealthy consortium seeking a space colony that could support millions of people. Now design it, within parameters, including the universal laws of science. Colonies, the written assignment said, 'will need to provide artificially all the resources found on earth if the colonists are to have a high-level technological civilization.'"[21]

Bania's course also addresses the issue of UFOs. He admits astronomers "universally assent to the certainty of life on other planets," then he asks: "So then the question is, 'Where are they?' as famed physicist Enrico Fermi [1901–1954, Italian-American renowned for being the creator of the world's first nuclear reactor, Chicago Pile-1] put it." At that point, Bania says he has about fifty possible answers to that question, including, "They are here… They were here… They are somewhere… and They are nowhere."[22]

I looked elsewhere for other possible impacts on the American academy should aliens be the UFO cause. Interestingly, a Reddit post entitled "UFOs and Academia" raises other insightful issues should the UFO cause be alien beings. That post argues that UFOs are not studied as much today because encounters "almost never result in physical evidence, limiting the extent to which the matter can be studied as a physical phenomenon." That being said, the "Redditor," the anonymous user posting on the American social news website, suggests perhaps UFOs could be studied much the same as the humanities. After all, "There is little physical evidence for many religious claims, yet people study religion."[23]

The disclosure of "genuinely convincing data" would change the academy's interest, alleges the Redditor. Specifically, a "soft-disclosure event," defined as the release of small amounts of information or data in support of the UFO phenomenon," might result in limited academic research, however. A "soft-disclosure," submits the Redditor, would not result in significant academic research, much less new journals or professorships dedicated to ufology.[24]

The academy's response would be quite different with a "hard-disclosure," which the Redditor defines "as a much larger release of information in support of the UFO phenomenon, the interpretation of which is not at all contentious." The writer also suggests this "hard-disclosure" would "have profound societal and scientific consequences," and would likely "permeate almost every aspect of society and pose new scientific questions."[25]

Evidently, many other academics like Professor Bania and the Redditor are enthusiastic about the possibility of researching UFOs, perhaps because such efforts mean fresh flows of grants from the public and private sectors. In fact, a 2023 poll of academics found that almost four in ten (37 percent) are interested in researching UFOs and a sizable minority (19 percent) have either witnessed or know someone who has witnessed a UFO.[26]

That study, published in the peer-reviewed academic journal, *Humanities and Social Sciences Communications*, conducted the survey of 39,984 academics across 144 different American universities. Four percent of the respondents said they had done academic research on UFOs. Yet, more than half (55 percent) said they would be more likely to conduct research if there is funding, and nearly half (43 percent) said they would do so, especially if there was a reputable academic scholar in their field who did, too.[27]

Nonetheless, when most academics are asked about UFOs, they tend to laugh off the question. For example, they are inclined to align themselves with astrophysicist Neil deGrasse Tyson, who said "he would only take the idea seriously when aliens send him a dinner invite."[28]

Commercial Response to UFO Cause(s)

Elon Musk was asked what he thought about the US Navy pilots' description of UFOs that displayed advanced technology beyond our understanding. Speculation at the time was that the pilots saw evidence of an alien craft. However, Musk said, "Honestly, I think I would know if there were aliens." His response likely reflects the view of many other prominent industry figures.[29]

These leaders will probably be genuinely skeptical about UFOs until there is solid evidence of their cause(s) and perhaps physical confirmation. Once the evidence is affirmed, if ever, then expect these giants of industry to jump at the opportunity to make a buck by harnessing emergent opportunities thanks to presumed alien-provided technologies.

Just consider the impact each of the possible causes for UFOs might have on the commercial space.

"New" physics would likely mean a host of new products, even though it will take time to develop and manufacture them. Certainly, new technology would spark a revolution in discovery and application, something that excites the entrepreneur.

Confirmation of UFOs attributed to spiritual beings will accelerate certain businesses such as fortune telling, reading the stars, and horoscopes, and the all-purpose spiritual adviser will become especially popular. Although most people will turn to various religious leaders and theologians to help them understand the spirits, others will arise promising to interpret the spiritual realm for a fee. Much of this will be quackery, but that is part of humankind's ongoing efforts to fool and manipulate the gullible. What is clear on this front is that government will provide little assistance.

If there is confirmation that we are being visited by aliens, and despite Musk's skepticism, then a host of new opportunities will emerge for the entrepreneur. For example, there will be all sorts of professional services and business opportunities—that is, if the aliens cooperate. How will we trade goods and services with aliens? Will there be a galaxy-wide common currency, stock markets, and banks, or something like cryptocurrency for humans and aliens alike?

Will the aliens be hostile to earthlings? Threatening aliens will create a boon for the defense industry, especially if those non-earthlings introduce super-advanced weapons, and some entrepreneurs will try to capitalize on those advances, assuming the aliens are willing to sell. What is the price for such technology, and who gets it first? Naturally, it remains to be determined whether the aliens would require precious tangible assets in exchange for access to the technology, which might be a price we are unwilling to pay.

What about entertainment? There is already widespread interest in make-believe alien movies. How might collaboration between earthlings and real aliens impact television, movies, and music? Would alien entertainment be acceptable to humans, and vice versa?

It is hard not to imagine that, once alien beings are confirmed, cottage industries teaching about space, selling telescopes, satellites, clothing lines, and space travel will come on the scene.

Just perhaps the aliens will help us mine distant planets, build space-based colonies, introduce us to new worlds and their inhabitants and much more.

Of course, all of this is totally fictitious, at least for the moment. We do not know what these notional aliens would be like, their motivation for visiting Earth, and our reaction. However, for the businessperson, the opportunities are truly out of this world.

Conclusion

Confirmation of the cause(s) of the UFO phenomenon will potentially and dramatically affect our key institutions by stretching our collective imaginations. If we find UFOs are spirits and/or aliens, the changes could well promise to remake our world beyond our wildest imaginations.

240

CHRISTIANS, SPIRITS, ALIENS, AND END TIMES

*Then I saw three impure spirits that looked like frogs; they came
out of the mouth of the dragon, out of the mouth of the beast and
out of the mouth of the false prophet. They are demonic spirits that
perform signs, and they go out to the kings of the whole world, to
gather them for the battle on the great day of God Almighty.*

REVELATION 16:13–14 (NIV)

Should Christians believe there are alien beings? Would Scripture support such a view? If so, what would that mean for
end-times prophecy? This final section of *Out of This World*
addresses those topics.

Chapter 15 addresses the question: Should Christians
believe there are alien beings? After all, as indicated in the previous section, I observed at least three possible explanations
for UFOs: alien beings, "new" physics, and spirits. I believe
humankind is surrounded by a mostly unseen spiritual world
that occasionally manifests itself to people through their senses.
They could well be part of what we call UFOs. Regarding, the
possibility of "new" physics, there are likely many things we
have yet to discover about our universe's laws of nature, and I
see nothing in the Bible to discount that possibility. The issue
at hand, though, is whether Christians should believe our universe has other living beings, call them aliens, who might have

come to Earth in the past or perhaps could visit here in the future—or the other way around.

Chapter 16 assumes there are manifestations of UFOs in terms of spirits—angels and demons—and possibly alien beings, not spiritual creatures. We have for ages seen evidence of UFOs that might include both spirits and alien beings. How does that work in end-times prophecy? What roles might they play?

CHRISTIANS, SPIRITS, AND ALIENS

All these people were still living by faith when they died.
They did not receive the things promised; they only saw them
and welcomed them from a distance, admitting that they
were foreigners and strangers on earth.

HEBREWS 11:13 (NIV)

New facts about our vast universe are being discovered all the time, yet even modern science does not understand certain aspects of this world, such as the invisible, spiritual realm. Therefore, for the Christian who relies on the Scriptures (the Bible), I combine what we know from God's Word with the collection of humanity's changing understanding of the universe, which helps the reader draw conclusions about unidentified flying objects.

Our formula for understanding UFOs and other paranormal events is based on a biblical perspective, which means we turn to the Bible for discernment about the spiritual realm. If the Bible is to be believed, and it is, it is likely that some of what we call UFOs are in fact spirits. However, there is a very slight chance other unknown objects in our earthly environment could possibly be alien beings or their technological proxies (robots) probing Earth in high-technology craft. Of course, the existence of invading/visiting aliens, although not mentioned per se in the Bible, creates theological problems for Christianity, most which are beyond the scope of this book.

Below, in two sections, I will examine both possibilities from a biblical perspective: UFOs are spirits and/or alien beings.

What should the Christian who relies on the Bible understand about our universe?[1]

"Spirits": Part of the Inexplicable Cornucopia of UFOs

The late Michael Heiser (1963–2023), a biblical scholar with a PhD in Hebrew Bible and Semitic languages, spent decades studying UFOs and the Bible. He asked the Christian rhetorically: How should we process UFO information?[2]

"This takes us right into the unseen world, of angels and demons and gods and God himself—biblical stuff…the spiritual world," said Dr. Heiser in 2021. He offered that there is an intersection between the UFO phenomenon and biblical theology "because people want to know what the truth is—who they are, why they are here, and whether God exists," writes the author of the article featuring Heiser.[3]

Yes, Scripture tells us there is a spiritual world. Our infinite God uses spirits for specific purposes and, unfortunately, there are also spirits that seek to undermine God's purposes: Satan and his army of demons. Given this as a starting point, we can understand that these immaterial beings—spirits—have powers to manifest themselves to be perceived by humankind at their convenience, as demonstrated

244

by a number of biblical passages. Further, there is no reason to believe these "spirits," which were active in biblical times, are not busy today appearing or manifesting themselves to humans for much the same reasons they did in biblical times.

We read in the Bible that some spirits appeared to humans as God's messengers; others, demons, appeared as warriors for Satan's cause. Why couldn't both be recognized today as UFOs? After all, the immaterial manifesting themselves, albeit momentarily to communicate with humans, is the very definition of a UFO.

In 1975, evangelist Billy Graham was one of the first to write an entire book about spirits, more specifically *Angels: God's Secret Agents*. That book is quite useful regarding a Christian, biblical perspective about the nature of these unseen beings.[4]

Angels is about both good spirits, angels, and rebellious spirits, Satan's army of demons. Understanding these spiritual beings from a biblical and experiential perspective helps us to best discern how these spirits might be part of the mystery of UFOs.

Dr. Graham cites two well-known theologians to begin describing the phenomenon. John Calvin (1509–1564), a French theologian and reformer during the Protestant Reformation, wrote in his *Institutes of the Christian Religions*:

> Angels are the dispensers and administrators of the divine beneficence toward us. They regard our safety, undertake our defense, direct our ways, and exercise a constant solitude that no evil befalls us.[5]

Martin Luther (1483–1546), the German theologian and seminal figure of the Protestant Reformation, wrote in *Tabletalk* that "an angel is a spiritual creature without a body created by God for the service of Christendom and the church."[6]

What's clear from both theologians is that angels are God's ambassadors to protect the Christian believer. Dr. Graham illustrates that role by advancing a number of accounts about angels, such as one attributed to Reverend John C. Paton, a missionary at the time in the New Hebrides Islands (now the Republic of Vanuatu, an island country in Melanesia, located in the South Pacific Ocean). Reverend Paton told a story involving the protective care of angels. Dr. Graham recounted the event:

> Hostile natives surrounded his [Paton's] mission headquarters one night, intent on burning the Patons out and killing them. John Paton and his wife prayed all during that terror-filled night that God would deliver them. When daylight came, they were amazed to see the attackers unaccountably leave.[7]
>
> A year later, the chief of the tribe was converted to Jesus Christ, and Mr. Paton, remembering what had happened, asked the chief what had kept him and his men from burning down the house and killing them. The chief replied in surprise, "Who were all those men you had with you there?" The missionary answered, "There were no men there; just my wife and I." The chief argued that they had seen many men standing guard—hundreds of big men in shining garments with drawn swords in their hands. They seemed to circle the mission station so that the natives were afraid to attack. Only then did Mr. Paton realize that God had sent his angels to protect them.[8]

Dr. Graham shared another account of angelic beings that occurred in the early days of World War II, when Britain's air force saved that nation from a likely Nazi invasion and defeat. This incident is attributed to the book, *Tell No Man*, written by Adela Rogers St. Johns, who describes the strange events of the air war. Ms. St. Johns describes a post-war celebration to honor Air Chief Marshall Lord Hugh Downing. Evidently, the Air Chief at the time recounted:

[The] story of his legendary conflict where his pitifully small complement of men rarely slept, and their planes never stopped flying. He told about airmen on a mission who, having been hit, were either incapacitated or dead. Yet their planes kept flying and fighting; in fact, on occasion pilots in other planes would see a figure still operating the controls. What was the explanation? The Air Chief Marshall said he believed angels had actually flown some of the planes whose pilots sat dead in their cockpits.[9]

For many Christians, especially those like Mr. and Mrs. Paton and Air Marshall Downing, angels are real, not what some secularists label evidence of "the ravings of the lunatic fringe," as described by Dr. Graham. In fact, the same society that rejects Christian talk about angels is quick to demonstrate a morbid fascination with the occult. "Occultism" is defined by *Encyclopedia Britannica* as:

Various theories and practices involving a belief in and knowledge or use of supernatural forces or beings. Such beliefs and practices—principally magical or divinatory—have occurred in all human societies throughout recorded history, with considerable variations both in their nature and in the attitude of societies toward them.[10]

Graham noted that modern society is enthralled by all things associated with the occult, the devil, Satan worship, and demon possession. Hollywood and television studios push these dark concepts and pretend Satan and his demonic army are laughable inventions. Not true!

The Bible is clear about Satan. He is a real being and works with his helpers (demons) against the people on this planet. In fact, as we learn in God's Word, the acceleration of demonic activity may in fact indicate the Second Coming of Jesus Christ is close at hand.[11]

Some Christian writers speculate that UFOs "could very well be part of God's angelic host who preside over the physical affairs of universal creation," wrote Dr. Graham. After all, it is true today as when Dr. Graham wrote *Angels* that "some people are now seeking some type of supernatural explanation for these [UFO] phenomena."[12]

In fact, some Christians who are grounded in the Bible "contend that these UFOs are angels. But are they? These people," continued Graham, "point to certain passages in Isaiah, Ezekiel, Zechariah and the book of Revelation, and draw parallels to the reports of observers of alleged UFO appearances."[13]

Dr. Graham illustrated the point in *Angels*. He cited the example of a highly credible airline crew's detailed description of a UFO and compared that alongside Ezekiel 10, which states:

Each of the four cherubim had a wheel beside him—"The Whirl-Wheels," as I heard them called, for each one had a second wheel crosswise within, sparkled like chrysolite, giving off a greenish-yellow glow…and when they rose into the air the wheels rose with them, and stayed beside them as they flew. When the cherubim stood still, so did the wheels, for the spirit of the cherubim was in the wheels. (Ezekiel 10:9–13, 16–17, TLB)

Dr. Graham stated, "I am convinced that these heavenly beings exist and that they provide unseen aid on our behalf. I do not believe in angels because someone has told me about a dramatic visitation from an angel, impressive as such rare testimonies may be." Rather, "I believe in angels because the Bible says there are angels; and I believe the Bible to be the true word of God." He added, "I also believe in angels because I have sensed their presence in my life on special occasions."[14]

Angels, according to the Bible, were created by God. Colossians 1:16 (NIV) states: "For in him all things were created…visible and invisible." Angels, said Graham, "are among the invisible things made by God." He continued, "It seems that angels have the ability to change their appearance and shuttle in a flash from the capital glory of heaven to earth and back again." That fits in part with many reported descriptions of some UFOs.[15]

Angels are nonmaterial, as we see in Genesis 6:2 and Hebrews 1:14. Although "they do not possess physical bodies they may take on physical bodies when God appoints them to special tasks," Graham wrote. These angels are mentioned directly or indirectly nearly three hundred times in the Bible.[16]

General William Booth, founder of the Salvation Army, "describes a vision of angelic beings, stating that every angel was surrounded with an aurora of rainbow light so brilliant that were it not withheld, no human being could stand the sight of it." Ezekiel 28 adds to General Booth's description of angels, about which Graham wrote: "They are exotic to the human eye and mind. Apparently, angels have a beauty and variety that surpass anything known to men." Further, angels "enjoy far greater power than men." Specifically, 2 Thessalonians 1:7 (NIV) states the "Lord Jesus is revealed from heaven in blazing fire with his powerful angels." This description seems to be consistent with UFO profiles identified earlier in this book.[17]

Angels are God's means of transportation. Matthew Henry (1662–1714), the seventeenth-century nonconformist minister and author of the six-volume biblical commentary, *Exposition of the Old and New Testaments*, stated:

Angels are the chariots of God, his chariots of war, which he makes use of against his enemies, his chariots of conveyance, which he sends for his friends, as he did for Elijah (and Lazarus is said to be carried by the angels), his chariots of state, in the midst of which he shows his glory and power. They are vastly numerous: Twenty thousands, even thousands multiplied.[18]

Also, wrote Dr. Graham:

249

Angels speak. They appear and reappear. They feel with apt sense of emotion. While angels may become visible by choice, our eyes are not constructed to see them ordinarily any more than we can see the dimensions of a nuclear field, the structure of atoms, or the electricity that flows through copper wiring.[19]

Just as there are angels, godly spiritual beings, there are spiritual beings with malevolent intent, Satan and his demonic army. Graham said, "The Devil is alive and more at work than at any other time. The Bible says that he realizes his time is short, [thus] his activity will increase."[20]

According to Graham, the "greatest catastrophe in history" was "Lucifer's defiance of God and the consequent fall of perhaps one third of the angels who joined him (Satan) in his wickedness."[21]

The Apostle Paul addressed Satan's rebellion in the heavens when he identified Satan as the "ruler of the kingdom of the air, the spirit who is now at work in those who are disobedient" (Ephesians 2:2, NIV). Also, Ephesians 6:12 (NIV) speaks of the infighting between the kingdom of satanic darkness:

For our struggle is not against flesh and blood, but against the rulers, against the authorities, against the powers of this dark world and against the spiritual forces of evil in the heavenly realms.[22]

The spiritual warfare mentioned here impacts humanity. Thus, God's angels and Satan's demons engage in a deadly conflict, and humankind is in the mix. Those demons are known "by the discord they promote, the wars they start, the hatred they engender," wrote Dr. Graham.[23]

Therefore, given the above, what might explain spirits being UFOs? One explanation is offered in a 2013 post entitled "What Do UFOs Have to Do with Christians?" found at the website Jesus: The Deliverer Ministry.[24]

The post indicates the Bible speaks of three heavens: first, our atmosphere, the sky; second, "the powers of the air" (Ephesians 2:2); and third, the place of the throne of God, with His angels and the saints in Christ (2 Corinthians 12:2).[25]

The second and third heavens are spiritual. However, the first heaven, which includes Earth, is material, inside which the spirit can also operate. We humans are spirit (our souls) protected by a material body.[26]

Scripture is full of examples of references to clouds associated with the spiritual world. Specifically, in the context of UFOs, we often understand that UFOs come out of a cloud and then once again disappear into a cloud. The biblical references indicate that God appears in a cloud and is riding upon a cloud. Below are some examples of this phenomenon—featuring the cloud—identified by the Jesus: The Deliverer Ministry article.[27]

And the angel of God, which went before the camp of Israel, removed and went behind them; and the pillar of the cloud went from before their face, and stood behind them. (Exodus 14:19, KJV)

And it came to pass, as Aaron spake unto the whole congregation of the children of Israel, that they looked toward the wilderness, and, behold, the glory of the Lord appeared in the cloud. (Exodus 16:10, KJV)

And the Lord said unto Moses, Lo, I come unto thee in a thick cloud, that the people may hear when I speak with thee, and believe thee for ever. And Moses told the words of the people unto the Lord. (Exodus 19:9, KJV)

And the Lord came down in a cloud, and spake unto him, and took of the spirit that was upon him, and gave it unto the seventy elders: and it came to pass, that, when the spirit rested upon them, they prophesied, and did not cease. (Numbers 11:25, KJV)

And it came to pass, when the priests were come out of the holy place, that the cloud filled the house of the Lord, So that the priests could not stand to minister because of the cloud: for the glory of the Lord had filled the house of the Lord. (1 Kings 8:10–11, KJV)

Bless the Lord, O my soul. O Lord my God, thou art very great; thou art clothed with honour and majesty. Who coverest thyself with light as with a garment: who stretchest out the heavens like a curtain: Who layeth the beams of his chambers in the waters: who maketh the clouds his chariot: who walketh upon the wings of the wind: Who maketh his angels spirits; his ministers a flaming fire: (Psalms 104:1–4, KJV)

While he yet spake, behold, a bright cloud overshadowed them: and behold a voice out of the cloud, which said, This is my beloved Son, in whom I am well pleased; hear ye him. (Matthew 17:5–6, KJV)

And then shall appear the sign of the Son of man in heaven: and then shall all the tribes of the earth mourn, and they shall see the Son of man coming in the clouds of heaven with power and great glory. (Matthew 24:30, KJV)

Jesus saith unto him, Thou hast said: nevertheless I say unto you, Hereafter shall ye see the Son of man sitting on the right hand of power, and coming in the clouds of heaven. (Matthew 26:64, KJV)

And when he had spoken these things, while they beheld, he was taken up; and a cloud received him out of their sight. (Acts 1:9, KJV)

Then we which are alive and remain shall be caught up together with them in the clouds, to meet the Lord in the air: and so shall we ever be with the Lord. (1 Thessalonians 4:17, KJV)

Behold, he cometh with clouds; and every eye shall see him, and they also which pierced him: and all kindreds of the earth shall wail because of him. Even so, Amen. (Revelation 1:7, KJV)

Evidently, when the spiritual realm "touches the material realm, a cloud, or what appears to be a cloud, is formed." The cloud is evidence of a transition from the immaterial (spiritual) to the material. So, "not only can God move from one realm to the other, but also UFOs" can move from the immaterial to the material via something like a cloud. Thus, "being spirit they are exempt from our physical laws, save for manipulating them," states the article in Jesus: The Deliverer Ministry.[28]

Whether spirits—angels and demons—exist, much less fit into the broad category of UFOs, may not be perfectly clear for the secular world at the moment. However, there is significant evidence the unseen spiritual realm is real and fighting over the Earth and its inhabitants, especially for the Christian. Do spirits appear in a physical form to humans? Many of us believe they do and have since the creation of man in the Garden of Eden. Are they interacting with humans today? Yes. What we don't know is whether some of the UFOs reported by reputable personnel like US Navy pilots are spirits "coming in a cloud" that manifest themselves for unknown purposes, such as serving as a precursor to the Second Coming of Christ and the prophetic end times.

The biblical evidence appears to match with many UFO sightings to confirm that some of what we are experiencing today is evidence of spirits revealing themselves to humankind, but not necessarily.

Should Christians Believe Some UFOs Are Alien Beings?

I believe UFOs are likely from the unseen realm—spiritual beings, as explained above. Yet, I also accept that there is a remote possibility we have been or are being visited by alien beings.

This section considers three aspects of the possibility that Earth is being visited by alien beings. First, the scientific issues associated with any alien visitors make the possibility seem very remote, but not impossible. Second, the Scriptures make the likelihood of aliens seem nonexistent. Finally, the theological issues, addressed earlier in this book regarding the existence of alien beings, pose some very tough challenges—especially for Christianity.

Science Makes Alien Visits Unlikely

There are reasons not to embrace the extraterrestrial hypothesis as the cause behind UFOs. However, the primary argument made by the pro-alien-cause crowd is that because UFOs are not explained by earthly means, the only logical explanation is to default to an alien origin. That view presents some serious challenges for advocates.[29]

Interstellar travel for the presumed aliens is incredibly hard to embrace. Hugh Ross, a former astronomer and co-author of *Lights in the Sky and Little Green Men*, argues that interstellar travel from distant planets or galaxies would require multigenerational travel as well as incredible amounts of energy, and would be a very dangerous trip given the debris in space and the necessary speed of the spacecraft.[30]

French astronomer and ufologist Jacques Vallée, introduced earlier in this book, provides a number of arguments against the view that aliens are the source of UFOs as well.

Mr. Vallée argues the numbers of UFOs seen are quite significant: many thousands over the recent decades alone. Why, he asks, would extraterrestrials have to make so many visits—much less, as he argues, to allegedly take samples of things like soil?

He also calls out the rudimentary technology aliens have reportedly used to experiment on humans, as some "abductees" claim, which seems to be odd at best. Earlier we discussed cases in which humans said they had been abducted by aliens and examined or used for experiments.[31]

There is also the issue that so-called aliens evolved in the same way as humans. Vallée argues that, as a naturalist and evidently a Darwinian evolutionist, aliens would not "arise from random chance with such similar structures [like humans]...[the probability of such an outcome] is basically zero." So, aliens would certainly be radically different from humans.[32]

There is also the issue that aliens purportedly can violate the known laws of physics (a topic examined in a previous chapter); travel at extremely fast speeds; make incredibly quick turns at [high] speed; and use craft capable of transmedium operations, which means "they can fly through space, air, and water without being affected...can change shape and size, and are seemingly impervious to being hit with bullets."[33]

Believing in alien beings that visit planet Earth takes more faith than believing UFOs are the result of spiritual beings.

The Bible Doesn't Support the Existence of Alien Beings

Reverend Billy Graham stated:

> The Bible doesn't say anything about the possibility of life on other planets. Its main concern is with human life on this planet, including our problems and our future. This doesn't mean life can't exist on other planets, for it well might; the Bible simply doesn't tell us.[34]

Not all theologians agree there might be aliens, even though there is no evidence in the Bible. Ken Ham, the founder and chief executive officer of Answers in Genesis and its popular attractions, the Creation Museum and Ark Encounters, makes a scriptural argument against the existence of alien beings. Mr. Ham responds when asked whether he believes in UFOs: "Absolutely! Any flying object that can't be identified is a UFO." However, he quickly follows with the statement: "But do I believe in UFOs piloted by Vulcans, Klingons, or Cardassians [the fictional extraterrestrial species from the television series *Star Trek*]? The answer is a definite no."[35]

Mr. Ham writes that, even though there are a seemingly endless number of theories about the possibilities of intelligent life beyond earth, "I believe a Christian worldview, built on the Bible, rejects such a possibility." Then he explains why.[36]

Mr. Ham points out from Genesis 1 that God made Earth as a very special place—"it is center stage," and the balance of the universe is related to the Earth.[37]

The Old Testament makes a distinction between Earth and the balance of the universe. After all, Psalm 115:16 (KJV) states, "The heaven, even the heavens, are the Lord's: but the earth has He given to the children of men." That means people on Earth are special to God, which is further echoed by Isaiah 66:1 (KJV), which states: "Thus says the Lord, the heaven is my throne, and the earth is my footstool."

Therefore, the Earth, according to Ham:

...is to be considered separate and special when compared with the rest of the universe, so they suggest that the earth alone was created for life. So far, based on man's limited exploration of space and the solar system, this certainly holds true.

Also, according to Ham, "There is a theological reason I believe rules out the possibility of intelligent life in outer space."[38]

That reason is found in Romans 8:22 (KJV), which states the "whole creation groaneth" because of Adam's sin. Ham explains that when Adam sinned, "the entire universe was affected." Not only this Earth and humankind are impacted by the original sin, but every known and unknown being (even presumed aliens if they exist) inherited Adam's sin. Fortunately, God's word states, "One day in the future, there will be 'a new heaven and a new earth: for the first heaven and the first earth were passed away'" (Revelation 21:1, KJV). Certainly, a similar idea is expressed in Isaiah 34:4 (KJV):

And all the host of heaven shall be dissolved, and the heavens shall be rolled together as a scroll: and all their host shall fall down, as the leaf falls off from the vine, and as a falling fig from the fig tree.[39]

The problem with alien beings on other planets and from other galaxies, according to Ham, is that:

...they would have been affected by the fall of Adam because the whole creation was affected. So, these beings would have to die because death was the penalty for sin. One day their planet will be destroyed by fire during God's final judgement, but they cannot have salvation because that blessing is given only to humans.

Therefore, Ham notes, "If intelligent beings lived on other planets, they would suffer because of Adam's sin but have no opportunity to be saved through Christ's sacrifice."[40]

He continues, "Jesus didn't become a 'God-Klingon,' a 'God-Vulcan,' or a 'God-Cardassian,' He became the God-man. It wouldn't make sense theologically for there to be other intelligent, physical beings who suffer because of Adam's sin but cannot be saved."[41]

"Now, regarding animal life and plants," writes Ham, "we cannot be so dogmatic because the Bible does not state whether life exists elsewhere in the universe. Based on the passages about the heavens and earth, however, I strongly suspect that life does not exist elsewhere."[42]

It should be clear that a dogmatic belief in extraterrestrial life simply is not supported by the Bible. As one source argued, God directed people to spread the gospel of Jesus Christ to the "uttermost parts of the earth (Acts 1:8)," "not to the uttermost regions of the galaxy or universe."[43]

Theological Issues if There Are Alien Beings

Although the Bible gives no reason to believe there is alien life, the speculation even among some theologians is significant. Perhaps that is why in 2014, NASA hired the Center for Theological Inquiry (CTI), in Princeton, New Jersey, an ecumenical research institute, to study "the societal implications of astrobiology," and, more specifically, the implications of the discovery of microbial life outside of Earth for the nation's various faith communities.[44]

Reverend Andrew Davidson, a British priest and a Starbridge Lecturer in Theology and Natural Science at the University of Cambridge, explained his work for CTI:

> I am researching and writing a survey of the main topics in Christian belief—what is sometimes called "systematic theology"—from the perspective of life elsewhere in the universe. I am thinking about its bearing on the doctrines of creation, sin, the person and work of Jesus, redemption, revelation, eschatology, and so on.[45]

The broad-based curiosity about the possible impact of ETs on religion was previously mentioned in this book, as you may recall. Specifically, I mentioned in an earlier chapter the late astrophysicist Carl Sagan, who pointed out in his out-of-print book *The Cosmic Question* that "space exploration leads directly to religious and philosophical questions." Also, I called out the relatively new discipline named "exotheology," a term defined by Ted Peters, professor emeritus in theology at Pacific Lutheran Theological Seminary, which refers to "speculation on the theological significance of extraterrestrial life."[46]

Exotheology addresses the tough questions about humanity's uniqueness and the principles of nature's uniformity, plenitude (everything that is possible will be realized), and mediocrity (the view that Earth isn't a special place). Of course, Christian evangelicals have a difficult time with the possibility of extraterrestrials because we tend to be scriptural literalists; Scripture is silent on the issue and these "principles" are not up for debate.

The theological issues most often raised by exotheologists includes topics like incarnation that tend to be especially difficult for Christians. After all, the existence of alien beings is troubling, given the Christian view of the concept of incarnation, the belief that God was fully and uniquely present in Jesus of Nazareth, and that salvation can only be achieved through His death and resurrection. How might this apply to notional aliens somewhere else in this vast universe who are completely unaware of Jesus?

Thomas Paine, an American founder, addressed that issue in his 1794 *Age of Reason*, which was cited in chapter 8, to argue that an infinite plurality of the world renders "the Christian system of faith at once little and ridiculous and scatters it in the mind like feathers in the air." Paine, a self-proclaimed monotheist who disdained all organized religion, explained, "If Christian salvation is only possible to creatures whose worlds have experienced an Incarnation from God, then that means God's life is spent visiting the many worlds throughout the cosmos where he is promptly crucified and resurrected."[47]

Some theologians also ask whether notional alien beings might be made in the "image of God" like humans. That reference is not about physical appearance—that is, aliens look like us—but about our conscience, which refers to God's being—rationality, morality, and sociability. That's an impossible issue to examine without an alien to compare with a human, however.[48]

Alternatively, Robert Letham writes in *Systematic Theology* the existence of aliens "would be no threat to the [Christian] faith, since all it would entail is that such Extraterrestrial Intelligent Life would be incidental to God's purposes for the human race." These beings, he explained, could be angels, demons, or unidentified living creatures around the throne of God mentioned in Revelation 4:8.[49]

Of course, Bible-believing evangelicals warn that the "idea of extraterrestrial life stems largely from a [blind] belief in evolution," writes Rick Pidcock for *Baptist News Global*. Pidcock continues, saying Christian salvation has no room for aliens because "intelligent alien beings cannot be redeemed. God's plan of redemption is for human beings: those descended from Adam."[50]

The realm of theological speculation about the existence of alien beings is probably a moot point, as demonstrated earlier in this chapter. After all, the UFO phenomenon is most likely a spiritual issue—and besides, as science demonstrates, the probability that ETs are here or have visited is incredibly remote but not impossible, as Dr. Graham acknowledged.

Conclusion

This chapter considers the UFO phenomenon from a biblical point of view to conclude that the spiritual realm is the most likely explanation for many unexplained sightings. Still, there is a remote chance our vast universe includes alien beings, life—albeit perhaps microscopic or far more advanced—other than spirits that probe our Earth in their high-technology craft.

The final chapter in *Out of This World* considers the prophetic end times and the role, if any, for UFOs, spirits, and aliens.

END-TIMES SPIRITS
DECEIVE AS UFOS

*Dear friends, do not believe every spirit, but test the spirits
to see whether they are from God, because many false prophets have
gone out into the world. This is how you can recognize the Spirit
of God: Every spirit that acknowledges that Jesus Christ has come
in the flesh is from God, but every spirit that does not acknowledge
Jesus is not from God. This is the spirit of the antichrist, which you
have heard is coming and even now is already in the world.*

(1 JOHN 4:1–3, NIV)

There is compelling reason to believe some, if not all, of the UFOs
are spiritual beings, not space aliens. Their appearance will grow
more frequent, if the cause is spiritual beings, as we draw closer to
the prophetic end times—primarily because of Satan's deception plan,
his last-ditch effort to disrupt God's plan for humankind. This effort
began with the biblical book of Genesis and the contamination of the
human gene pool by the "sons of God," the entities that led to hybrid
offspring, the product of "fallen angels" and human women.

In three parts, I outline Satan's plan to disrupt God's design for
humankind from the time of Genesis by "seeding" the world with
Satan's demonic angels, who are evident today. Secondly, those
demonic offspring, who are half human, are made to appear as alien
beings today in order to deceive people into uniting behind the coming

Antichrist to create a global religious movement that ushers in the prophetic end times and the Second Coming of Jesus Christ. Finally, the third part of this chapter explains why demonic spirits—the seed of those fallen angels mentioned in Genesis 6—fit the profile for what we often identify today as UFOs.

1. Demonic Spirits behind UFO Phenomenon

Up to this point in *Out of This World*, I have provided an overview of the UFO phenomenon. Certainly, in a number of chapters I have considered the source of UFOs, which includes the possibility that they are caused by "new" physics, spirits, and/or aliens from space. What's clear to me from all efforts to date regarding UFOs is that we have no definitive answer about the cause(s) of many UFOs, but desperately want to know. As stated previously, I don't totally discount the possibility of alien beings created by God that live in distant places in our universe. Like Billy Graham said, though, and I agree:

> There may be intelligent life on other planets—but if so, the Bible doesn't mention it. If there is, it is because God put them there (just as He put us here), and their purpose is to glorify and serve God (just as ours is).[1]

What follows, however, in an abbreviated fashion, is an explanation of the origin of demonic spirits that could very well explain the cause of some, if not all, ancient and contemporary UFOs. It is based on both biblical and extrabiblical sources to suggest that long ago Satan hatched a plan that may now become a reality as we approach the prophetic end times. In fact, this explanation will sound bizarre, but I assure you, it is no stranger than other explanations from scientists, ufologists, and the like regarding UFOs and, in fact, it is based on some pretty compelling rationale.

There is compelling reason to believe some, if not all, UFOs are spiritual beings, not space aliens.[2]

Missler's *Alien Encounters*

The following perspective is mostly attributed to the interpretation of UFO events from a book titled *Alien Encounters* by the late Charles "Chuck" W. Missler (1934–2018), an American author, evangelical Christian, Bible teacher, and engineer.[3]

Missler indicated that Satan, from the earliest time, had a plan to "seed" the world with his demonic angels in order to disrupt God's plan for humankind. This account dates back to humanity's earliest times, recorded in the book of Genesis. Missler began his analysis with a critical question: Why did God judge humankind by sending the Flood? The answer to that question could have grave consequences for our present time and especially for the coming prophetic end times.

We begin this storyline with a statement made by Jesus in Matthew 24. Specifically, the Lord reminds us, "Of that day [the coming end times] and hour no one knows, not even the angels of heaven, nor the Son, but the Father alone" (Matthew 24:36, NAS). Then He states, "For the coming of the Son of man will be just like the Days of Noah." What does this mean for us today?

We need to digest the phrase "Days of Noah" to begin this journey of discernment. Let me refresh your memory. You will recall from Genesis 6 the situation that led to the global Flood in the time of Noah that erased all but eight lives—Noah, his wife and their three sons and their wives. That biblical passage states:

> When human beings began to increase in number on the earth and daughters were born to them, the sons of God saw that the daughters of humans were beautiful, and they married any of them they chose. Then the Lord said, "My Spirit will not contend with humans forever, for they are mortal; their days will be a hundred and twenty years." (Genesis 6:1–4, NIV).

The stand-out phrase in this passage is "sons of God," which in Hebrew is *B'nai HaElohim*, an Old Testament term for "angels." Evidently, according to Missler, the third-century Greek translation of the Hebrew Torah rendered the term "angels" as well.[4]

Even the Book of Enoch, which was authored by Enoch, the biblical figure and patriarch prior to Noah's Flood, "treats these strange events as involving angels," according to Missler. Specifically, the reader will recall from Genesis 5:24 (NIV) that Enoch lived 365 years before he was taken by God: "Enoch walked faithfully with God; then he was no more, because God took him away." The Book of Enoch treats the events in Genesis 6—"sons of God" and daughters of man—as involving fallen angels and human women. Although Enoch's book is not considered part of the "inspired" canon, it is respected as authentic. The passage in question refers to "supernatural beings intruding upon the planet earth," Missler wrote.[5] Genesis 6:2 states "the daughters of men," which refers to the natural female descendants of humankind, mated with the "sons of God," and they produced unnatural "superhuman offspring"—what Genesis 6:4 calls "giants," the Hebrew translation of the word "Nephilim," which literally means "the fallen ones."

Scripture portrays these unnatural offspring of women and fallen angels, the "Nephilim," as monstrous. It appears that they are similar to Greek demigods. After all, as Missler pointed out, in Greek mythology, "We find that intercourse between the gods and women yielded half-god, half-man titans, demigods, or heroes, which were partly terrestrial and party celestial," such as Hercules, and there is also mention of so-called ancient giants in the records of the great pyramid near Cairo. (Hercules is the Roman version of the Greek divine hero Heracles, who according to classical mythology, was the son of Jupiter [the Roman sky god] and the mortal Alcmena. Hercules is known for his strength and his many adventures.)[6]

Thus, we are faced with the question posed by Missler: "Why was the presence of the Nephilim so great a threat that God would resort to such an extreme measure as the worldwide Flood?" After all, in the very next verse, Genesis 6:5 (NAS), we read: "Then the Lord saw that the wickedness of man was great on the earth, and that every intent of the thoughts of his heart was only evil continually."[7]

Threat That Prompted the Flood

The answer to that question is found in Genesis 6:9 (NIV): "This is the account of Noah and his family. Noah was a righteous man, blameless among the people of his time, and he walked faithfully with God." The key term here is "family," or, in other translations, "generations," which in the text refers to genealogies, "a line of descent traced continuously from an ancestor."[8] Further, Noah is labeled "a righteous man," or "perfect," which means "without blemish, sound, healthful, without spot, unimpaired," wrote Missler. This appears to mean Noah's family was not tarnished by the intrusion of the fallen angels, "the sons of God" mentioned in Genesis 6:2.

This account, explained Missler, is "well documented in both ancient Jewish rabbinical literature and early church writings." For example, Josephus Flavius (AD 37–100), a Roman-Jewish historian and author of *The Jewish War*, stated:

> They made God their enemy; for many angels of God accompanied with women, and begat sons that proved unjust, and despisers of all that was good, on account of the confidence they had in their own strength, for the tradition is that these men did what resembled the acts of those whom the Grecians call giants.[9]

Even early church fathers, according to Missler, understood the phrase "sons of God" as identifying angels. The Apostle Peter and Jude comment on the issue. Second Peter 2:4–5 (KJV) states:

> For if God spared not the angels that sinned, but cast them down to hell, and delivered them into chains of darkness, to be reserved unto judgment; And spared not the old world, but saved Noah the eighth person, a preacher of righteousness, bringing in the flood upon the world of the ungodly.

Missler explained that Peter's use of the word "hell" is translated *Tartarus*, a Greek term for "dark abode of woe," "the pit of darkness in the unseen world." Similarly, in Greek mythology, some of the demigods who rebelled were condemned to *Tartarus* as well.[10]

Peter, in his first book, identified the angels' fall as "in the days of Noah." Specifically, in 1 Peter 3:19–20 (KJV) the apostle states:

> By which also [Christ] went and proclaimed unto the spirits in prison; which sometime were disobedient, when once the long-suffering of God waited in the days of Noah, while the ark was a preparing, wherein few, that is, eight souls were saved by water.

Jude says much the same in Jude 6–7 (KJV):

And the angels which kept not their first estate, but left their own habitation, he hath reserved in everlasting chains under darkness unto the judgment of the great day. Even as Sodom and Gomorrah, and the cities about them in like manner, giving themselves over to fornication, and going after strange flesh, are set forth for an example, suffering the vengeance of eternal fire.

The word "habitation" in Jude, according to Missler, is a reference to "heavenly bodies from which they had disrobed." The term appears two times in the New Testament (Jude 6 and 2 Corinthians 5:2) and each is a reference to "a dwelling place for the spirit." Further, the reference to "first estate," also in Jude, is a reference from where they (the fallen angels) came from, in the presence of God before their fall with Satan.[11]

In chapter 15 of this book, I profiled some of the characteristics of angels that apply to demons as well. Missler called out a few others for context. Specifically, we know these spirits (both angels and demons) can materialize into our space-time; they can speak to humans, eat a meal, take us by the hand, and fight. In fact, in Hebrews 13:2 (NIV), we are told some of us have "shown hospitality to angels without knowing it."

Unlike the "sons of God" in Genesis 6, we understand that godly angels cannot marry. We read in Luke 20:35–36 (KJV):

But they which shall be accounted worthy to obtain that world, and the resurrection from the dead, neither marry, nor are given in marriage: Neither can they die any more: for they are equal unto the angels; and are the children of God, being the children of the resurrection.

Therefore, by inference, godly angels do not procreate. However, "fallen angels" "can aspire to degeneracy," wrote Missler. After all, angels and, by association, demons are identified in the Scripture as masculine and, although disturbing, it is clear they were the objects of lust for the men of Sodom (Genesis 19:5).[12]

Perhaps the Nephilims' "Genes" Didn't Perish

It is possible that the "seed" of the "sons of God," the Nephilim (Genesis 6:4), perhaps weren't totally destroyed by the Flood because they reappear "also afterward," as it states in Genesis 6:4. After all, we find evidence in the Bible elsewhere of giants after the Flood, such as those in Canaan. In fact, numerous tribes had "giants," and, according to Deuteronomy 7:2 (NIV), Joshua told the Israelites to "utterly destroy" those tribes—the Canaanites, Amorites, Hittites, Jebusites, Hivites, Perizzites, and Girgashites.

There are two possible explanations for the continuation of the Nephilim "seed" after the Flood. An article published by *Knowing Scripture*, "Giants in the Land: A Biblical Theology of the Nephilim, Anakim, Rephaim (and Goliath)," states that those possible explanations for the seed of Nephilim after the Flood include: "(1) The same event [Genesis 6:4] transpired later in history, as spirit beings again bred with women and produced more Nephilim; (2) Nephilim genes were passed down through Noah's [three] daughters-in-law." On the second account, keep in mind that the wives of Ham, Shem, and Japheth were not blood descendants from Noah, thus they potentially had Nephilim genes.[13]

There is much biblical history about giants—perhaps the result of the seed of the Nephilim—after the Flood. Recall from Numbers 13:17 that Moses sent out twelve spies to reconnoiter the promised land of Canaan. They reported back to Moses (Numbers 13:26–29, NIV):

> They came back to Moses and Aaron and the whole Israelite community at Kadesh in the Desert of Paran. There they reported to them and to the whole assembly and showed them the fruit of the land. They gave Moses this account: "We went

into the land to which you sent us, and it does flow with milk and honey! Here is its fruit. But the people who live there are powerful, and the cities are fortified and very large. We even saw descendants of Anak there. The Amalekites live in the Negev; the Hittites, Jebusites and Amorites live in the hill country; and the Canaanites live near the sea and along the Jordan."

A little further into Numbers 13 at verse 33 (NIV), we read that the spies reported: We saw the Nephilim there (the descendants of Anak come from the Nephilim). We seemed like grasshoppers in our own eyes, and we looked the same to them.

The result of the report about the Nephilim is found in Numbers 14:1 (NIV): "That night all the members of the community raised their voices and wept aloud." Why? The Nephilim terrified the Israelites, and, as a result, they kept wandering in the wilderness for another thirty-eight years.

Once Moses died and the mantel of leadership passed to Joshua, the Israelites were finally ready to enter the Promised Land. However, as they entered, Joshua provided explicit orders (Joshua 6:21) to utterly destroy every man, woman, and child in Jericho. That begs the question: Why did Joshua order such a harsh judgment from God? Evidently, observes Missler, the intent was to utterly destroy the "gene pool problem" of the Nephilim who were present in the Promised Land. "These Rephaim, Nephilim, seem to have been established as an advance guard to obstruct Israel's possession of the promised land," said Missler. "Was this also a stratagem of Satan?"

We know from the Scripture that "no Anakites were left in Israelite territory; only in Gaza, Gath and Ashdod did any survive" (Joshua 11:22, NIV). Why? It's not clear. However, the consequence of that disobedience was significant. The article from *Knowing Scripture* states: "First, this means the task that God gave Israel to drive out the Canaanites was not complete (Judges 1–2). Second, the Philistines, with whom the Anakim remained, became Israel's chief enemy during the time of Samuel. And third, the Philistines' champion [Goliath] in 1 Samuel 17 was from Gath."[14]

Arguably, the seed of the Nephilim proliferated and perhaps continues to plague Israel today in terms of its many enemies such as those in the Gaza Strip.

Giants and Demons in the Time of Christ

Another alternative perspective regarding the spirits of the Nephilim is proposed in Missler's book, *Alien Encounters*. He stated, "Numerous ancient rabbinic and early church texts, when the Nephilim died [presumably in the Flood] their spirits became disembodied and roamed the earth, harassing mankind and seeking embodiment!"[15]

Certainly, that view of the spirits of the Nephilim seems to fit in New Testament times. Specifically, it is curious that demons, at the time of Christ, "seem desperate to seek embodiment," according to Missler. He cited Christ's power over demons in Matthew 8:28–34, to illustrate that angels and demons are quite different.

In Matthew 8, Jesus calms the sea and then lands His boat in the country of the Gadarenes (eastern side of the Sea of Galilee), where He is approached by "two men who were demon-possessed" and "extremely violent." The demons inside the men ask Christ, "Have you come here to torment us before the appointed time?" (Matthew 8:29, NIV). Christ did not answer them before the demonic spirits said, "If you drive us out, send us into the herd of pigs" (Matthew 8:30, NIV).

The pregnant question from this passage is how this text about Christ casting out demons at the Galilee juxtaposes with the presumed drowning of the Nephilim in the Flood of Genesis 7. Evidently, according to Missler, the spirits of the Nephilim survived the Flood and settled into tribes that surrounded Israel in the Promised Land, and continued to be present even in the New Testament era. In fact, it was Missler's view that those same disembodied spirits are quite evident as UFOs today.

2. Nephilim Spirits Mimic UFOs

Gordon Craighton (1908–2003), a former British diplomat and the former editor of the British periodical, *Flying Saucer Review*, admitted:

> There seems to be no evidence yet that any of these [UFO] craft or beings originate from Outer Space. The whole phenomenon involves a mass of features that conflict with modern science, and many researchers now believe that more than one type of being may be involved, some of them originating from Outer Space and some of them of an 'interdimensional' nature, and consequently possibly from some unknown aspect of our own World.[16]

The problem for much of the scientific and secular world today is with the whole interdimensional nature of UFOs, because that line of investigation contributes to a host of reports about angels, demons, fairies, incubi, and other supernatural entities. In fact, Jacques Vallée, the French astronomer and ufologist introduced earlier in this book, admits in his book, *Passport to Magonia*, "I am also tempted to accept as a working hypothesis that in times remote contact occurred between human consciousness and another consciousness, variously described as demonic, angelic, or simply alien."[17]

The whole concept of an interdimensional (spiritual) cause for UFOs "seems incompatible with prevailing scientific and religious paradigms," writes Missler. He continues, "To many 'naturalists' this thought is anathema because it introduces the very real possibility of angels, demons, and God forbid, GOD!"[18]

We may never persuade some scientists and otherwise skeptics there is an interdimensional component to UFOs. Yet, at present, there is no other reasonable explanation unless you have faith in the absolute remote prospect that aliens are the cause of UFOs. Perhaps both "causes" require faith, but certainly the alien cause requires far more than the time-tested spiritual cause.

3. Great End-times Deception: Spirits as Alien UFOs

Now that I've established, using Dr. Missler's work, that disembodied demonic spirits are part of human history, we come to the question: What role do these spirits play, if any, as UFOs in ushering in the prophetic end times?

Certainly, Jesus provided several examples of events to precede the prophetic end times that might be attributed to demonic spirits. For example, in Luke 21:10–11 (NIV), our Lord said:

Nation will rise against nation, and kingdom against kingdom. There will be great earthquakes, famines and pestilences in various places, and fearful sights and great signs from heaven.

What does Jesus mean by "fearful sights and great signs from heaven"? Does that mean asteroids, space junk, and solar flares, or does it mean demonic spirits that create UFO scares? All of these are possible.

Keep in mind humankind has experienced UFO sightings for thousands of years, as indicated in chapter 2 of this book. Today, our culture continues to explore the possible causes of UFOs. What seems to be clear is something is happening that includes what Jesus predicted: "fearful sights and great signs from heaven." (Luke 21:11, KJV). Perhaps what we are seeing today is an example of the coming great deception associated with the end times. After all, the UFO phenomenon is likely demonic in nature and deceives us behind the lie that the threat is something else, perhaps aliens from outer space, albeit doubtful, given the explanation of the extraordinary parameters for such visitations provided in chapter 15.

Alternatively, we need to appreciate what the Lord states in Matthew 24:24 (NIV): "For false messiahs and false prophets will appear and perform great signs and wonders to deceive, if possible, even the elect." That deception may well mean demonic beings are presented as so-called aliens, promising much to win our allegiance.

We have already seen this Scripture played out in history. Specifically, keep in mind that demonic beings presented themselves as angels of light to Joseph Smith, the founder of Mormonism, and Muhammad, the founder of Islam. Both oppose the gospel of Christ. Therefore, it's not hard to imagine that demonic beings, Satan's proxies, could present themselves as alien beings to deceive the world.

As established earlier in this book, the Bible does not address the existence of alien beings. However, it does tell us about visitors from another world—the spiritual realm—and they will tempt humankind with their superior wisdom to ensnare us. Unfortunately, we are gullible and must be careful not to be deceived by these spirits.

When these spiritual deceivers come, they will unite at the prophetic end times with most of humankind under the power and influence of the Antichrist. The coming Antichrist, presumably Satan (or his human surrogate), certainly has many characteristics attributed to the fictional accounts of alien beings that might visit Earth. For example, as some alien accounts suggest, those beings will promise a nirvana on Earth: globalism, ecumenism, personal immortality, pantheism (Genesis 3:15), and moral relativism, and they will declare the Bible is false. Not surprisingly, these beliefs match Satan's agenda as seen throughout Scripture and promote "the coming global confederacy [one-world government under the Antichrist]," as addressed by Missler.[19]

Of course, as a ruse, the Antichrist may well pretend to be an alien with the powers just outlined, but he will not attribute them to God. Rather, to secure the support of the majority of people, the alien pretending to be the Antichrist (or a proxy) will "boast of a connection with the powerful, god-like alien entities who have, it is believed, helped [humankind] overcome the problems of poverty, famine, disease, war, and the pain of cultural and religious division," wrote Missler.[20]

Not surprisingly, this demonic Antichrist will offer a plan to "unify humankind" by providing answers to our global mess as outlined above. And of course, this Antichrist "savior" will demonstrate power, like so many UFOs do by "[superseding] the laws of physics and perform, in effect supernatural signs and wonders," wrote Missler. This Antichrist will also provide, according to Missler, a deceptive and winsome "message of love, unity, and peace, along with answers we need backed up by supernatural signs and wonders, the peoples of the world will willingly set aside their differences, lay down their weapons to follow him, and even worship him as god!"[21]

Today, as we anticipate the prophetic end times, according to Missler, we are surrounded by demonic beings, the "seed" of the Nephilim, disembodied spirits that contribute to UFOs and other paranormal activities, which act as the Antichrist's advance guard preparing the way for him by distracting and deceiving humankind.

Don't believe that is possible?

Keep in mind that the skills attributed to Satan and his cohort to masquerade as extraterrestrials includes their ability and power not only to distract and deceive, but also to manipulate matter within our space-time domain. Like the UFOs described in earlier chapters of this book, these demons, the disembodied Nephilim, can come and go in the blink of an eye; appear to be under intelligent control (which they are—Satan); although mostly invisible, they do appear and bring messages; they can't be proven by our science to exist but can alter space and time; and much more.

Another indicator of end-times prophecy is the Antichrist's ability to create a global religious following. Can demonic alien pretenders generate "a global ecumenical religious belief system," something akin to what we expect in the end times? Yes, because already the UFO phenomenon inspires people across the world to join in religion-like belief and the related fear of the unknown is a strong motivator as well.

In fact, that outcome is a foregone conclusion.

We see in Revelation 13:8 (NIV):

All inhabitants of the earth will worship the beast—all whose names have not been written in the Lamb's book of life, the Lamb who was slain from the creation of the world.

Then Daniel 7:25 (NIV) indicates that Antichrist is a cultic leader: "He shall speak against the Most High and oppress his holy people and try to change the set times and the laws." Further, we read in 2 Thessalonians 2:4 that Antichrist "will oppose and will exalt himself over everything that is called God or is worshiped, so that he sets himself up in God's temple, proclaiming himself to be God." Therefore, we can rightly conclude, Antichrist accepts the worship of people across the world.

Even the secular world confirms as much. Louis Whitley Strieber, an American author of fiction and advocate of paranormal concepts, addresses the implications of the UFO phenomenon to promote the worship of the coming Antichrist, as cited by Missler. Strieber wrote:

> It is a social issue of the utmost importance, because it has all the potential of a truly powerful idea to enter unconscious mythology and there to generate beliefs so broad in their scope and deep in their impact that they emerge with religious implications for the surrounding culture. The only thing now needed to make the UFO myth a new religion of remarkable scope and force is a single undeniable sighting.[22]

French astronomer and ufologist Jacques Vallée concurs that the power of the UFO phenomenon can indeed inspire a widespread religious following. He states:

> I think the stage is set for the appearance of new faiths, centered on the UFO belief. To a greater degree than all the phenomena modern science is confronting, the UFO can inspire awe, the sense of the smallness of man, and an idea of the possibility of contact with the cosmic. The religions we have briefly surveyed began with the miraculous experiences of one person, but today there are thousands for whom the belief in otherworldly contact is based on intimate conviction, drawn from what they regard as personal contact with UFOs and their occupants.[23]

This strong delusion of the end times is mentioned in 2 Thessalonians 2:9–12 (NIV):

> The coming of the lawless one will be in accordance with how Satan works. He will use all sorts of displays of power through signs and wonders that serve the lie, and all the ways that wickedness deceives those who are perishing. They perish because they refused to love the truth and so be saved. For this reason, God sends them a powerful delusion so that they will believe the lie and so that all will be condemned who have not believed the truth but have delighted in wickedness.

How Demonic Spirits Fit the UFO Profile

Finally, below I briefly address why demonic spirits satisfy the UFO profile as opposed to other possible causes like "new" physics and alien beings visiting Earth.

This connect-the-dots effort is not intended to be exhaustive, but suggests demonic spirits do appear to answer a lot of our questions about UFOs. Like Dr. Graham, I accept the possibility that God made other beings outside of the Earth, but because of the challenges outlined in chapter 15, I doubt any of those presumed aliens, if they exist, have yet visited this planet for the reasons stated earlier in this book.

Religious history records significant spirit-related events, and some also embrace the possibility of aliens. Most faith groups acknowledge the existence of an unseen (spiritual) realm that interacts with humankind. Those faith groups are inclined to believe UFOs are caused by spirits. Meanwhile, some of the same people are open to the possibility that God created—or if you are an evolutionist, life evolved—living beings elsewhere across this massive universe. However, the possibility that life from other places has visited Earth is viewed skeptically by many of those same people.

The UFO phenomenon is global. The number of UFO sightings has waxed and waned throughout history. Although most are eventually explained as natural phenomena, there remains a significant number that are inexplicable, and the profile of that cohort tends to be consistent across time. Further, based on Luis Elizondo's Pentagon reports, the unexplainable have common traits that seem to fit with the spiritual realm. Those include, as outlined earlier in this book:[24]

Anti-gravity propulsion: Evidently, many UFOs have an anti-gravity propulsion system that allows them to travel at significant speeds, disappear quickly, or hover silently.

Sudden and instantaneous acceleration: Some UFOs are tracked at speeds thirty times the speed of sound and others appear to effortlessly transition from one medium like air into another like water. They also hover and make turns that, according to one US Navy F-18 pilot, would turn any human body into paste.[25]

Hypersonic speeds without signatures: UFOs leave no vapor trails, nor do they create sonic booms. That means they operate in an atmosphere-free environment and use an anti-gravity propulsion system.

Unclear images: UFO sightings, even when caught on radar or by cameras, never present a clear, detailed view. In fact, there seems to be a glow or haze (perhaps a cloud) around the objects. That explains why most sightings are described as "bright lights or bright glows" and are never described in detail.

Navigation across different mediums—space, air, and water: UFOs move easily in and between different environments.

Spiritual beings are capable of displaying all of these traits. These UFO characteristics that track back thousands of years defy our laws of physics and aerodynamics, yet very much parallel the capabilities associated with spiritual beings discussed in the previous chapters. Both angels and demons are described as strong and powerful. They are capable of tremendous speeds that defy our physics. They can appear to people but tend to be invisible most of the time. Although angels do not possess physical bodies, disembodied demonic spirits, as explained above, do seek to possess human flesh. Outlandish? Not at all! Recall the case of Jesus confronting "two men who were demon-possessed" (Matthew 8, NIV). Those demons begged Jesus to embody them in the herd of pigs rather than leave them in a disembodied spiritual state.

US government in possession of "biologics": The disembodied demonic spirit issue might explain, if true, the allegation made by David Grusch, a former military intelligence officer, in his July 26, 2023, testimony before a US House of Representatives oversight committee. He alleged the government "absolutely" has "biologics" of "non-human origins." The "biologics" allegation might be explained by the dead body of a human or animal that had previously been possessed by a demonic spirit and associated with what remains labeled a UFO.[26]

Alien abduction or possession: Alien abduction is evidently, according to the Roper Center for Public Opinion Research, a real phenomenon. Nevertheless, it is associated with a variety of mental issues, according to the scientific world. It can also be explained by demonic possession and/or manipulation.[27]

The scientific world has few useful explanations for the capabilities evidenced by the often-chronicled UFO traits and observations above. Until there are better explanations, I conclude that some of the UFOs across time should be attributable to spiritual beings.

Conclusion

In the twenty-first century, interest in UFOs is spiking. Biblical history indicates there is good reason to believe the seed of fallen angels who mated with female humans (Genesis 6) might have survived the Flood or restarted after that event to once again produce monstrous offspring via disembodied spirits that could very well be evident as UFOs today. Those spirits could be Satan's mechanism to deceive humankind as our world rushes headlong into the prophetic end times. Further, the Antichrist, perhaps a faux alien, intends to force humanity to abandon God and embrace the false promises of a global religion, the greatest deception in history, which ushers in the Second Coming of Christ.

AFTERWORD

For we wrestle not against flesh and blood, but against
principalities, against powers, against the rulers of the darkness
of this world, against spiritual wickedness in high places.

(EPHESIANS 6:12, KJV)

This is perhaps my most important work to date because of the long-term geopolitical, scientific, and spiritual implications. After all, the UFO phenomenon is arguably the most complex, enduring challenge we face that potentially touches every aspect of our lives. Yet, at this point, and after thousands of years of sightings with many incidents still inexplicable, no one has any credible answers.

UFOs might present an existential threat to humankind or they could be evidence of the unseen realm providing a glimpse of the coming prophetic end times. It is hard to know what to believe, because the government seems to be quite evasive on the topic and many UFO-related bizarre stories and conspiracy theories are deeply embedded in our culture. Truth in this realm seems to be elusive.

The bottom line for humankind regarding this issue is the loaded question: Are we alone in this vast universe? Further, for many of the spiritually minded readers of *Out of This World*, there are critical questions that must be addressed as well: Did the God of the Bible create other beings elsewhere in this massive universe? If there are other beings (aliens), are they reaching out to us, and if so, how should we relate to them? What are the answers to tough doctrinal issues about the evidence of aliens' existence might raise, such as regarding salvation? Alternatively, we must ask: Are UFOs evidence of the battle in the spiritual realm that occasionally lifts its invisible veil to allow humanity to catch a glimpse of the metaphysical, and is their appearance a precursor to the coming prophetic end times?

Are we alone in this vast universe?[1]

Below consider a review of the content of *Out of This World* and some of the conclusions along the pathway that have brought us to this point.

In the first section, we considered the metaphysical and paranormal issues UFOs raise, followed by an overview of the ancient records of some of these incidents; and, for the Christian, we briefly examined what the Bible has to say on the issue, which isn't much.

The conclusions from this section are that the complex milieu of abstract terms like "metaphysical" and "paranormal" are part of the UFO verbal landscape, which must be understood in order to sort out fact from fiction. Further, UFO sightings made in both ancient secular and religious history have remarkable parallels with modern sightings, suggesting perhaps the same causes are evident today. Also, although the Bible includes hundreds of references to angels and demons, evidence of "alien" beings is absent from the Scriptures.

Section two explores the record of UFO sightings after World War

II, the way those incidents are documented, and government programs and the research approaches used to catalog and study the phenomenon. Unfortunately, most of those efforts haven't seriously dealt with the subject in a credible, standardized, scientific manner; as a result, most people across the globe are understandably skeptical about the assurances their governments and the scientific community offer.

Some of the most inexplicable UFO incidents, what some people label as absolutely bizarre, are profiled in this book, including what makes them so extraordinary. Though, as I point out, the vast majority of UFOs are eventually identified as being caused by either natural phenomena, like weather or meteors, or by man-made objects like satellites and aircraft. The minority remain truly inexplicable, and such sightings began coming to humanity's attention thousands of years ago—and similar sightings are reported across every corner of the Earth even today.

This section concludes with the often-repeated statement: The absence of evidence is not evidence of absence. In other words, the fact that we can't explain the cause(s) of many UFOs doesn't mean they are or are not aliens, spirits, or evidence of "new" physics. In fact, we can't answer the question, because our UFO sighting documentation is poor and we too often fail to expose those incidents to rigorous scientific analysis. Besides, until recently, few officials took the subject seriously and discouraged thoughtful study by associating these incidents with a stigma.

Section Three elaborates on what key institutions of society as well as the general population think about UFOs and what, if anything, they do or want to do about the phenomenon. It is noteworthy that our scientific community is fickle about the issue, primarily because of the age-old stigma associated with these incidents and the prevalence of wacko conspiracy theories steeped in UFO folklore. Yes, there are some scientists addressing the UFO challenge, but most avoid it like the plague. Even theologians from all religious backgrounds are not unified about the mystery, while the interest on the issue among the general population is exploding.

I concluded this section by stating that our scientific community isn't totally aboard with investigating UFOs, and we haven't yet provided those few who are willing to undertake legitimate investigations with sufficient resources, much less encourage broad-scale collaboration and require sound research standards. Also, our religious communities remain divided, especially over the issues with metaphysical and doctrinal implications. However, it's clear that a significant number of people around the world believe UFOs are evidence of alien life, according to surveys, although many citizens remain skeptical.. Perhaps that is because, thanks to corrupted media, they are not hearing the truth from the scientific community and our various governments.

It is indeed unfortunate the US government until recently has tended to treat this mystery as a distraction that must be addressed using public relations ploys, nothing more. Therefore, as explained in section four, instead of taking this issue seriously, our authorities have in the past fed us excuses and assaulted our intelligence by dismissing some of the most troubling incidents. Of course, it doesn't help that members of the news and entertainment media make a game of these sightings and fuel speculation about the worst possibilities. Hollywood in particular too often jokingly sees this as an opportunity to exploit gullible people in order to line their own pockets.

Section five recommends not only five "take-aways" based on the information and data about UFOs presented in the first eleven chapters of *Out of This World*, but then recommends a strategy for the government to address the matter. Further, that strategy considers implications for each of the five "take-aways," as well as how government ought to recruit key public institutions to help discover and publicize the truth about the issue.

I conclude that section to recommend Project UFO, a whole-of-government commitment to find the cause(s) of UFOs, something akin to the 1960s' Project Apollo, America's program to put a man on the moon. Anything short of a similar herculean effort will be insufficient, because too much is at stake.

Section six primarily addresses the Christian public. What should be the Christian response to the issue? Then we consider the possible prophetic end-times role of UFOs, with an emphasis on the spiritual manipulation of the widespread view that aliens are a reality.

I concluded this final section affirming that I believe many of the UFOs across history have a spiritual origin; others are likely natural phenomena. However, I don't dismiss the remote possibility that God created life elsewhere in this vast universe. Further, I believe the spirits behind UFOs are mostly demonic; perhaps they are traceable to the Nephilim first introduced in Genesis 6:4 and are now building a head of steam to usher in the prophetic end times.

Thus, the challenge for all of us is to answer the question: Are UFOs evidence of far-superior alien beings visiting from planets light years away, or are they tangible evidence of the increased activity in the spiritual realm preparing perhaps to usher in the prophetic end times? I believe, as stated above, they are more likely spirits as opposed to aliens, and I doubt many of the yet-to-be-explained incidents are evidence of "new" physics, but I am willing to be proven wrong on that cause as well.

So far, however, most scientists and government agents have naively discarded the paranormal, the spiritual possibility as a cause in favor of the alien alternative. I consider that a mistake, because believing in the evolution of alien beings from non-life material—evidence of a belief in the Darwinian theory of life—is far more difficult to embrace than believing in a supernatural life-giver, the creator God, especially given thousands of years of biblical evidence.

Therefore, in these tenuous times, we need a serious effort across government and the scientific and religious communities to attack this issue with a maximum effort—such as the recommended Project UFO—because these inexplicable incidents could well present a truly existential threat for all of us. Further, and even though the atheists and agnostics will object, the Bible that I believe speaks of the end times, identifying future incidents and entities remarkably similar to many descriptions of the unidentified flying objects that span humanity's history on Earth.

Let me conclude *Out of This World* with a special warning for the evangelical church, which has been taken captive by the UFO craze much as has the balance of society. That's a tragic mistake and dishonors our God!

The truth is, in the twenty-first century, and even among Bible-believing Christians, we no longer put weight in God's Word. In fact, as David F. Wells, a professor at Gordon-Conwell Theological Seminary, writes in his book, *God in the Wasteland*:

> It is one of the defining marks of Our Time that God is now weightless. I do not mean by this that he is ethereal but rather that he has become unimportant. He rests upon the world so inconsequentially as not to be noticeable. He has lost his saliency for human life.[2]

Dr. David Schrock, my pastor, applied Wells' "weightless" allegation to evangelicals and how many of us share anxiety about distractions like UFOs. He explained that we "have little ballast to hold" us in place, "and little grace and truth to see how much culture has shaped" our lives "and how little Christ has."[3]

"What the church needs more than anything today is a vision of a holy and loving God, sovereign over all life," which includes potentially when we face frightening issues associated with UFOs—alien beings, spirits, and the like. More specifically, what the twenty-first century Christian needs today is "to recapture the glory of God, or better we need to be captured by God's glory," wrote Dr. Schrock.[4]

Appendix A

SIGNIFICANT UFO SIGHTINGS AND AREAS ASSOCIATED WITH UAPS

B elow are some of the most tantalizing examples of humanity's search for signs of extraterrestrial life and the paranormal, a supplement to those identified in chapter 5. In this list are some places across the globe associated with frequent UFO sightings and alleged evidence of extraterrestrial life. Each example includes a link to a publicly available video of UAPs or an explanation of the UFO-related location.

US Government's Area 51
Groom Lake, Nevada

This is the most famous spot often associated with UFOs and extraterrestrial life, perhaps because it is closed to the public. There are rumors the US government holds at this desert facility, eighty-five miles north of Las Vegas, Nevada, crashed alien craft and out-of-this world "biologics" of strange creatures and technologies light years more advanced than ours.[1] A video introducing Area 51 is found at this link: https://www .youtube.com/watch?v=ki1m0z3v1kc&ab_channel=AmericanEye.

UFO Capital of the World
San Clemente, Chile

Hundreds of UFO sightings have been reported near San Clemente, Chile, in recent decades. The site is so popular the Chilean tourism board established an official trail—the UFO Trail—in 2008. A video

introducing Chile's UFO capital is found at this link: https://www
.youtube.com/watch?v=fV_QZKqwRs4&ab_channel=EVIDEN-
CIAYt%C3%BAquecrees%3F

Perm Anomalous Zone
Molebka, Russia

This mysterious, isolated area—Russia's "Area 51"—is known for
reports that wristwatches stop dead at the site; people visiting Molebka
hear strange, rushing sounds emanating from the heavens; visitors claim
to see UFOs around the zone; and some observers even report seeing actual alien creatures. A video profiling Russia's Perm Anomalous
Zone is available at this link: https://www.youtube.com/watch?v=S3f-
55hTG79Y&ab_channel=UFONEARSUN-myunhauzen74.

UFO Capital of Australia
Wycliffe Well, Australia

Evidently, Wycliffe Well, Australia, has become famous for sightings
of UFOs for decades. The area is populated by alien-themed manne-
quins resting outside many commercial establishments, thus giving
the town an amusement park feeling. A video highlighting the UFO
capital of Australia is available at this link: https://www.youtube.com
/watch?v=IACvBqNOYGA&ab_channel=WhyGoTravel.

International UFO Lab
Fukushima, Japan

The International UFO Lab opened on June 24, 2021, to collect,
analyze, and disclose information on sightings of UFOs around the
world. UFOs have long been reported near Senganmori Mountain, a
cone-shaped pinnacle located half an hour's drive from the Fukushima
city center.[2] Further, it likely is not a coincidence that UFO sightings are quite common near nuclear facilities such as the famous
Fukushima Daiichi Nuclear Power Plant, which was severely damaged by an earthquake on March 11, 2011.[3] A video profiling the

International UFO Lab is available at this link: https://video.search.yahoo.com/search/video?fr=mcafee&ei=UTF-8&p=youtube+on+International+UFO+Lab%2C+Fukushima%2C+Japan&type=E211US-0G0#id=1&vid=990e6758a78335b7087c0a67f0c1c224&action=click.

US Navy Encounters with UFOs

In 2019, the US Navy released three videos depicting UFO sightings. A spokesman for the Navy said, "The three videos (one from 2004 and two from 2015) show incursions into our military training ranges by unidentified aerial phenomena [UAPs]." He continued, "The Navy has characterized the observed phenomena as unidentified."[4] The Navy's three videos are available at this link: https://www.youtube.com/watch?v=PkPn-YMp9vI&ab_channel=TheTelegraph.

Civilian Reports of UFOs

Many individual civilian reports of UFO sightings are rather sobering. Here are a few examples of alleged UFO encounters that are inexplicable and are provided for context.

Minnesota Deputy Sheriff Encounters UFO

At approximately 2 a.m. on August 27, 1979, Marshall County Deputy Sheriff Val Johnson was patrolling Minnesota Highway 220 near the town of Stephen, Minnesota, when he saw a beam of light hovering above the otherwise dark road ahead. Soon the light engulfed Johnson and his patrol car, then the thirty-five-year-old deputy lost consciousness for thirty-nine minutes. When he awoke, he was bruised and had eye irritation, which the emergency room physician compared to "welder's burns." His vehicle's windshield was shattered and the radio antenna was bent 90 degrees. The clock on his dashboard mysteriously had somehow lost fourteen minutes.[5] A video report about this is found at the following link for an article by Katie Wermus, "Mysterious UFOs: A Look at Sightings in Minnesota," Fox 9, September 14, 2022: https://www.fox9.com/news/mysterious-ufos-minnesota-2022.

Saucer-shaped Craft Hovers above O'Hare's Gate C17

On November 7, 2006, United Flight 446 was preparing to depart Chicago's O'Hare International Airport for North Carolina when United Airline employees on the tarmac near the aircraft noticed a dark gray metallic craft hovering overhead. At least twelve United employees and others outside the airport spotted the craft around 4:15 p.m. They stated the vehicle hovered for about five minutes before launching out of sight. News of the strange object was reported in a number of media outlets. A Federal Aviation Administration spokesperson said that, because the craft was not detected by radar, there was no investigation.[6] A YouTube program that addresses the event is found at the following link: https://www.youtube.com/watch?v=nntr4rB6F4M&ab_channel=FindingUFO.

British Woman Photographs Unusual Object in the Sky

An East Yorkshire, United Kingdom, woman noticed the unusual object outside her home at 9 p.m. on September 5, 2022. "There were oval-shaped lights next to each other horizontally, and it was very silent," she said. "My first thoughts were that I didn't know what they are, and I thought, 'are my eyes playing tricks on me?'" The woman sent a photo of the object to her friend, Leslie Kean, an investigative journalist and the author of the book *UFOs: Generals, Pilots and Government Officials Go on the Record*. Ms. Kean concluded the encounter was "most likely a UFO sighting."[7] A picture of the object is available at the following link: https://www.hulldailymail.co.uk/news/hull-east-yorkshire-news/ufo-sighting-cottingham-woman-records-7630527.

UFO Near Miss with Passenger Jet at 35,000 Feet over Colombia

In 2023, a passenger on a domestic flight from Bogota to Salento in Colombia recorded a mysterious, black object gliding past. The video can be viewed at this link: https://video.search.yahoo.com/search/video?fr=mcafee&p=Classic+Flying+Saucer+Shaped+UFO+Sighted+During

+A+Commercial+Flight+Over+Colombia.+-+YouTube&type=E210
US0G0#id=1&vid=bb3fb19ee8305e5cde1505c43ff0f02e&action=click.

UFOs in the Bible: Analysis of UFOs in the Bible by the Aetherius Society

According to this group's website, it is "an international spiritual organization dedicated to spreading, and acting upon, the teachings of advanced extraterrestrial intelligences."[8] Founder George King claimed to have contacted extraterrestrial intelligences, whom he referred to as "cosmic masters."[9] The video at this link argues that the Bible is one of the best sources of UFOs: https://www.aetherius.org/evidence /ufos-in-the-bible/.

Mutual UFO Network Case #130602: April 26, 2023, New Brunswick, Canada

MUFON collects UFO reports across the world, such as the following 2023 incident occurring over the city of Moncton, New Brunswick, Canada. The MUFON report states:

> The witness did draw a pencil sketch of what they saw and provided a short narrative as follows: "Travelling east on Killam Drive in Moncton NB, I was near the overpass for Wheeler Blvd in my car. I am not exactly sure what I spotted in the sky above the coliseum, cloud cover was low. Object was all white with two windows that I could see, at first, I thought a plane but it was far too low in the sky and was not moving. I continued watching as I approached the coliseum parking lot, the object eventually faded out of site or into the clouds by the time I approached Millenium Drive. I would estimate it was 500 ft above the ground, approximately 70 ft in width, appeared to have wings at first glance."[10]

A 2018 video taken by a drone also over New Brunswick, Canada shows another UFO over the city of Moncton. The witness description states:

Caught on video while flying my drone. Drone was at approx. 30m heading in a NW direction. I am located in North West Moncton New Brunswick and on June 4th, 2018 I was flying my DJI Phantom 4 Advanced drone at an altitude of 30 meters (100 ft) and at 54kph (30mph) while capturing video footage. The video had been on my hard drive since then and on Feb. 18, 2019 I was reviewing the footage and came across this interesting "UFO" as it ascended in front of a distant tree line and sped towards and pass my drone. At first, I thought it was a bird, so I rewound the clip for a second look and was amazed at the speed it was travelling. I am submitting 2 video clips; one at the recorded speed and one that I slowed down. I believe that at the speed it is going it is impossible for it to be a bird or drone. Although I was just 100 m. from the drone at the time I did not hear any sound from it in passing.

The video of the UFO is available here: https://www.youtube .com/watch?v=EHnAuuFHuLY&ab_channel=4KRelaxationChannel.

Appendix B

UFO RESOURCES

There are many resources related to matters regarding UFOs, especially documents released by the US government. A few websites that list journal articles and other references are identified below. Further, many other UFO-related websites and references are cited throughout this book.

"An Extensive List of Peer Reviewed Scientific Papers on UFOs over the Last 40 Years. What Have I Missed?" See that list once you sign in at:

> **Scientific and scholarly articles about UFOs:** Canadian ufologist Chris Rutkowski provides a list of peer-reviewed articles on UFOs at his blogspot. He writes, "Despite what you may have heard from skeptics and believers alike, science has taken the subject of UFOs seriously on many, many occasions. Dozens of scholarly and academic articles have appeared in peer-reviewed journals all along." See the list at: https://uforum. blogspot.com/2022/01/scientific-and-scholarly-articles-about. html?fbclid=IwAR1dU9OxUP-32DBZHwvRvYj9UStBaku-VTK1_THGHwFCqoiyCMQUcGTctJ_w.

Galileo Project:

> The goal of the Galileo Project is to bring the search for extraterrestrial technological signatures of Extraterrestrial Technological Civilizations (ETCs) from accidental or anecdotal

observations and legends to the mainstream of transparent, validated and systematic scientific research. This project is complementary to traditional SETI, in that it searches for physical objects, and not electromagnetic signals, associated with extraterrestrial technological equipment.[1]

The founder of the Galileo Project is Avi Loeb, the...

...chair of Harvard's astronomy department, director of the Institute of Theory and Computation at the Harvard-Smithsonian Center for Astrophysics, founding director of the Black Hole Initiative, author of four books and more than 700 scientific papers, [and] one of *Time* magazine's 25 most influential people in space science in 2012."[2] The website for the Galileo Project is found at https://projects.iq.harvard.edu/galileo/home.

Barry Greenwood's UFO Archive: The website featuring this archive states:

What we wish to do here is provide some basics on unidentified flying objects and related aerial peculiarities, coupled with bringing into the open obscure, hard-to-find bits of UFO history from the backwaters of this much maligned topic. This comes from nearly fifty years of our close involvement monitoring the various forms odd aerial phenomena have taken, from aerolites, to airships, to mystery aeroplanes, to ghost rockets, to flying saucers and to the modern views of UFOs. See http://www.greenwoodufoarchive.com/.

The National UFO Reporting Center Online Database: UFO reports are accessed at NUFORC's website based on event date, state/country, shape of UFO and date posted. See the link at https://nuforc .org/databank/.

Declassified UFO-related Records from the CIA: Approximately 2,780 pages of CIA documents detailing US government findings on UFOs are available to read and download at the Black Vault's collection here:

https://www.theblackvault.com/documentarchive/ufos-the-central-intelligence-agency-cia-collection/.

The US government's "All-domain Anomaly Resolution Office (AARO)": The Pentagon's AARO leads the US government's...

...efforts to address Unidentified Anomalous Phenomena (UAP) using a rigorous scientific framework and a data-driven approach. Since its establishment in July 2022, AARO has taken important steps to improve data collection, standardize reporting requirements, and mitigate the potential threats to safety and security posed by UAP. See https://www.aaro.mil/.

Mutual UFO Network (MUFON): MUFON provides an online database of UFO sightings for its membership. The website outlines MUFON's goals:

I. Investigate UFO sightings and collect the data in the MUFON Database for use by researchers worldwide. II. Promote research on UFOs to discover the true nature of the phenomenon, with an eye towards scientific breakthroughs, and improving life on our planet. III. Educate the public on the UFO phenomenon and its potential impact on society.

See https://mufon.com/mission-statement-and-goals%e2%80%8b/.

MuckRock Uses FOIA (Freedom of Information Act) to Promote Transparency:

MuckRock is a non-profit, collaborative news site that brings together journalists, researchers, activists, and regular citizens to request, analyze, and share government documents, making politics more transparent and democracies more informed."

MuckRock's website includes a number of declassified UFO-related US government documents secured through FOIA requests. See https://www.muckrock.com/talk/ufo/.

List of Reported UFO Sightings: Wikipedia hosts a list of UFO sightings beginning with antiquity to the present. These entries are well-documented here: https://en.wikipedia.org/wiki/List_of_reported_UFO_sightings#cite_note-8.

List of UFO Sightings in the U.S., 1942–2023: "UFO Sightings in the United States," accessed October 29, 2023, https://en.wikipedia.org/wiki/UFO_sightings_in_the_United_States.

UFO Files: This site claims that "this is quite possibly the largest collection of publicly accessible UFO documents in the world, drawing from as many sources and countries as possible." See https://that1archive.neocities.org/subfolder1/ufo-files.

List of Reported UFO Sightings, Antiquity to Twenty-first Century: Wikiwand reports:

> This is a list of notable reported sightings of unidentified flying objects (UFOs) and related claims of close encounters or abductions. UFOs are generally considered to include any perceived aerial phenomenon that cannot be immediately identified or explained. Upon investigation, most UFOs are identified as known objects or atmospheric phenomena, while a small number remain unexplained.
>
> See https://www.wikiwand.com/en/List_of_UFO_sightings.

The UFO Chronicles: This website advertises itself as "UFO News: Current & Historic Reports from Around the World." It provides ready access to an assortment of recent and historic materials related to UFOs. See the link at https://www.theufochronicles.com/.

Appendix C

NOTABLE UFO HOAXES

UFO hoaxes give serious ufologists and the entire effort to investigate the phenomenon a bad name and understandably are a significant distraction. Unfortunately, UFO hoaxes are part of the reality of our culture. Why? People seek to believe something extraordinary. There is a human desire, as explained in the preface of this book, to fill a void in our lives. However, if we don't invite the true God of creation into our hearts, we fill it with things like UFO hoaxes, and there are plenty to consider.

Keith Kloor wrote an opinion article on UFO hoaxes for *Scientific American* titled "Why We Can't Quit Them." He concluded the piece with the following paragraph:

> Pop culture needs a consistent diet of this junk food to meet our incessant UFO hunger. Will we ever kick the habit? UFO promoters obviously don't think so. In recent days, the 'whistleblower' has spoken out more to say that the multiple space alien crafts retrieved by the U.S. military are the size of football fields and held by unnamed U.S. defense contractors. Additionally, he suggested that the Vatican is involved in the cover-up and that, oh, by the way, people have been murdered to keep all this hushed up.[1]

Below are a few examples of UFO hoaxes that have captivated the masses.

War of the Worlds: Arguably the most famous UFO-related hoax was the 1938 mastermind of American actor and filmmaker Orson Welles, which created near mass hysteria. On October 30, 1938, Welles' radio broadcast began with an "introduction presenting the Mercury Theater's update of writer H. G. Wells' science fiction novel *The War of the Worlds,* but unfortunately, many people were listening to a popular ventriloquist on another station" until moments prior and "therefore missed the disclaimer." An article in the *Readers' Digest* explained:

Welles' take on Wells' Martian invasion tale started with a weather report and a concert live from the Hotel Park Plaza before news alerts about explosions on Mars, a meteor crashing into a New Jersey farm, and eventually aliens with tentacles, heat rays, and poisonous gas broke in. Terrified announcers were then saying cylinders had landed in Chicago and St. Louis, 7,000 National Guardsmen had been wiped out, and that people were fleeing.[2]

The writer of the article on hoaxes elaborated:

Only the panic part turned out to be real as potentially a million listeners thought Earth was under attack. People crowded the highways, armed themselves, begged police for gas masks, requested their power be shut off so the aliens wouldn't see them, and were treated for shock at hospitals. A woman ran into an Indianapolis church during evening service to proclaim, "New York has been destroyed. It's the end of the world. Prepare to die!" When CBS got wind of hysteria, Welles went on the air as himself to remind listeners that it was fiction. The FCC investigation found no wrongdoing but networks agreed to be more cautious regarding programming going forward. The attention scored Welles a Hollywood contract, which enabled him to write, direct, and star in his 1941 masterpiece, *Citizen Kane.*[3]

Other famous hoaxes: Some of the most famous UFO hoaxes are identified by the website Viral Ventura, which states, "As much as people tell you they are not interested in UFOs as soon as there is a 'sighting' everyone is suddenly a believer." Below are three examples of UFO hoaxes profiled by Viral Ventura."[4]

Ease of faking UFO photos:

Michael Shermer, the editor of *Skeptic* magazine, released a short video showing his investigation of how easy it can be to fake UFO photos. He had children "make" UFOs using household items, glue, and silver paint, then had the kids photograph their creations hanging by a fishing line against a backdrop of a grey sky.[5]

Eight crop circles:

Strange patterns have appeared in fields for decades, but the most famous outbreak of crop circles happened in England during the 1980s and 90s. When two "con-men in their sixties" stepped forward claiming responsibility for the circles in 1991, the cereal scam appeared to have been exposed. "They called us 'superior intelligence' and this was the biggest laugh of all," said David Chorley, who claimed to have pulled off the hoax with his best mate Doug Bower.[6]

1995 "Alien Autopsy": Spyros Melaris, the producer of the 1995 production "Alien Autopsy," said, "For me, it was just a joke, a bit of fun but I have learned my lesson." The video was promoted as a secret government film from the 1947 Roswell incident. In 2017, Melaris said, "I would like to say now that there is a big part of me that feels remorse" for making the video. "I underestimated the response. The reality is that everybody in the UFO community took this film as the smoking gun, proof of UFOs and aliens."[7] See the film at this link:

https://www.youtube.com/watch?v=CtrR84jboT4&ab_channel=DMAXUK.

Ten-foot alien appears from Las Vegas UFO, 2023: A 2023 video widely shown on social media purported to show a giant creature linked to a "UFO crash" in a residential area of Las Vegas, Nevada. The video, filmed in the night mode, shows a "10ft tall" extraterrestrial, explained an eyewitness.[8]

The article on the incident indicates it is likely a hoax. Specifically, "The audio-video mismatch is often a red flag when it comes to verifying dubious or manipulated content." Further, the alleged alien video shows the date of recording as "2023/05/26," which conflicts with the police report made almost a month later.[9]

The best evidence that the clip is not genuine is that it appears to be a digital creation by a visual effects artist with the TikTok handle "owltreestump," and there is evidence the creator used open-source computer graphics software.[10]

A number of other significant UFO hoaxes are outlined at The UFO Chronicles, https://www.theufochronicles.com/search/label/Hoax.

USE THE QR-CODE BELOW TO ACCESS
MANY SPECIAL DEALS AND PROMOTIONS
ON BOOKS AND FILMS FEATURING DISCOVERY,
PROPHECY, AND THE SUPERNATURAL!

NOTES

Frontmatter

1 Robert Oppenheimer and Albert Einstein, Draft document entitled "Relationships with Inhabitants of Celestrial Bodies," Princeton, New Jersey, June 1947, https://www.academia.edu/7482539/Relationships_with_Inhabitants_of_Celestrial_Bodies_by_Oppenheimer_and_Einstien.

2 Chris Melore, "UFO Sightings in America: Report Reveals Which States Have Most 'Alien' Encounters," StudyFindings, October 22, 2022, https://studyfinds.org/ufo-sightings-usa-most-reports/.

3 Bill Chappell, "The Pentagon Got Hundreds of New Reports of UFOs in 2022, a Government Report Says," NPR, January 13, 2023, https://www.npr.org/2023/01/13/1149019140/ufo-report.

4 Chen Liu, "Stars in the Sky During Night Time," Unsplash, https://unsplash.com/photos/stars-in-the-sky-during-night-time-jgt81f_UDuU.

Section One

1 James Hibberd, "Former Pentagon UFO Official Luis Elizondo to Reveal 'Shocking Details' in New Book," Hollywood Reporter, September 13, 2021, https://www.hollywoodreporter.com/lifestyle/arts/luis-elizondo-ufo-book-1235012266/#!.

Chapter 1

1 "A Compilation of UFO Facts and Quotes," History 101, NICAP.org, accessed October 17, 2023, http://www.nicap.org/history101.htm.

2 NASA, "View of Earth and Satellite," Unsplash, https://unsplash.com/photos/view-of-earth-and-satellite-yZygONrUBe8.

3 "Metaphysics," Stanford Encyclopedia of Philosophy, September 10, 2007, https://plato.stanford.edu/entries/metaphysics/.

4 "Metaphysics," Merriam-Webster.com, accessed October 17, 2023, https://www.merriam-webster.com/dictionary/metaphysics.

5 William Markowitz, "Unidentified Flying Objects: Reported UFOs Cannot Be under Extraterrestrial Control if the Laws of Physics Are Valid," *Science*, September 15, 1967, Vol. 157, Issue 3794, https://www.jstor.org/stable/1722149.

6 Ibid.

7 Ibid. Note: "Most of the energy that we put into rockets doesn't go into getting to space, it goes into staying in space. If you want to escape the gravitational clutches of the Earth altogether, you must achieve a speed of at least 25,000 mph (15,570

km/h), which is around 33 times the speed of sound." Cited from Paul Sutter, "Will We Ever Figure out How to Defy Gravity?" Astronomy, March 14, 2023, https://www.astronomy.com/science/will-we-ever-figure-out-how-to-defy-gravity/.

8 Ibid.

9 Ibid.

10 Ibid.

11 "Metaphysics," Britannica.com, accessed October 17, 2023, https://www.britannica.com/topic/ontology-metaphysics.

12 Ari Joury, "How Ontology and Data Go Hand-in-Hand," Built-In.com, February 1, 2023, https://builtin.com/data-science/ontology.

13 "List of Religious and Spiritual Traditions," Wikpedia, accessed October 17, 2023, https://en.wikipedia.org/wiki/List_of_religions_and_spiritual_traditions.

14 David Salisbury, "Belief in Alien Life Varies Widely by Religion," Futurity, September 30, 2014, https://www.futurity.org/extraterrestrial-life-religion-773862/.

15 Keith Cowing, "NASA's Search for Life: Astrobiology in the Solar System and Beyond," NASA, June 28, 2021, https://astrobiology.com/2021/06/nasas-search-for-life-astrobiology-in-the-solar-system-and-beyond.html.

16 Ling Xi, "Fast, the World's Largest Radio Telescope, Zooms in on a Furious Cosmic Source," Scientific American, October 13, 2021, https://www.scientificamerican.com/article/fast-the-worlds-largest-radio-telescope-zooms-in-on-a-furious-cosmic-source/.

17 "UFO Research: What Is Ufology? What Are Ufologists?" ufologyweb.com, accessed October 17, 2023, https://ufologyweb.com/ufo-research-what-is-ufology/.

18 "Occultism," Merriam-Webster.com, accessed October 17, 2023, https://www.merriam-webster.com/dictionary/occultism.

19 "Spiritualists," Merriam-Webster.com, accessed October 17, 2023, https://www.merriam-webster.com/dictionary/spiritualists.

20 Marco Margaritoff, "The 9 Most Convincing Alien Abduction Stories in Modern History," allthatsinteresting.com, October 7, 2020, https://allthatsinteresting.com/alien-abductions.

Chapter 2

1 Richard B. Stothers, "Unidentified Flying Objects in Classical Antiquity," The Classical Journal, October–November 2007, Vol. 103, No. 1, https://archive.org/details/stothers-2007-ufos.

2 Photo by Luca Giarelli on Creative Commons.

3 Frances Fontaine, Reader's Digest Mysteries of the Unexplained. (Pleasantville, NY: Reader's Digest Association, 1985). "UFO Sightings in Ancient Egypt, Rome, and the Middle Ages." Rense. Web. http://www.rense.com/general7/ages.htm.

4 Jake Carter, "UFOs in Ancient Egypt? The Mystery of the Tulli Papyrus," Anomalien.com, February 20, 2021, https://anomalien.com/ufos-in-ancient-egypt-the-mystery-of-the-tulli-papyrus/.

5 Zecharia Sitchin, The Stairway to Heaven, as cited by Carter, op. cit.

NOTES

6   Edward U. Condon, "Scientific Study of Unidentified Flying Objects," Vision Collection, 1970, https://archive.org/details/scientificstudyo0000cond/page/500/mode/2up?q=tulli.

7   Ibid. And "Boris de Rachewiltz," Wikipedia, accessed November 14, 2023, https://en.wikipedia.org/wiki/Boris_de_Rachewiltz.

8   Ibid. "*The Classical Journal* is the official publication of the Classical Association of the Middle West and South (CAMWS). Established in 1905, the quarterly, peer-reviewed *Classical Journal* features scholarly articles on the literature, culture, and history of Graeco-Roman antiquity. *CJ* also includes select book reviews and a Forum of shorter notes on pedagogical methodologies, technologies, and theory at all levels of classical education." https://press.jhu.edu/journals/classical-journal.

9   Ibid.

10 Ibid.

11 "Aurora," Wikipedia, accessed October 18, 2023, https://en.wikipedia.org/wiki/Aurora.

12 Stothers, op. cit.

13 Ibid.

14 Ibid.

15 Ibid.

16 Ibid.

17 Ibid.

18 Ibid.

19 Ibid.

20 "Ball Lightning," Wikipedia, accessed November 14, 2023, https://en.wikipedia.org/wiki/Ball_lightning.

21 Stothers, op. cit.

22 Ibid.

23 Ibid.

24 Ibid.

25 Mack Maloney, *UFOs in Wartime: What They Didn't Want You to Know.* (New York: Berkley, 2011). As cited in What Did the Ancients See? Unidentified Flying Objects that Made an Impact on Early History | Ancient Origins (ancient-origins.net).

26 Joanna Gillan, "The Mysterious Aboriginal Rock Art of the Wandjina Sky Beings," *Ancient Origins*, November 27, 2021, The Mysterious Aboriginal Rock Art of the Wandjina Sky Beings | Ancient Origins (ancient-origins.net).

27 Ibid.

28 Ibid.

29 John Black, "The Unidentified Flying Objects in the Sky of the Summer's Triumph Tapestry," *Ancient Origins*, December 13, 2013, The unidentified flying objects in the sky of the Summer's Triumph Tapestry | Ancient Origins (ancient-origins.net).

30 Ibid.

31 Daniela Giordano, "Ancient Artists Left Signs for us to Decode. Did They Witness UFOs?," *Ancient Origins*, September 9, 2019, Ancient Artists Left Signs For us to Decode. Did they Witness UFOs? | Ancient Origins (ancient-origins.net).

NOTES

32 "Quimbaya Artifacts," *Ancient Origins*, accessed October 18, 2023, Quimbaya Artifacts | Ancient Origins (ancient-origins.net).

Chapter 3

1 Billy Graham, "Answers," Billy Graham Association, June 19, 2006, https://billy graham.org/answer/what-does-the-bible-say-about-life-on-other-planets-or-does-it -forbid-us-to-believe-there-might-be-intelligent-life-elsewhere-in-the-universe/.

2 "Sanskrit," Merriam-Webster, accessed October 18, 2023, https://www.merriam -webster.com/dictionary/Sanskrit.

3 Enrico Baccarini, "Vimanas in Sanskrit literature," Vaimānika Shāstra, November 3, 2012, https://vaimanika.com/vimanas-in-sanskrit-literature/#:~:text=%E2%80%9CWhen%20morning%20dawned%2C%20Rama%2C%20taking%20the%20Celestial%20Car,sound%20as%20it%20coursed%20along%20its%20airy%20way.%E2%80%9D

4 Ibid.

5 Ibid.

6 John Nail, "Stonehenge England," Pexels, https://www.pexels.com/photo/stonehenge -england-1448136/.

7 Seth Rogovoy, "The Secret Jewish History of UFOs (and Why Ezekiel Might Have Had a Close Encounter)," *Forward*, February 3, 2023, https://forward.com/culture /470977/the-secret-jewish-history-of-ufos-and-why-ezekiel-might-have-had-a-close/.

8 Ibid.

9 Ibid.

10 Ibid.

11 Ibid.

12 Ibid.

13 Rick Pidcock, "With All This Talk of UFOs, What's a Christian to Think?" *Baptist News Global*, June 8, 2021, https://baptistnews.com/article/with-all-this-talk-of-ufos -whats-a-christian-to-think/.

14 In fact, there are ten "words" spoken in Genesis 1. See Genesis 1:3, 6, 9, 11, 14, 20, 24, 26, 28, 29.

15 For a full statement on the one God as three persons, see the Athanasian Creed. Available online at https://www.crcna.org/welcome/beliefs/creeds/athanasian-creed.

16 Dr. David Schrock, "Beholding the Glory of God [sermon title]," Occoquan Bible Church, November 5, 2023.

17 Ibid.

18 Job 38:7, *Ellicott's Commentary*, accessed October 18, 2023, https://biblehub.com /job/38-7.htm.

19 Monami Mukherjee, "Rebel Angels in *Paradise Lost*: Milton's Myth Making in Book 1," Nibble Pop, December 14, 2020, https://nibblepop.com/rebel-angels-in -paradise-lost/.

20 Edward Antonio, "Who Are the Nephilim in the Bible? 4 Origin Theories," Christianity.com, August 17, 2023, https://www.christianity.com/wiki/angels -and-demons/who-were-the-nephilim-in-the-bible.html#google_vignette.

21 Ibid.

22 Tim Callahan, "Ezekiel's Spaceships," *Skeptics Society*, Vol. 12, Nu. 1, 2005, https://www.skeptic.com/eskeptic/05-07-28/.

23 Marcus Lowth, "10 Historic Paintings That Clearly Show UFOs," ListVerse, April 24, 2016, https://listverse.com/2016/04/24/10-historic-divine-paintings-that-clearly -show-ufos/.

24 Ibid.

25 Ibid.

26 Ibid.

27 Ibid.

28 Starbrite A. Sparkles, "Could Jesus Christ Be One of the First Alien Hybrids, the Son of an Extraterrestrial and an Earthly Woman?," *UFO Digest*, April 8, 2012, Could Jesus Christ Be One Of The FIrst Alien Hybrids, The Son Of An Extraterrestrial And An Earthly Woman? - UFO Digest.

Section Two

1 "Stephen Hawking," GreetingIdeas, accessed October 18, 2023 https://greetingideas .com/popular-ufo-quotes-sayings/.

Chapter 4

1 Jeffrey Clark, "UFO Whistleblower Unhappy with Christie Response to Debate Question: 'Americans Deserve Answers…Not Jokes,'" Fox News, August 24, 2023, UFO whistleblower unhappy with Christie response to debate question: 'Americans deserve answers…not jokes' | Fox News.

2 Haziq Mehboob, "A Group of People Standing in Front of a House," Unsplash, https://unsplash.com/photos/a-group-of-people-standing-in-front-of-a-house-HyCO q0772zI.

3 Greg Wehner, "Pentagon to Release Declassified UFO Photos, Videos and Reports on New Website," Fox News, August 31, 2023, https://www.foxnews.com/politics /pentagon-release-declassified-ufo-photos-videos-reports-website.

4 "All-domain Anomaly Resolution Office (AARO)," Department of Defense, accessed October 18, 2023, AARO Home.

5 Stephanie Pappas, "Declassified Military Video Shows 'UFO' Off East Coast," LiveScience.com, March 12, 2018, Declassified Military Video Shows 'UFO' Off East Coast | Live Science.

6 Christopher Wilson, "UFO Hearing: Whistleblower Testifies Government 'Absolutely' Has Possession of 'Nonhuman' Craft," Yahoo News, July 26, 2023, https:// news.yahoo.com/ufo-whistleblower-hearing-house-oversight-non-human-craft-uap -navy-pilots-171759861.html?fr=sycsrp_catchall.

7 Jeffrey Kluger, "The U.S. Government's Long-Awaited UFO Report Is Here. Its Findings?" Time.com, June 4, 2021, https://time.com/6071397/ufo-study/.

8 Jeffrey Kluger, "Congress Is Finally Taking UFOs Seriously, 50 Years after Its Last Hearing on the Mysterious Subject," Time.com, May 17, 2022, https://time.com /6177650/congress-ufo-hearings/.

NOTES

9 Leah Crane, "NASA's UFO Team Discusses Its Findings Publicly for the First Time," *New Scientist*, May 31, 2023, https://www.newscientist.com/article/2376425-nasas -ufo-team-discusses-its-findings-publicly-for-the-first-time/.

10 Ibid.

11 Kluger, "The U.S. Government's Long-Awaited UFO Report Is Here," op. cit.

12 Ibid.

13 Travis Greene, "Data Analysis: Everything You've Ever Wanted to Know about UFO Sightings," *Medium*, July 2, 2018, https://towardsdatascience.com/data-analysis -everything-youve-ever-wanted-to-know-about-ufo-sightings-e16f2ed34151.

14 Ibid.

15 Chris Melore, "UFO Sightings in America: Report Reveals Which States Have Most 'Alien' Encounters," StudyFindings, October 22, 2022, https://studyfinds .org/ufo-sightings-usa-most-reports/.

16 Marek N. Posard, Ashley Gromis, and Mary Lee, "Not the Files," RAND Corporation, 2023, https://www.rand.org/content/dam/rand/pubs/research_reports/RRA 2400/RRA2475-1/RAND_RRA2475-1.pdf.

17 "RAND Corporation," RAND website, accessed October 18, 2023, https://www. rand.org/about.html.

18 Ibid.

19 Ibid.

20 Ibid.

21 Ibid.

22 Ibid.

23 Greg Daughterty and Missy Sullivan, "These 5 UFO Traits, Captured on Video by Navy Fighters, Defy Explanation," History.com, June 5, 2019, https://www .history.com/news/ufo-sightings-speed-appearance-movement.

24 Gideon Lewis-Krause, "How the Pentagon Started Taking U.F.O.s Seriously," *New Yorker*, April 30, 2021, https://www.newyorker.com/magazine/2021/05/10/how -the-pentagon-started-taking-ufos-seriously.

25 Warren Aguis, "5 Characteristics Typical of a UFO Sighting," Llewellyn, March 19, 2021, https://www.llewellyn.com/journal/article/2897

26 "Five Characteristics Unique to UAP's," To The Stars, accessed January 25, 2024, https://tothestars.media/blogs/press-and-news/five-characteristics-unique-to-uaps

27 Daughterty and Sullivan, Op Cit.

28 For further explanation of Elizondo's "Five Observables," see: "You Should Know: Luis Elizondo's Five Observables," The Other Topic, November 7, 2023, You Should Know: Luis Elizondo's Five Observables (substack.com).

29 Ted Roe, "A Preliminary Examination of the Flight Dynamics of Four Profiles of Unidentified Aerial Phenomena, UAP, Commonly Associated with Aviation Safety Incidents as Reported by Pilots," NARCAP.org, October 2019, https://www.narcap .org/blog/flightdynamicsofuap.

30 "Existence of UFOs 'Beyond Reasonable Doubt', Former Pentagon Official Says," *The Independent* (London, England), December 26, 2017.

31 Adam Janos, "Why Have There Been So Many UFO Sightings Near Nuclear Facilities?," History.com, June 23, 2019, https://www.history.com/news/ufos-near-nuclear-facilities-uss-roosevelt-rendlesham.

32 Ibid.

33 Ibid.

34 Ibid.

35 Eric Levenson, "Aliens, Flying Discs and Sightings—Oh My! A Short History of UFOs in America," CNN, September 20, 2019, https://www.cnn.com/2019/09/20/us/ufo-sightings-history-scn-trnd/index.html.

36 Brandon Specktor, "UFOs Left 'Radiation Burns' and 'Unaccounted for Pregnancies,' New Pentagon Report Claims," LiveScience, April 5, 2022, https://www.livescience.com/ufo-report-human-biological-injuries.

37 Ibid.

38 Emma Parry, "UFO Encounters Left Witnesses with Radiation Burns, Brain Problems & Damaged Nerves, Claims Pentagon Docs," *The US Sun*, April 5, 2022, UFO encounters left witnesses with radiation burns, brain problems & damaged nerves, claims Pentagon docs | The US Sun (the-sun.com).

39 Ibid.

40 Jeffrey Kluger, "America's Best Astrophysicists Are Taking UFOs Seriously. Maybe You Should Too," Time.com, June 10, 2022, https://time.com/6186451/nasa-ufo-study/.

Chapter 5

1 "Preliminary Assessment: Unidentified Aerial Phenomena," Office of the Director of National Intelligence, June 25, 2021, a report provided in response to the provision in Senate Report 116-233, accompanying the Intelligence Authorization Act (IAA) for fiscal year 2021. https://www.dni.gov/files/ODNI/documents/assessments/Prelimary-Assessment-UAP-20210625.pdf.

2 Joe Bills, "Are We Alone?" *Yankee*, August 31, 2023, https://newengland.com/yankee/magazine/are-we-alone-a-closer-look-at-new-englands-long-ties-to-the-unexplained/.

3 "The SETI Institute," accessed October 18, 2023, https://www.seti.org/about.

4 Krista Carothers, "9 UFO Sightings No One Can Explain," *Reader's Digest*, August 23, 2023, https://www.rd.com/list/ufo-sightings-no-one-can-explain/.

5 Danie Franco, "A Group of People Standing in Front of a Lighted Archway," Unsplash, https://unsplash.com/photos/a-group-of-people-standing-in-front-of-a-lighted-archway-OF2Jr51vxiI.

6 N. Currie, "'See Something, Say Something': UFO Reporting Requirements, Office of Military Government for Bavaria, Germany May 1948," National Archives, July 5, 2017, https://text-message.blogs.archives.gov/2017/07/05/see-something-say-something-ufo-reporting-requirements-office-of-military-government-for-bavaria-germany-may-1948/.

7 Ibid.

8 Ibid.

9 Ibid.

10 Ibid.

11 Ibid.

12 Ibid.

13 Ibid.

14 Ibid.

15 Ibid.

16 Stefanie Waldek, "History's Most Infamous UFO Sightings of the Modern Era," History.com, December 8, 2020, https://www.history.com/news/historys-most-in-famous-ufo-sightings.

17 "20 UFO Sightings Investigated by the US Government." *International Business Times*, April 27, 2023. This account is recorded in Gray Baker's 1956 book, *They Knew Too Much About Flying Saucers*, https://www.goodreads.com/book/show/2415847.They _Knew_Too_Much_about_Flying_Saucers.

18 Ibid.

19 Natasha Frost, "When Dozens of Korean War GIs Claimed a UFO Made Them Sick," History.com, September 27, 2023, https://www.history.com/news/korean -war-us-army-ufo-attack-illness.

20 Ibid.

21 Ibid.

22 Ibid.

23 "The Strange George Adamski UFO Incident," Coolinterestingstuff.com, November 21, 2018, https://coolinterestingstuff.com/the-strange-george-adamski-ufo-incident.

24 Ibid.

25 Daniel Loxton, "Flying Saucer 'Space Brothers' from Venus!?" *Skeptic*, 2015, Vol. 20, Issue 4.

26 Ibid.

27 Meghan Gunn, "UFO Sightings No One Can Explain," *Newsweek*, September 1, 2021, https://www.newsweek.com/2021/09/10/modern-day-ufo-sightings-no-one -can-explain-1624722.html.

28 Ibid.

29 Ibid.

30 Ibid.

31 Waldek, op. cit.

32 Gunn, op. cit.

33 Waldek, op. cit.

34 Ibid.

35 Gunn, op. cit.

36 Ibid.

37 Chuck Missler, *Alien Encounters*, book excerpt, (Koinonia House Publishing, May 1, 2017) https://khouse.org/articles/2017/1297/.

38 Ibid.

39 "UFOs Sighted, Filmed over Carteret, New Jersey," July 15, 2001, accessed October 23, 2023, https://ufocasebook.com/2008c/cateretnj2001.html#:~:text=CART

ERET%2C%20New%20Jersey%20-%20A%20large%20UFO%20was,2001.%20
Sighting%20on%20Sunday-7%2F15%2F01%2012%3A20%20AM-%2012%3A
30%20AM.

40 Gunn, op. cit.

41 Ibid.

42 Karoun Demirjian, "Pentagon Will Track Unexplained Airborne Objects through New Intelligence Group," *The Washington Post*, November 24, 2021, https://www.washingtonpost.com/national-security/2021/11/24/ufos-pentagon/.

43 Belinda Palmada, "US Government Receives More Than 500 UFO Reports with Hundreds Unexplained," News.com.au, January 15, 2023, https://www.news.com.au/technology/science/space/us-government-receives-more-than-500-ufo-reports-with-hundreds-unexplained/news-story/0667fa5f2cd6524cfa3a4bfd7d6b0fe6.

44 Op. cit., "Preliminary Assessment: Unidentified Aerial Phenomena."

45 Ibid.

46 Ibid.

47 Ibid.

48 J. Allen Hynek, *The UFO Experience: A Scientific Inquiry*,(Da Capo Press, 1998). https://www.amazon.com/UFO-Experience-Scientific-Inquiry/dp/156924782X.

49 Ibid.

50 Suzie Dundas, "Are UFOs Real? Close Encounters of the First, Second and Third Kinds," Howstuffworks.com, September 30, 2021, https://science.howstuffworks.com/space/aliens-ufos/ufo-classification.htm.

51 Ibid.

Chapter 6

1 Julian E. Barnes, "The Truth Has Not Always Been out There," *New York Times*, June 24, 2021, https://www.nytimes.com/2021/06/24/us/politics/ufo-report-us-pentagon.html.

2 Lawrence H. Larsen, "United States Air Force Efforts to Investigate UFOs: Great Plains Encounters," *South Dakota History*, South Dakota State Historical Society, pp. 17–31, 1982, https://www.sdhspress.com/journal/south-dakota-history-12-1/united-states-air-force-efforts-to-investigate-ufos-great-plains-encounters/vol-12-no-1-united-states-air-force-efforts-to-investigate-ufos.pdf.

3 Ibid.

4 Ibid.

5 John Uri, "60 Years Ago: President Kennedy Proposes Moon Landing Goal in Speech to Congress," NASA, May 25, 2021, https://www.nasa.gov/feature/60-years-ago-president-kennedy-proposes-moon-landing-goal-in-speech-to-congress.

6 Keith Kloor, "UFOs Won't Go Away," *Issues in Science and Technology*, Spring 2019, pp. 49–56, https://issues.org/ufos-wont-go-away/.

7 Christopher Dean Hopkins and Giles Snyder, "The Military's UFO Database Now Has Info from about 400 Reported Incidents," NPR, May 17, 2022, https://www.npr.org/2022/05/17/1099410910/ufo-hearing-congress-military-intelligence.

NOTES

8 Ibid.

9 Ibid.

10 Ibid.

11 Photo in public domain: originally published in the United States between 1928 and 1963 and any initial copyright registration with the U.S. Copyright Office was not maintained and/or renewed by *Roswell Daily Record* for the July 8, 1947 issue; section 15 U.S.C. § 1115(b)(4) of the Lanham Act recognizes Fair Use of a newspaper trademark in educational, editorial, and informational media, when cited and to describe the original product or service, under the First Amendment of the United States Constitution regarding freedom of speech and of the press: front page containing headline "RAAF Captures Flying Saucer On Ranch in Roswell Region: No Details of Flying Disk Are Revealed," *Roswell Daily Record* (Roswell, New Mexico; July 8, 1947).

12 Larsen, op. cit., p.20.

13 Ibid.

14 Ibid.

15 Ibid.

16 Ibid.

17 Ibid, p. 22.

18 Evan Andrews, "How the U.S. Air Force Investigated UFOs During the Cold War," History.com, January 15, 2020, https://www.history.com/news/u-s-air-force-closes-the-book-on-ufos-45-years-ago.

19 Ibid.

20 Ibid. And Larsen, op. cit., p. 25.

21 Lewis-Krause, op. cit.

22 Ibid.

23 Ibid.

24 Ibid.

25 Larsen, op. cit., p. 31.

26 Elizbeth Howell, "UFO Watch: 8 Times the Government Looked for Flying Saucers," LiveScience, January 2, 2018, https://www.livescience.com/61310-ufo-government-alien-investigations.html.

27 Ibid.

28 Ibid.

29 Ibid.

30 "President Clinton Statement Regarding Mars Meteorite Discovery," Office of the Press Secretary, The White House, August 7, 1996, https://www2.jpl.nasa.gov/snc/clinton.html///.

31 "Jupiter's Europa Harbors Possible 'Warm Ice' or Liquid Water," NASA, Release 96-164, August 13, 1996, https://www2.jpl.nasa.gov/galileo/status960813.html#:~:text=Tantalizing%20new%20images%20of%20Jupiter%27s%20moon%20Europa%20from,still%20exists%20today%20beneath%20Europa%27s%20cracked%20icy%20crust.

32 "NASA Is Hiding Evidence of Life on Mars Claims Scientist Who Says Has Evidence," Ancient-Code.com, April 20, 2022, https://www.ancient-code.com/nasa-is-hiding-evidence-of-life-on-mars-claims-scientists-who-says-has-evidence/.

33 Ibid.

34 Ibid.

35 Ibid.

36 Elizabeth Howell, "We May Not Be Alone, Former Pentagon UFO Investigator Says," Space.com, December 20, 2017, We May Not Be Alone, Former Pentagon UFO Investigator Says | Space.

37 Howell, "UFO Watch," op. cit.

38 Ryan Morgan, "CIA Declassifies Hundreds of UFO Documents—Here's Where to Find Them," *American Military*, January 14, 2021, https://americanmilitarynews.com/2021/01/the-cia-declassifies-hundreds-of-new-ufo-documents-heres-where-to-find-them/.

39 Hopkins, op. cit.

40 "Fiscal Year 2023 Consolidated Annual Report on Unidentified Anomalous Phenomena," Office of the Director of National Intelligence and The Department of Defense, October 17, 2023.

41 Ibid.

42 Ibid.

43 Ibid.

44 Ibid.

45 Kyla Guifoil, "Pentagon Launches UFO Reporting form," NBC News, November 1, 2023, Pentagon launches UFO reporting form (nbcnews.com).

46 Ibid.

47 Ibid.

48 Ibid.

49 "Unidentified Flying Objects and Air Force Project Blue Book," USAF Fact Sheet 95-03, June 1995, https://www.nsa.gov/portals/75/documents/news-features/declassified-documents/ufo/usaf_fact_sheet_95_03.pdf.

50 "UFO Files," accessed October 18, 2023, https://that1archive.neocities.org/subfolder1/ufo-files.

51 David Tormsen, "10 Official Government Programs That Studied UFOs," ListVerse, March 23, 2015, https://listverse.com/2015/03/23/10-official-government-programs-that-studied-ufos/

52 Ibid.

53 Ibid.

54 Ibid.

55 Ibid.

56 Ibid.

57 Ibid.

58 "National UFO Reporting Center," https://nuforc.org/.

59 "Mutual UFO Network," https://mufon.com/.

NOTES

Section Three

1   Albert Einstein, AZ Quotes, accessed January 25, 2024, https://www.azquotes.com/author/4399-Albert_Einstein

Chapter 7

1   Sarah Lewin, "Winston Churchill on Aliens: 1939 Essay Discovered," LiveScience, February 15, 2017, Winston Churchill on Aliens: 1939 Essay Discovered | Live Science.

2   "What Were Neil Armstrong's Famous First Words on the Moon?," AroundtheO.com, July 16, 2019, https://around.uoregon.edu/content/what-were-neil-armstrongs-famous-first-words-moon.

3   James E. McDonald, "Science in Default: Twenty-Two Years of Inadequate UFO Investigations," noufors.com, December 27, 1969, http://noufors.com/Documents/scienceindefault.pdf.

4   Ibid.

5   Austrian National Library, "Two Men Near Machines," Unsplash, https://unsplash.com/photos/two-men-near-machines-dzXWHBXzYz4.

6   Howell, "UFO Watch," op. cit

7   McDonald, op. cit.

8   Ibid.

9   "Scientist: I Want to Believe in UFOs. Prove Me Wrong." CNN Wire, June 17, 2021, https://www.cnn.com/2021/06/17/opinions/pentagon-ufo-report-opinion-lincoln/index.html.

10   Ibid.

11   Ibid.

12   Jeff Miller, "Evolutionists Have a Blind Faith," *Reason & Revelation*, Apologetics Press, November 2017, https://apologeticspress.org/evolutionists-have-a-blind-faith-5485/.

13   Ibid.

14   Ibid.

15   Ella Morton, "The *X-Files* 'I Want to Believe' Poster's Origin Story," *The New Republic*, December 29, 2015, https://newrepublic.com/article/126715/x-files-i-want-believe-posters-origin-story.

16   Liz Kruesi, "Why Some Scientists Want Serious Research into UFOs," *Science News*, May 19, 2022, https://www.sciencenews.org/article/ufo-science-research-uap-congress-pentagon.

17   Ibid.

18   Ibid.

19   Ibid.

20   Aaron Reichmay, "UFOs Becoming Increasingly Attractive to US Academics—Study," *Jerusalem Post*, May 28, 2023, https://www.jpost.com/science/article-744416#:~:text=Over%20a%20third%20%2837%25%29%20of%20US%20academics%20are,unidentified%20aerial%2Fanomalous%20phenomena%20%28UAPs%29%2C%20a%20new%20study%20revealed.

21 Ibid.
22 Alexander Wendt and Raymond Duvall, "Sovereignty and the UFO," *Political Theory*, Vol. 36, No. 4, August 2008, https://journals.sagepub.com/doi/epdf /10.1177/0090591708317902.
23 Ibid.
24 Reichmay, op. cit.
25 Ibid.
26 Joe Bills, "Are We Alone?" *Yankee*, August 31, 2023, https://newengland.com /yankee/magazine/are-we-alone-a-closer-look-at-new-englands-long-ties-to-the -unexplained/.
27 Ibid.
28 "SALT," accessed November 17, 2023, https://www.salt.org/about/. "SALT is a global thought leadership forum encompassing finance, technology and public policy."
29 Reichmay, op. cit.
30 "Scientific and Scholarly Articles about UFOs," January 24, 2022, https://uforum .blogspot.com/2022/01/scientific-and-scholarly-articles-about.html.
31 Leonard David, "Scientists Try to Get Serious about Studying UFOs. Good Luck with That," *Scientific American*, February 3, 2023, https://www.scientificamerican .com/article/scientists-try-to-get-serious-about-studying-ufos-good-luck-with-that/.
32 Ibid.
33 Ibid.
34 Ibid.
35 Ibid.
36 Ibid.
37 Katrina Miller, "Scientist's Deep Dive for Alien Life Leaves His Peers Dubious," *New York Times*, July 24, 2023, https://www.nytimes.com/2023/07/24/science /avi-loeb-extraterrestrial-life.html.
38 Ibid.
39 Ibid.
40 Ibid.
41 Ibid.
42 Ibid.
43 Ibid.
44 Ibid.

Chapter 8

1   Brandon Ambrosino, "If We Made Contact with Aliens, How Would Religions React?," BBC, December 16, 2016, https://www.bbc.com/future/article/20161215- if-we-made-contact-with-aliens-how-would-religions-react#:~:text=As%20Carl%20 Sagan%20has%20pointed%20out%20in%20%28the,it%20should%20shake%20 our%20beliefs%20to%20the%20core.
2   Courtney Kennedy and Arnold Lau, "Most Americans Believe in Intelligent Life beyond Earth; Few See UFOs as a Major National Security Threat," Pew Research

Center, June 30, 2021, https://www.pewresearch.org/short-reads/2021/06/30/most
-americans-believe-in-intelligent-life-beyond-earth-few-see-ufos-as-a-major-national
-security-threat/#:~:text=As%20an%20unprecedented%20U.S.%20intelligence%20
report%20brings%20new,just%20before%20the%20release%20of%20the%20
government%20assessment.

3   Klaus Brasch, "Do We Really Want to Believe in UFOs? Is Belief in UFOs
    Reassuring to Those Who Fear We Might be Alone in an Otherwise Godless or
    Purposeless Universe?," *Skeptical Inquirer*, Vol. 39, Issue 4, July–August 2015.

4   Jeff Hilles, "There is a God-shaped vacuum in the heart of each man which can-
    not be satisfied by any created thing but only by God the Creator, made known
    through Jesus Christ," *Biblical Christian Worldview*, December 30, 2022, https://
    www.bcworldview.org/there-is-a-god-shaped-vacuum-in-the-heart/.

5   Walter Staggs, "The Pedagogy of Ancient Aliens," *The Christian Century*, September
    2023, https://www.christiancentury.org/article/features/pedagogy-ancient-aliens.

6   Jonathan Martin Pisfil, "A Sign That Says the Truth Is Out There," Unsplash,
    https://unsplash.com/photos/a-sign-that-says-the-truth-is-out-there-NodE_jxsjp0

7   Ibid.

8   Ibid.

9   Richard R. Lingeman, "Erich von Daniken's Genesis," *New York Times*, March 31,
    1974, https://www.nytimes.com/1974/03/31/archives/erich-von-danikens-genesis
    .html

10 Ibid.

11 Ibid.

12 Ibid.

13 Ibid.

14 Staggs, op. cit.

15 Ibid.

16 Anthony Wood, "Former Intelligence Officer Claims U.S. Has Been Recovering
    Non-Human Technology For Decades," IGN, June 7, 2023, https://www.ign.com
    /articles/ufo-non-human-technology-comment.

17 Sean Illing, "The New American Religion of UFOs," Vox, June 4, 2019, https://
    www.vox.com/culture/2019/6/4/18632778/ufo-aliens-american-cosmic-diana
    -pasulka.

18 John A. Saliba, "The Study of UFO Religions," *The Journal of Alternative and
    Emergent Religions*, Vol. 10, Issue 2, November 2006, https://www.jstor.org/stable
    /10.1525/nr.2006.10.2.103.

19 Ninian Smart, *Dimensions of the Sacred: An Anatomy of the World's Beliefs*, (Univer-
    sity of California Press, 1996; as cited in Saliba).

20 Saliba, op. cit.

21 Ibid.

22 Benjamin E. Zeller, "At the Nexus of Science and Religion: UFO Religions," One
    Compass Many Directions, November 1, 2011, https://compass.onlinelibrary
    .wiley.com/doi/abs/10.1111/j.1749-8171.2011.00313.x

23 Ibid.

24 Anthony Wood, "Former Intelligence Officer Claims U.S. Has Been Recovering Non-Human Technology For Decades," IGN.com, June 7, 2023, https://www.ign .com/articles/ufo-non-human-technology-comment.

25 Ibid.

26 Ibid.

27 Ibid.

28 Ibid.

29 Zeller, op. cit.

30 Ibid.

31 Ibid.

32 Ibid.

33 Juli Cragg Hilliard, "Written in the Stars," *Publishers Weekly*, February 10, 2023, https://www.publishersweekly.com/pw/print/20030210/18255-written-in-the-stars .html.

34 Ibid.

35 Ibid.

36 Salbia, op. cit., p. 112.

37 Ibid.

38 Ibid.

39 "Division Overview," NASA, accessed November 17, 2023, https://www.nasa.gov /space-science-and-astrobiology-at-ames/division-overview/.

40 Salbia. op. cit., p. 118.

41 Sarah Pulliam Bailey, "Highly Religious Americans Are Less Likely to Believe Intelligent Life Exists on Other Planets, Survey Says," *The Washington Post*, August 19, 2021, https://www.washingtonpost.com/religion/2021/08/19/religious-americans -intelligent-life-ufos/.

42 Ibid.

43 Ibid.

44 Ibid.

45 Ibid.

46 Ibid.

47 Ambrosino, op. cit.

48 Ibid.

49 Ibid.

50 Ibid.

51 Ibid.

52 Ibid.

53 Ibid.

54 Ibid.

55 Ibid.

56 Ibid.

57 Paul Davies, "E.T. and God," *The Atlantic*, September 2003, https://www.theatlantic .com/magazine/archive/2003/09/et-and-god/376856/.

58 Ibid.
59 Ibid.
60 Ibid.
61 Gerald E. Nora and Nils Blatz, in "Letters to the Editor, Readers Respond to Paul Davies's article, 'E.T. and God,'" *Atlantic Monthly*, September 2003 Issue, November 2003, Vol. 292, Issue 4, pp. 23–30, https://www.theatlantic.com/letters/archive /2018/12/years-must-read-letters-editor/578257/.
62 Ibid.
63 Ibid.
64 Ibid.
65 Ibid.
66 Ibid.
67 Ibid.
68 Ibid.
69 Ibid.
70 Ibid.
71 Ibid.

Chapter 9

1 Quotation of the Day: "NASA's U.F.O. Chief Also an Unidentified Phenomenon," *New York Times*, September 15, 2023, Quotation of the Day: NASA's U.F.O. Chief Also an Unidentified Phenomenon - The New York Times (nytimes.com).
2 Lydia Saad, "Do Americans Believe in UFOs?" Gallup, August 20, 2021, https://news.gallup.com/poll/350096/americans-believe-ufos.aspx.
3 Miriam Kramer, "65% of Americans Believe in Aliens, New Poll Finds," Axios.com, July 6, 2021, https://www.axios.com/2021/07/06/aliens-exist-poll.
4 Iain Marlow and Roxana Tiron, "UFO Sightings Aren't for 'Kooks' Anymore, Lawmaker Says," Bloomberg.com, May 17, 2022, https://www.bnnbloomberg.ca /ufo-sightings-aren-t-for-kooks-anymore-lawmaker-says-1.1767264.
5 Ibid.
6 Jackie Wattles, "Independent Group of Experts and Scientists Releases 33-page Report on UFOs," CNN, September 14, 2023, https://www.cnn.com/2023/09/14 /world/ufo-nasa-uap-report-research-scn/index.html.
7 Ibid.
8 Martha McHardy, "'Alien Corpses' Shown in Mexico Raise Eyebrows among Scientists," *Independent*, September 15, 2023, https://www.aol.com/news/alien-corpses -shown-mexico-raise-191118545.html.
9 Lydia Saad, "Americans Skeptical of UFOs, but Say Government Knows More," Gallup News, September 6, 2019, https://news.gallup.com/poll/266441/americans -skeptical-ufos-say-government-knows.aspx.
10 Ibid.
11 Ibid.
12 Leo, "Gray Scale Photo of Human Face," Unsplash, https://unsplash.com/photos /gray-scale-photo-of-human-face-sMPRCsoUM4A.

13 Viren Swami, et al, "The Truth Is out There: The Structure of Beliefs about Extra-terrestrial Life among Austrian and British Tespondents," *Journal of Social Psychology*, 2008, 148(2), 2008, https://pubmed.ncbi.nlm.nih.gov/19245046/.

14 Ibid.

15 Ibid.

16 Ibid.

17 Ibid.

18 Ibid.

19 Ibid.

20 Ibid.

21 Ibid.

22 Phillip J. Hutchison and Herbert J. Strentz, "Journalism Versus the Flying Saucers: Assessing the First Generation of UFO Reportage, 1947–1967," *American Journalism*, 36:2, 150–170, 2019. https://www.tandfonline.com/doi/abs/10.1080/08821127.2019.1602418.

23 Ibid.

24 Ibid.

25 Ibid.

26 Ibid.

27 Ibid.

28 Ibid.

29 Ibid.

30 Ibid.

31 Ibid.

32 "Mutual UFO Network," accessed October 20, 2023, MUFON – Mutual UFO Network.

33 Gregory L. Little, "Educational Level and Primary Beliefs about Unidentified Flying Objects Held by Recognized Ufologists," *Psychological Reports*, Vol. 54, Issue 3, 1984, https://journals.sagepub.com/doi/abs/10.2466/pr0.1984.54.3.907.

34 Ibid.

35 Ibid.

36 Ibid.

37 Rebecca Caldwell, "Subcultures: Ufologists: The Truth Is Still out There," *Globe & Mail* (Toronto, Canada), February 22, 2003.

38 Ibid.

39 Ibid.

40 Ibid.

41 Ibid.

42 Dave Roos, "How Do You Become a Ufologist?," How Stuff Works.com, undated, https://science.howstuffworks.com/science-vs-myth/unexplained-phenomena/do-become-ufologist.htm.

43 Ibid.

44 Ibid.

45 Christopher C. French, "Open Skies, Closed Minds: For the First Time a Government UFO Expert Speaks Out," *Skeptical Inquirer*, vol. 21, no. 1, January–February 1997, pp. 50+, https://books.google.com/books/about/Open_Skies_Closed_Minds.html?id=6tcOAAAACAAJ

46 Ibid.

47 Ibid.

48 Roos, op. cit.

49 "Ufology Degree," IMHS Metaphysics Institute, accessed October 21, 2023, Ufology Degree - IMHS Metaphysics Institute.

50 "Ufology Degree," Thomas Francis University, accessed October 21, 2023, TFU: Ufology Degree (tfuniversity.org).

51 Ibid.

52 Mick West, "The Military-UFO Complex," *Reason*, Vol. 54, Issue 7, December 2022, https://reason.com/2022/11/15/the-military-ufo-complex/.

53 Ibid.

54 Ibid.

55 Helene Cooper, Ralph Blumenthal, and Leslie Kean, "Glowing Auras and 'Black Money': The Pentagon's Mysterious U.F.O. Program," *New York Times*, December 16, 2017, https://www.nytimes.com/2017/12/16/us/politics/pentagon-program-ufo-harry-reid.html.

56 Ibid.

57 Ibid.

58 Ibid. And Lewis-Kraus, op. cit.

59 Ibid.

60 Robert W. Balch and David Taylor, "Seekers and Saucers: The Role of the Cultic Milieu in Joining in UFO Cult," *American Behavioral Scientist*, Vol. 20, No. 6, July/August 1977, https://journals.sagepub.com/doi/10.1177/000276427702000604.

61 Ibid.

62 Ibid.

63 Ibid.

64 "10 Famous Cults in the World," Spiritual Ray, accessed October 21, 2023, 10 Famous Cults in the World - Spiritual Ray.

65 Ibid.

66 Ibid.

67 Isabel Carraco, "The UFO Cult That Murdered 19 Boys Because They Thought They Were Evil," CulturaColectiva.com, March 17, 2023, https://culturacolectiva.com/en/history/superior-universal-alignment-ufo-cult-murders/ and Beth Elderkin, "6 Lesser-Known Cults That Will Give You More Nightmares Than *American Horror Story*," gizmodo.com, September 11, 2017, 6 Lesser-Known Cults That Will Give You More Nightmares Than American Horror Story (gizmodo.com).

68 Ibid.

69 Katharine J. Holden and Christopher C. French, "Alien Abduction Experiences: Some Clues from Neuropschology and Neuropsychiatry," *Cognitive Neuropsychiatry*, 2002, 7(3), https://www.tandfonline.com/doi/abs/10.1080/13546800244000058

70 Ibid.

71 Neil Dagnall and Ken Drinkwater, "Scientific Explanations to Debunk Alien Abductions," RealClear Science, Not Dated, Scientific Explanations to Debunk Alien
Abductions | RealClearScience.

72 Ibid.

73 Ibid.

74 Ibid.

75 Ibid.

76 Anne Skomorowski, "Alien Abduction or 'Accidental Awareness'?" *Scientific American*,
November 11, 2014, https://www.scientificamerican.com/article/alien-abduction-or
-accidental-awareness/.

77 Ibid.

78 Ibid.

Section Four

1   Michael Mitsanas, "Here Are the 5 Most Memorable Moments from Congress'
UFO Hearing," NBC News, July 26, 2023, https://www.nbcnews.com/politics
/congress/are-5-memorable-moments-congress-ufo-hearing-rcna96476.

Chapter 10

1   Jake Carter, "Astronaut Quotes about UFOs and Extraterrestrial Life," anomalien
.com, October 16, 2019, https://anomalien.com/astronaut-quotes-about-ufos-and
-extraterrestrial-life/.

2   Lydia Saad, "Americans Skeptical of UFOs, but Say Government Knows More,"
Gallup, September 6, 2019, https://news.gallup.com/poll/266441/americans
-skeptical-ufos-say-government-knows.aspx.

3   Oliver Pacas, "Stop Sign," Unsplash, https://unsplash.com/photos/stop-sign-gCZ
DPYWG9sY.

4   "Center for the Study of Extraterrestrial Intelligence (CSETI)," accessed October 21,
2023, https://www.ipsgeneva.com/en/directory/science/194-center-for-the-study-of
-extraterrestrial-intelligence-cseti#:~:text=Center%20for%20the%20Study%20of%20
Extraterrestrial%20Intelligence%20%28CSETI%29,include%20the%20CE-5%20
Initiative%20and%20the%20Disclosure%20Project.

5   The Disclosure Institute, accessed October 21, 2023, https://www.disclosureinstitute
.org/testimony/.

6   Steven Greer, Disclosure Institute, 2001 National Press Club Event, accessed October 21, 2023, https://www.youtube.com/watch?v=4DrcG7VGgQU&ab_channel=
Dr.StevenGreer.

7   Mick West, "About Metabunk," Metabunk.org, July 8, 2013, https://www.metabunk
.org/threads/about-metabunk.1966/.

8   Ibid.

9   Guido Lombardi and Conrado Rodriguez Martin, "Fake and Alien Mummies,"
The Handbook of Mummy Studies, Springer Link, November 19, 2021, https://link
.springer.com/referenceworkentry/10.1007/978-981-15-3354-9_36.

10 Micah Hanks, "It Isn't Ours. Marco Rubio Says the Government Is Taking Unidentified Aerial Phenomena Seriously," Debrief, March 24, 2021, https://thedebrief .org/it-isnt-ours-marco-rubio-says-the-government-is-taking-unidentified-aerial -phenomena-seriously/.

11 Chris Ciaccia, "Former CIA Director Says Unexplained Phenomenon 'Might… Constitute a Different Form of Life,'" Fox News, December 21, 2020, https:// www.foxnews.com/science/former-cia-director-unexplained-phenomenon-different -form-of-life.

12 Patrick Thornton, "The 'Majestic 12': A Secret UFO Committee, or an Elaborate Hoax Created by a Disinformation Agent?," Ranker, November 29, 2021, https:// www.ranker.com/list/majestic-12-fact-or-fiction/patrick-thornton.

13 "Majestic 12," FBI Records: The Vault, accessed October 21, 2023, https://vault .fbi.gov/Majestic%2012.

14 David Howard, "The Truth Is Out There. So Is Lue Elizondo," *Popular Mechanics*, May/June 2023.

15 Joel Mathis, "What We Know from Decades of UFO Government Investigations," *National Geographic*, July 6, 2023, https://www.nationalgeographic.com/science /article/ufo-alien-spacecraft-investigation-timeline.

16 Ibid.

17 Ibid.

18 Nick Rufford, "We Are Not Alone; the US Government Has Channeled Millions to an *X-Files* Hangar in the Nevada Desert," *Sunday Times*, August 12, 2018.

19 Ibid.

20 Howard, op. cit.

21 Ibid. And Bill Whitaker, "UFOs Regularly Spotted in Restricted U.S. Airspace," *60 Minutes*, August 29, 2021, https://www.cbsnews.com/news/ufo-military-intelligence -60-minutes-2021-08-29/.

22 Ibid.

23 Ibid.

24 Ibid.

25 Howard, op. cit.

26 Rufford, op. cit.

27 Ibid.

28 Cooper, op. cit.

29 Rufford, op. cit.

30 Howard, op. cit.

31 Ibid.

32 Ibid.

33 Keith Kloor, "The Media Loves This UFO Expert Who Says He Worked for an Obscure Pentagon Program. Did He?" The Intercept, June 1, 2019, https://the intercept.com/2019/06/01/ufo-unidentified-history-channel-luis-elizondo-pentagon/.

34 Howard, op. cit.

35 Mathis, op. cit.

NOTES

36 "Establishment of Unidentified Aerial Phenomena Task Force," US Department of Defense Press Release, August 14, 2020, https://www.defense.gov/News/Releases /Release/Article/2314065/establishment-of-unidentified-aerial-phenomena-task-force/.

37 Akshita Jain, "Pentagon Confirms Leaked Video of UFO 'Buzzing' Navy Warships Is Genuine," *The Independent*, April 13, 2021, Pentagon confirms leaked video of UFO 'buzzing' Navy warships is genuine | The Independent.

38 Mathis, op. cit.

39 Ibid.

40 "2022 Annual Report on Unidentified Aerial Phenomena," Reports, Office of the Director of National Intelligence, 2022, https://www.dni.gov/index.php/newsroom /reports-publications/reports-publications-2023/3667-2022-annual-report-on -unidentified-aerial-phenomena.

41 Mathis, op. cit.

42 Lewis-Kraus, op. cit.

43 Ibid.

44 Ibid.

45 Ibid.

46 Nick Pope email interview with author, September 26, 2023.

47 Rufford, op. cit. and https://www.nytimes.com/2017/12/16/us/politics/pentagon-program-ufo-harry-reid.html.

48 Ibid.

49 Tim McMillan, "Bob Lazar Says the FBI Raided Him to Seize Area 51's Alien Fuel. The Truth Is Weirder," Vice.com, November 13, 2019, https://www.vice.com /en/article/evjwkw/bob-lazar-says-the-fbi-raided-him-to-seize-area-51s-alien-fuel-the -truth-is-weirder.

50 Bob Lazar, "Bob Lazar: Area 51 & Flying Saucers," *Larry King Now*, January 20, 2019, What's ELEMENT 115? - Larry King - Get ready to learn a lot - kinda a behind the scenes of my film - Bob Lazar : Area 51 & Flying Saucers 👽👽 Watch the... | By Bob Lazar : Area 51 & Flying Saucers | Facebook.

51 Ibid.

52 McMillan, op. cit.

53 Ibid.

54 Cynthia McCormick Hibbert, "Crashed UFOs" Non-human 'Biologics'? Professor Asks: Where's the Evidence? *Northeastern Global News*, July 28, 2023, https://news .northeastern.edu/2023/07/28/congress-holds-hearing-on-ufos/.

55 Ibid.

56 Adam Gabbatt and Joan E. Greve, "House of Representatives to Hold Hearing on Whistleblower's UFO Claims," *The Guardian*, June 8, 2023, https://www.theguardian .com/world/2023/jun/08/ufo-house-representatives-hearing-investigation.

57 Lewis-Kraus, op. cit.

58 Vanessa Romo and Bill Chappell, "U.S. Recovered Non-human 'Biologics' from UFO Crash Sites, Former Intel Official Says," NPR.org, July 27, 2023, https:// www.npr.org/2023/07/27/1190390376/ufo-hearing-non-human-biologics-uaps.

59 Pope, op. cit.

60 "Ret. US Army SGT: US Govt. Has over 50 Species of Aliens Cataloged, Wanted to Testify Before Congress," New UFO—Aliens, accessed October 22, 2023, http://newsnow24hrs.com/2022/07/26/ret-us-army-sgt-us-govt-has-over-50-species-of-aliens-cataloged-wanted-to-testify-before-congress/#:~:text=In%20the%20world%20of%20UFO%20research%2C%20the%20name,UFO%20or%20E.T.%20parts%2C%20alien%20bodies%2C%20and%20artifacts.

61 Ibid.

62 "1979 Bluefly & Moondust," Document #41, UFO Info Service, dated September 30, 1986, FOIA from Department of the Air Force, August 20, 1979, cufon.org/cufon/foia_009.htm.

63 "Ret. US Army SGT: US Govt. Has over 50 Species of Aliens Cataloged, Wanted to Testify Before Congress," op. cit.

64 Rufford, op. cit.

65 "Existence of UFOs 'Beyond Reasonable Doubt', Former Pentagon Official Says," The Independent (London, England), December 26, 2017.

66 Elizabeth Kim and Amelia Davidson, "Close Encounters with UFOs Described to Congressional Committee," Bloomberg, July 26, 2023.

67 Adam Gabbatt and Leonie Chao-Fong, "UFO Hearing Key Takeaways," The Guardian, July 26, 2023.

68 Ibid.

69 Hibbert, op. cit.

70 Kim and Davidson, op. cit.

71 Rennenkampff, op. cit.

72 Ibid.

73 Abraham Loeb and Sean Kirkpatrick, "Physical Constraints on Unidentified Aerial Phenomena," draft version March 7, 2023, LK1.pdf (harvard.edu).

74 Rennenkampff, op. cit.

75 https://www.rand.org/blog/2023/09/ufo-research-is-only-harmed-by-antigovernment-rhetoric.html.

76 Ibid.

77 Ibid.

78 Ibid.

79 Ibid.

Chapter 11

1 Matt Berg, "NASA Calls on the American Public to Help in the Hunt for UFOs," Politico, September 14, 2023, https://www.politico.com/news/2023/09/14/nasa-to-americans-help-us-find-ufos-00115896.

2 Julius Silver, "Saint Basils Cathedral," Pexels, https://www.pexels.com/photo/saint-basil-s-cathedral-753339/.

3 "No Doubt That UFOs Exist Says Pentagon's Alien Hunter," Daily Mail, December 26, 2017, https://www.dailymail.co.uk/news/article-12175675/Pentagon-UFO-expert-says-aliens-crash-landed-Earth.html.

4 Lewis-Kraus, op. cit.
5 Paul D. Shinkman, "The U.S. Is about to Change the Way the World Thinks about UFOs," *U.S. News & World Report*, June 25, 2021, https://www.usnews.com /news/national-news/articles/2021-06-24/the-us-is-about-to-change-the-way-the -world-thinks-about-ufos
6 Ibid.
7 Ibid.
8 Ibid.
9 Ibid.
10 Ibid.
11 Ibid.
12 "Qigong," Wikipedia, accessed, November 27, 2023, https://en.wikipedia.org/wiki /Qigong.
13 "China's UAP Research Associations," Enigma, May 2, 2023, https://enigmalabs.io /library/30848c73-c9f2-447f-b09a-340b5b5f725c.
14 Ibid.
15 Ibid.
16 Ibid.
17 Ibid.
18 Ibid.
19 Shinkman, op. cit.
20 Greg Eghigian, "'A Transatlantic Buzz': Flying Saucers, Extraterrestrials and America in Postwar Germany," *Journal of Transatlantic Studies*, Vol. 12, Issue 3, July 2014, https://www.tandfonline.com/doi/abs/10.1080/14794012.2014.928032.
21 Ibid.
22 "*Sendboten ferner Welten*," Hamburger Abendblatt 169 (July 24–25, 1954): 16 as cited in Eghigian, op. cit.
23 Ibid.
24 Ibid.
25 Sabrina P. Ramet, "UFOS over Russia and Eastern Europe," *Journal of Popular Culture*, Vol. 32, Issue 3, Winter 1998, https://onlinelibrary.wiley.com/doi/10.1111/j .0022-3840.1998.3203_81.x.
26 Ibid.
27 Ibid.
28 Ibid.
29 Ibid.
30 Ibid.
31 Ibid.
32 Ibid.
33 Ibid.
34 Ibid.
35 Ibid.
36 Ibid.

37 Ibid.

38 David Tormsen, "10 Official Government Programs That Studied UFOs," List-Verse, March 23, 2015, https://listverse.com/2015/03/23/10-official-government -programs-that-studied-ufos/.

39 Ibid.

40 Ibid.

41 Ibid.

42 Gideon Lewis-Kraus, "How the Pentagon Started Taking U.F.O.s Seriously," *The New Yorker*, April 30, 2021, https://www.newyorker.com/magazine/2021/05/10 /how-the-pentagon-started-taking-ufos-seriously

43 Tormsen, op. cit.

44 Ibid.

45 Ibid.

46 Jacques Vallée, *Confrontations—A Scientist's Search for Alien Contact*, hardcover ed., (Ballantine Books, March 1990). p. 134. ISBN 0-345-36453-8.

47 Tormsen, op. cit.

48 "Foo Fighters: World War II UFOs Before and After," accessed October 22, 2023, https://sped2work.tripod.com/foo_fighters.html#:~:text=England%20entered%20 the%20war%20long%20before%20the%20U.S.,several%20month%20lull%20in %201943%2C%20throughout%20the%20war.

49 Tormsen, op. cit.

50 Ibid.

51 Christopher C. French, "Open Skies, Closed Minds: For the First Time a Government UFO Expert Speaks Out." *Skeptical Inquirer*, vol. 21, no. 1, Jan.-Feb. 1997, pp. 50+, https://skepticalinquirer.org/authors/chris-french/.

52 Ibid.

53 Ibid.

54 Nick Pope, email interview with author, September 21, 2023.

55 Ibid.

56 Ibid.

Section Five

1 Benjamin R. Rich, accessed October 22, 2023, https://greetingideas.com/popular -ufo-quotes-sayings/.

Chapter 12

1 Edgar Mitchell, accessed October 22, 2023, https://www.brainyquote.com/quotes /edgar_mitchell_585512?src=t_ufo.

2 Paolo Boaretto, "UFO Parking Sign," Pexels, https://www.pexels.com/photo/ufo -parking-sign-16794996/.

3 Sophie Lewis, "There May Be More Than 36 Intelligent Alien Civilizations in the Milky Way, Scientists Say," *CBS News*, June 18, 2020, https://www.cbsnews.com /news/alien-civilizations-intelligent-milky-way-study/ and Tom Westby and Christopher J. Conselice, "The Astrobiological Copernican Weak and Strong Limits for

Intelligent Life," *The Astrophysical Journal*, Vol. 896, No. 1, June 15, 2020. The Astrobiological Copernican Weak and Strong Limits for Intelligent Life - IOP-science.

4 Ibid.

5 Ibid.

6 Ibid.

7 Pallab Ghosh, "Machine Finds Tantalising Hints of New Physics," BBC, March 23, 2021, https://www.bbc.com/news/science-environment-56491033.

8 Ibid.

9 Ibid.

10 Ibid.

11 Louis Markos, "The Truth about Angels and Demons Is Staring Us in the Face," *Christianity Today*, June 2020, https://www.christianitytoday.com/ct/2020/june-web -only/michael-heiser-angels-demons-unseen-realm.html.

12 Ibid.

13 Glory Dy, "How Do We Know That Angels Are Real?" Christianity.com, April 8, 2022, https://www.christianity.com/wiki/angels-and-demons/how-do-we-know-that -angels-are-real.html.

14 Michael Moran, "Bible-reading Pentagon Commanders Halted UFO Research 'over Fears Aliens Were Demons'," *Daily Star*, September 29, 2023, https://www .dailystar.co.uk/news/weird-news/bible-reading-pentagon-commanders-halted -31060240.

15 Alan Steinfeld, "Making Contact: Preparing for the New Realities of Extraterrestrial," St. Martin's Essentials, May 4, 2021, https://www.amazon.com/Making-Contact -Preparing-Realities-Extraterrestrial/dp/1250773946.

16 Robert L. Maginnis, "The Bible's Explainer on UFOs," Fox News, August 6, 2023, https://www.foxnews.com/opinion/the-bibles-explainer-on-ufos.

17 Ibid.

18 Ibid.

19 Ibid.

20 Ibid.

21 Ibid.

22 Ibid.

23 Adam Gabbatt, " 'Something's Going On': UFOs Threaten National Security, US Polilticians Warn," *The Guardian*, June 17, 2021, https://www.theguardian.com /us-news/2021/jun/17/ufos-us-report-national-security-concerns.

24 Ibid.

25 Ibid.

26 "The Dragons of Eden," Wikipedia, accessed November 8, 2023, https://en.wikipedia .org/wiki/The_Dragons_of_Eden.

27 Avi Loeb, "What We Can Learn from Studying UFOs," *Scientific American*, June 24, 2021, https://www.scientificamerican.com/article/what-we-can-learn-from -studying-ufos/#:~:text=A%20fresh%20scientific%20study%20that%20offers%20

reproducible%20evidence,will%20enhance%20the%20public%E2%80%99s%20
confidence%20in%20evidence-based%20knowledge.

28 Ibid.

29 Ibid.

30 Cassie Buchman, "Poll: Many Believe Government Hiding What It Knows on UFOs," *News Nation*, July 11, 2023, https://www.newsnationnow.com/space/ufo/poll-government-hiding-what-it-knows-ufos/.

31 Michael Matsanas, "Lawmakers Call for Greater Transparency on UFOs Urging House Oversight," *NBC News*, July 26, 2023, https://www.nbcnews.com/politics/congress/house-oversight-committee-hold-hearing-ufos-rcna96154.

32 Ibid.

33 Mark von Rennenkampff, "'Aliens,' or a Foreign Power? Pentagon UFO Chief Says Someone Is in Our Backyard," The Hill, November 10, 2023, https://thehill.com/opinion/national-security/4301944-aliens-or-a-foreign-power-pentagon-ufo-chief-says-someone-is-in-our-backyard/.

Chapter 13

1 Mitsanas, op. cit.

2 "The Decision to Go to the Moon: President John F. Kennedy's May 25, 1961 Speech before a Joint Session of Congress," NASA, accessed October 22, 2023, https://www.nasa.gov/history/the-decision-to-go-to-the-moon/.

3 Ibid.

4 Used by permission from NASA.

5 "Unified Land Operations," ADRP 3-0, US Department of the Army, May 2012, chrome-extension://efaidnbmnnnibpcajpcglclefindmkaj/https://www.moore.army.mil/infantry/DoctrineSupplement/ATP3-21.8/PDFs/adrp3_0.pdf.

6 Alan Steinfeld, "Making Contact: Preparing for the New Realities of Extraterrestrial," St. Martin's Essentials, May 4, 2021, https://www.amazon.com/Making-Contact-Preparing-Realities-Extraterrestrial/dp/1250773946.

7 Ibid.

8 Ibid.

9 Ibid.

10 Ibid.

11 Ibid.

12 Ibid.

13 Ibid.

Chapter 14

1 Ronald Reagan, Space Quotations, accessed October 22, 2023, https://spacequotations.com/quotes-about-ufo/.

2 Dre Erwin, "Photo of Aurora and the Northern Lights," Unsplash, https://unsplash.com/photos/a-long-exposure-photo-of-the-aurora-and-the-northern-lights-bod CEGgfaK4.

3 "'Fake News,' Lies and Propaganda: How to Sort Fact from Fiction, University of Michigan Library, accessed October 22, 2023, https://guides.lib.umich.edu/c.php?g=637508&p=4462444

4 "Video & Highlights: Faith in Journalism—How News Organizations Can Build Trust with Religious Americanism," Journalism Institute, May 18, 2022, https://www.pressclubinstitute.org/event/faith-in-journalism-how-news-organizations-can-build-trust-with-religious-americans/.

5 "Mendel's Law," Merriam-Webster.com, accessed October 22, 2023, https://www.merriam-webster.com/dictionary/Mendel%27s%20law.

6 Jacques Vallée, *Revelations: Alien Contact and Human Deception* (Alien Contact Trilogy Book 3). Anomalist Books. Kindle Edition, 1991, https://www.amazon.com/REVELATIONS-Alien-Contact-Deception-Trilogy-ebook/dp/B00J4WWY9A.

7 Lynn E. Catoe, *UFOs and Related Subjects: An Annotated Bibliography*, Prepared by the Library of Congress Science and Technology Division for the Air Force Office of Scientific Research Office of Aerospace Research, USAF Arlington, Virginia 22209.

8 Dr. Pierre Guerin, FSR Vol. 25, No. 1, p. 13-14

9 R. Alan Street, *The Invaders: A Biblical Study of UFOs*, 1975, pp. 16–17

10 "Public Praises Science; Scientists Fault Public, Media," Pew Research Center, July 9, 2009, https://www.pewresearch.org/politics/2009/07/09/public-praises-science-scientists-fault-public-media/.

11 Greg Eghigian and Christian Peters, "It's Time to Hear from Social Scientists about UFOs," *Scientific American*, October 2, 2023, https://www.scientificamerican.com/article/its-time-to-hear-from-social-scientists-about-ufos/.

12 Ibid.

13 Ibid.

14 Ibid.

15 Ibid.

16 Ibid.

17 Ibid.

18 Neil Gross, "How Religious Are America's College and University Professors?" Solon Simmons Publishing, SSRC, February 6, 2007, chrome-extension://efaidnbmnnnibpcajpcglclefindmkaj/http://religion.ssrc.org/reforum/Gross_Simmons.pdf.

19 Rich Barlow, "Astronomy Class Ponders Life Beyond Earth Course Explores Everything from Human Colonies in Space to UFOs," *States News Service*, March 3, 2023, https://www.bu.edu/articles/2023/astronomy-class-ponders-life-beyond-earth/.

20 Ibid.

21 Ibid.

22 Ibid.

23 "UFOs and Academia," Reddit, accessed October 22, 2023, https://www.reddit.com/r/UFOs/comments/bncyg7/ufos_and_academia/?rdt=60914.

24 Ibid.

25 Ibid.

26 Aaron Reich, "UFOs Becoming Increasingly Attractive to US Academics—study," *Jerusalem Post*, May 28, 2023, https://www.jpost.com/science/article-744416.

27 Ibid.

28 Rizwan Virk, "The U.S. Military Takes UFOs Seriously. Why Doesn't Silicon Valley or Academia?" NBC News, April 16, 2021, https://www.nbcnews.com/think/opinion/u-s-military-takes-ufos-seriously-why-doesn-t-silicon-ncna1264107.

29 Ibid.

Chapter 15

1 Pixabay, "Person Standing under a Rock Formation on a Starry Night," Pexels, https://www.pexels.com/photo/person-standing-under-a-rock-formation-on-a-starry-night-33688/.

2 Karen Engle, "Aliens, UFOs, and the Bible: Should Christians Study the Unseen Realm?", Logos.com, May 24, 2021, https://www.logos.com/grow/aliens-ufos-and-the-bible/.

3 Ibid.

4 Billy Graham, *Angels: God's Secret Agents*, (New York: Doubleday & Company, 1975).

5 Ibid.

6 Ibid.

7 Ibid.

8 Ibid.

9 Ibid.

10 "Occultism," Britannica.com, accessed October 30, 2023, https://www.britannica.com/topic/occultism.

11 Graham, op. cit.

12 Ibid.

13 Ibid.

14 Ibid.

15 Ibid.

16 Ibid.

17 Ibid.

18 As cited in Graham, Matthew Henry, Psalm 68, *Commentaries*, accessed October 22, 2023, https://www.biblestudytools.com/commentaries/matthew-henry-complete/psalms/68.html.

19 Graham, op. cit.

20 Ibid.

21 Ibid.

22 Ibid.

23 Ibid.

24 "What Do UFOs Have to Do with Christians?" Deliverance Ministry, March 16, 2013, http://www.jesusthedeliverer.org/what-do-ufos-have-to-do-with-christians-part-i/.

25 Ibid.

26 Ibid.

27 Ibid.

28 Ibid.

29 J. Brian Huffling, "UFOs, Aliens, and Christianity," Southern Evangelical Seminary and Bible College, November 7, 2022, https://ses.edu/ufos-aliens-and-christianity/.

30 Ibid.

31 Ibid.

32 Ibid.

33 Ibid.

34 Billy Graham, "Answers," Billy Graham Evangelical Association, February 1, 2018, https://billygraham.org/answer/bible-say-anything-life-planets/.

35 Ken Ham, "Do I Believe in UFOs? Absolutely! Case against Alien Beings," *Answers Magazine*, December 5, 2007, https://answersingenesis.org/astronomy/alien-life/do -i-believe-in-ufos-absolutely/.

36 Ibid.

37 Ibid.

38 Ibid.

39 Ibid.

40 Ibid.

41 Ibid.

42 Ibid.

43 Ibid.

44 Brandon Ambrosino, "If We Made Contact with Aliens, How Would Religions React?" BBC, December 16, 2016, https://www.bbc.com/future/article/20161215 -if-we-made-contact-with-aliens-how-would-religions-react.

45 Madison Dapcevich, "Did NASA Fund Theological Research to Study How Humans Would React to Extraterrestrial Life?" Snopes.com, December 29, 2021, https://www.snopes.com/fact-check/nasa-24-theologians-research-aliens/.

46 Ibid.

47 Ambrosino, op. cit.

48 Ibid.

49 Rick Pidcock, "With All This Talk of UFOs, What's a Christian to Think?" *Baptist News*, June 8, 2021, https://baptistnews.com/article/with-all-this-talk-of-ufos-whats -a-christian-to-think/.

50 Ibid.

Chapter 16

1 Billy Graham, "Answers," Billy Graham Evangelical Association, June 19, 2006, https://billygraham.org/answer/what-does-the-bible-say-about-life-on-other-planets -or-does-it-forbid-us-to-believe-there-might-be-intelligent-life-elsewhere-in-the -universe/.

2 Marek Piwnicki, "Silhouette of Mountain under Starry Night," Unsplash, https:// unsplash.com/photos/silhouette-of-mountain-under-starry-night-jPuTl4xsTkM.

3 Chuck Missler and Mark Eastman, *Alien Encounters: The Secret Behind the UFO Phenomenon*, (Koinonia House, January 1, 2003), https://www.amazon.com/Alien -Encounters-Secret-Behind-Phenomenon/dp/1578212057/ref=tmm_pap_swatch_0? _encoding=UTF8&qid=1697211867&sr=8-1.

4 Ibid.

5 Ibid.

6 Ibid.

7 Ibid.

8 "Genealogy," Merriam-Webster.com, accessed October 22, 2023, https://www.merriam-webster.com/dictionary/genealogy.

9 As cited by Missler, Flavius Josephus, *The Antiquities of the Jews*, Internet Archive, accessed October 22, 2023, https://archive.org/details/theAntiquitiesOfTheJews_507.

10 Ibid.

11 Ibid.

12 Ibid.

13 Zachery Garris, "Giants in the Land: A Biblical Theology of the Nephilim, Anakim, Rephaim (and Goliath)," Knowing Scripture, July 2, 2019, https://knowingscripture.com/articles/giants-in-the-land-a-biblical-theology-of-the-nephilim-anakim-rephaim-and-oliath#:~:text=Numbers%2013%20is%20the%20key%20passage%20on%20giants,in%20it%20are%20strong%20or%20weak%E2%80%9D%20%28Numbers%2013%3A18%29.

14 Ibid.

15 Ibid.

16 As cited by Missler. Gordon Creighton, *Flying Saucer Review* official position statement, 1996.

17 As cited by Missler, Jacques Vallée, *Dimensions* (Ballantine Books, 1988), p. 32.

18 Ibid.

19 Ibid.

20 Ibid.

21 Missler, op. cit.

22 Jacques Vallée, *Dimensions: A Casebook of Alien Contact* (Ballantine Books, 1989 edition).

23 Ibid., 192.

24 Greg Daugherty and Missy Sullivan, "These 5 UFO Traits, Captured on Video by Navy Fighters, Defy Explanation," History.com, June 5, 2019, https://www.history.com/news/ufo-sightings-speed-appearance-movement.

25 Lewis-Kraus, op. cit.

26 Christopher Wilson, "UFO Hearing: Whistleblower Testifies Government 'Absolutely' Has Possession of 'Nonhuman' Craft," Yahoo News, July 26, 2023, https://news.yahoo.com/ufo-whistleblower-hearing-house-oversight-non-human-craft-uap-navy-pilots-171759861.html?fr=sycsrp_catchall.

27 Holden, op. cit.

Afterword

1 Pixabay, "Blue and White Planet Display," Pexels, https://www.pexels.com/photo/blue-and-white-planet-display-87009/.

2 David F. Wells, God in the Wasteland (Grand Rapids: Eerdmans, 1994), 88.

3 David S. Schrock, "Divine Weightlessness: The Fundamental Problem in Evangelicalism," VIA EMMAUS, March 19, 2014, https://davidschrock.com/2014/03/19/divine-weightlessness-the-fundamental-problem-in-evangelicalism/.

4 Ibid.

Appendix A

1 "Area 51," Britannica, https://www.britannica.com/place/Area-51.

2 Shoko Rikimaru, "We Are Not Alone: Mystery-loving Fukushima Area Opens UFO Lab," The Asahi Shimbun, July 6, 2021, https://www.asahi.com/ajw/articles/14383617.

3 Adam Janos, "Why Have There Been So Many UFO Sightings Near Nuclear Facilities?" History.com, June 23, 2019, https://www.history.com/news/ufos-near-nuclear-facilities-uss-roosevelt-rendlesham.

4 Mosheh Gains and Phil Helsel, "Navy Confirms Videos Did Capture UFO Sightings, but It Calls Them by Another Name," NBC News, September 19, 2019, https://www.nbcnews.com/news/us-news/navy-confirms-videos-did-capture-ufo-sightings-it-calls-them-n1056201.

5 Dane Enerio, "UFO Spotted in Minnesota? Deputy's 1979 Experience Is 'Completely Genuine,' Says Investigator," *International Business Times*, September 15, 2022, https://www.ibtimes.com/ufo-spotted-minnesota-deputys-1979-experience-completely-genuine-says-investigator-3613168?utm_source=feeds_ibt&utm_medium=feed&utm_campaign=_content.

6 Robert Sapiro, "The 5 Most Credible Modern UFO Sightings," History.com, July 28, 2023, https://www.history.com/news/ufo-sightings-credible-modern.

7 "UFO Spotted in Yorkshire, England? Expert Says 'Bizarre' Lights 'Most Likely' A UFO." *International Business Times* [U.S. ed.], 28 Sept. 2022, p. NA. *Gale Academic OneFile*, link.gale.com/apps/doc/A719889501/AONE?u=wash92852&sid=ebsco&xid=654877cc. Accessed 11 Aug. 2023.

8 "UFOs in the Bible," Aetherius Society, accessed November 11, 2023, https://www.aetherius.org/evidence/ufos-in-the-bible/.

9 "Aetherius Society," Wikipedia, accessed November 11, 2023, https://en.wikipedia.org/wiki/Aetherius_Society.

10 Bob Spearing, "Were MUFON Cases # 130602 & 130105 a Stealth B-21 Raider?" MUFON, November 13, 2023, https://mufon.com/2023/11/13/were-mufon-cases-130602-130105-a-stealth-b-21-raider/.

Appendix B

1 The Galileo Project, Harvard University, accessed October 29, 2023, https://projects.iq.harvard.edu/galileo/home.

2 Joe Bills, "Are We Alone?" Yankee, August 31, 2023, https://newengland.com/yankee/magazine/are-we-alone-a-closer-look-at-new-englands-long-ties-to-the-unexplained/.

NOTES

Appendix C

1 Keith Kloor, "Why We Can't Quit Them," *Scientific American*, June 27, 2023, https://www.scientificamerican.com/article/ufos-keep-appearing-in-the-news-heres-why-we-cant-quit-them/.

2 Carrie Bell, "12 Famous Hoaxes That (almost) Fooled Everyone," *Readers Digest*, updated April 10, 2023, https://www.rd.com/list/famous-hoaxes-almost-fooled/.

3 Ibid.

4 "Top 10 Most Famous UFO Hoaxes Ever," Viral Ventura, accessed November 4, 2023, https://viralventura.com/ufo-hoaxes/.

5 Ibid.

6 Ibid.

7 "'Alien Autopsy' Filmmaker Regrets Hoax," *New York Post*, September 26, 2017, 'Alien autopsy' filmmaker regrets hoax (nypost.com).

8 Yevgeny Kuklychev, "Did Night Vision Footage Show '10ft Alien' from Las Vegas UFO Crash Report?" *Newsweek*, June 12, 2023, https://www.newsweek.com/did-night-vision-footage-show-alien-las-vegas-crash-report-1806008.

9 Ibid.

10 Ibid.